To the memory of William Teale,
whose suggestion it was that we develop a unifying focus
for the International Literacy Association
preconference research institute that served as the basis
for this edited collection

—M. R. K. and M. J. D.

To the memory of my mother and father,
who supported me every step of the way

And to my husband and son
for their patience as we undertook this book

—M. R. K.

To my husband and daughter
for their support and encouragement

—M. J. D.

About the Editors

Melanie R. Kuhn, PhD, is Professor and Jean Adamson Stanley Faculty Chair in Literacy at the Purdue University College of Education. In addition to reading fluency, her research interests include literacy instruction for struggling readers, and comprehension and vocabulary development. Formerly on the faculties of the Boston University School of Education and the Rutgers Graduate School of Education, Dr. Kuhn began her teaching career in the Boston public schools and worked as an instructor at an international school in England. She served as a member of the Literacy Research Panel for the International Literacy Association. Dr. Kuhn has published several books and numerous journal articles and book chapters.

Mariam Jean Dreher, PhD, is Professor in the Department of Teaching and Learning, Policy and Leadership at the University of Maryland, College Park. Previously she was an elementary classroom teacher and Title I specialist. Her research interests include ways to integrate informational text into literacy instruction to enhance students' comprehension, vocabulary, and motivation. Dr. Dreher has published numerous articles and books and has served on many editorial advisory boards, receiving the Outstanding Reviewer Award from the *Journal of Literacy Research*. She is a consultant to National Geographic Children's Books on a series of information books for young children. Dr. Dreher is a recipient of a Fulbright Senior Specialist Grant and was awarded an honorary doctorate from the University of Oulu, Finland.

Contributors

Richard C. Anderson, EdD, Department of Educational Psychology (Emeritus), University of Illinois at Urbana–Champaign, Champaign, Illinois

Estanislado S. Barrera IV, PhD, School of Education, Louisiana State University, Baton Rouge, Louisiana

Marco A. Bravo, PhD, Department of Education, Santa Clara University, Santa Clara, California

Jill Castek, PhD, Department of Teaching, Learning, and Sociocultural Studies, University of Arizona, Tucson, Arizona

Mariam Jean Dreher, PhD, Department of Teaching and Learning, Policy and Leadership, University of Maryland, College Park, Maryland

Maria Grant, EdD, Department of Secondary Education, California State University, Fullerton, Fullerton, California

Claire E. Hamilton, PhD, Center for Teaching and Learning, University of Massachusetts at Amherst, Amherst, Massachusetts

Sharon B. Kletzien, PhD, Literacy Department (Emerita), West Chester University of Pennsylvania, West Chester, Pennsylvania

Melanie R. Kuhn, PhD, College of Education, Purdue University, West Lafayette, Indiana

Catherine Lammert, PhD, Department of Teaching and Learning, The University of Iowa, Iowa City, Iowa

Diane Lapp, EdD, Department of Teacher Education, San Diego State University, San Diego, California

Stacia L. Long, PhD candidate, Department of Language and Literacy Education, University of Georgia, Athens, Georgia

Saúl I. Maldonado, PhD, Department of Dual Language and English Learner Education, San Diego State University, San Diego, California

Michael Manderino, PhD, Director of Curriculum and Instruction, Leyden High School District 212, Franklin Park, Illinois, and College of Education, Northern Illinois University, DeKalb, Illinois

Heidi Anne E. Mesmer, PhD, School of Education, Virginia Tech, Blacksburg, Virginia

Brian W. Miller, PhD, Department of Elementary Education, Towson University, Towson, Maryland

Pei-Yu Marian Pan, MA, Department of Educational Psychology, University of Illinois at Urbana–Champaign, Champaign, Illinois

Paula J. Schwanenflugel, PhD, Department of Educational Psychology (Emerita), University of Georgia, Athens, Georgia

Kim Skinner, PhD, School of Education, Louisiana State University, Baton Rouge, Louisiana

Jorge L. Solís, PhD, Department of Bicultural–Bilingual Studies, The University of Texas at San Antonio, San Antonio, Texas

Jeanne Swafford, PhD, Department of Early Childhood, Elementary, Middle, Literacy, and Special Education, University of North Carolina–Wilmington, Wilmington, North Carolina

Thomas DeVere Wolsey, EdD, Graduate School of Education, The American University in Cairo, Cairo, Egypt

Jo Worthy, PhD, Department of Curriculum and Instruction, The University of Texas at Austin, Austin, Texas

Foreword

Consider the themes of two texts: One describes how technological advances such as 3-D imaging have changed the study of mummies, while another illustrates how a stranded, juvenile white shark is prepared to survive in the wild by staff at an aquarium. The relevant passages demonstrate what fourth graders read on the National Assessment of Educational Progress (NAEP; National Center for Education Statistics, 2017) in 2013 and 2017. Policymakers and pundits frequently use the findings of the NAEP—which show that approximately two-thirds of a fourth-grade cohort fails to attain comprehension proficiency—to bemoan the status of American education. The interventions that educators initiate to ameliorate the situation invariably focus on word recognition skills. Summaries of students' word accuracy, however, indicate that all but the bottom 2–3% of a cohort are capable of recognizing the words in these texts (Gray, Warnock, Kaminski, & Good, 2018). Obviously, something else influences these performances.

Research has long pointed to one source for students' lackluster comprehension performances: background knowledge (Ahmed et al., 2016; Priebe, Keenan, & Miller, 2012). That is, comprehension of a text, such as either of the two NAEP passages above, is aided by knowledge about the text's topic. Furthermore, students' success in college, careers, and communities will rely heavily on background knowledge and knowing how to use texts to learn. Never before has the need to know and to use text to learn been more critical than in the digital–global world of the 21st century. As has been the case throughout humankind's history, knowledge is stored in texts. That pattern continues, even when that knowledge is stored in bytes rather than paperbound books.

Yet, when we visit English language arts (ELA) classrooms, we find little attention to developing the background knowledge that underlies comprehension and learning. Teachers assist students with the basic content required for a specific text, but an observer will often find that the information taught appears more conducive to playing Trivial Pursuit than to approaching content independently. For example, informational texts within a given level of a leveled text program include one on the history of soccer, another on the geography of France, and a third on Día de los Muertos (Reading A–Z, n.d.). Students get a smidgen of information on an array of topics but few opportunities to acquire knowledge and vocabulary on any one topic in depth.

This book advocates an alternative approach—one where attention to knowledge is central to the ELA curriculum. It is one of the first to bring together literacy scholars' work on knowledge and its role in ELA in a single volume. For classroom practices to change, forums are needed where knowledge is in the foreground. This book provides such a context, where multiple insights on the role of background knowledge and how it can be facilitated in classrooms are presented. From such exchanges, we learn from each other and also bring particular perspectives to the foreground.

The contents of this book address the means of increasing students' conceptual knowledge across the years of schooling from preschool to high school preparation for career and college. The chapter authors address a variety of strategies and contexts for fostering conceptual knowledge. The manner in which texts are used to develop and anchor knowledge is a theme that runs throughout the volume. Rich discussions occur when the ideas of text are worthy of students' time and effort. That is, the content of texts needs to be sufficiently complex for students to be challenged and engaged in concept development. Multimodal text sets and the variety of text types in digital environments mean that the forms of texts that can be the source for concept development are also varied and plentiful.

Another principle that resonates throughout the chapters is that concept development is not passive. Active involvement in interacting with ideas and producing responses to and interpretations of ideas characterizes knowledge building. Opportunities to use oral language to process and integrate knowledge are fundamental. Educators can use the carefully documented heuristics provided in this book to conduct discussions that foster concept development. Writing also provides a means for assimilating concepts. Models, including graphic organizers, are provided in the text to guide students in expressing and sharing concepts in a variety of forms that they will encounter in careers and communities.

Another theme coming out of this volume is the need for a focus on specific topics. That is, the "Trivial Pursuit" curriculum of many programs—especially in primary-level classrooms—will not develop the conceptual knowledge that is so essential for deep comprehension.

This book represents an important step if the literacy needs of students of this and future generations are to be facilitated in ELA classrooms. The authors of these chapters illustrate the kind of work that is required if knowledge is to be the "sixth pillar" of the ELA curriculum as Cervetti and Hiebert (2015) advocated. Yes, phonemic awareness, phonics, fluency, and vocabulary underlie comprehension, as the National Reading Panel's (2000) review showed. But without attention to the knowledge that is conveyed in text, students' reading proficiency will not be sufficient for the tasks of the 21st century.

It is hoped that this volume will serve as an inspiration and clarion call for other literacy scholars and educators to address the gaps in knowledge building in ELA classrooms. Numerous aspects of the knowledge enterprise remain to be addressed. As illustrated by the chapters in this book, a strong foundation has been laid on the means of supporting knowledge development through oral and written language. For the next generation of work on conceptual knowledge, we also need to address questions about *what* knowledge should be the focus. Teachers require support in the curation of materials for the rich experiences that underlie knowledge building and also in the identification of topics that are especially germane for specific developmental levels and school contexts. Literacy researchers have an important role in both of these processes.

One aspect of support that especially merits the attention of literacy scholars has to do with the role of narrative in knowledge building in ELA. Informational text provides particular kinds of knowledge and has rightfully become central to ELA curriculum. For example, a narrative that is set in the context of a bridge is unlikely to describe pylons and torsion, as Seymour Simon (2005) does in *Bridges*. However, literary texts such as *Pop's Bridge* (Bunting, 2006) and *Twenty-One Elephants and Still Standing* (Prince, 2005) can support understandings about the building and functions of bridges, while at the same time telling engaging stories. Indeed, psychological experiments have shown that people retain information in deeper ways when they need to make inferences in narrative texts than when the information is explicitly stated, as often occurs in informational texts (Chabris & Simons, 2011).

The contributors to this volume are addressing a critical gap in ELA curriculum and instruction. The key question facing literacy educators is: How can we build on this content and move ahead with the alacrity and vision that is required to prepare the current and next generations of students for the "knowledge age"?

ELFRIEDA H. HIEBERT, PhD
TextProject

REFERENCES

Ahmed, Y., Francis, D. J., York, M., Fletcher, J. M., Barnes, M., & Kulesz, P. (2016). Validation of the direct and inferential mediation (DIME) model of reading comprehension in grades 7 through 12. *Contemporary Educational Psychology, 44*, 68–82.

Bunting, E. (2006). *Pop's bridge*. Orlando, FL: Harcourt.

Cervetti, G. N., & Hiebert, E. H. (2015). The sixth pillar of reading instruction: Knowledge development. *The Reading Teacher, 68*(7), 548–551.

Chabris, C. F., & Simons, D. J. (2011). *The invisible gorilla: And other ways our intuitions deceive us*. New York: Crown.

Gray, J. S., Warnock, A. N., Kaminski, R. A., & Good, R. H. (2018). *Acadience™ reading national norms 2014–2015* (Technical Report No. 23). Eugene, OR: Dynamic Measurement Group.

National Center for Education Statistics. (2017). *National Assessment of Educational Progress (NAEP): 1992–2017 reading assessments*. Washington, DC: Institute of Education Sciences, U.S. Department of Education. Retrieved from *www.nationsreportcard.gov/reading_2017*.

National Reading Panel. (2000). *Report of the National Reading Panel*. Washington, DC: National Institute of Child Health and Human Development.

Priebe, S. J., Keenan, J. M., & Miller, A. C. (2012). How prior knowledge affects word identification and comprehension. *Reading and Writing, 25*(1), 131–149.

Prince, A. J. (2005). *Twenty-one elephants and still standing*. New York: HMH Books for Young Readers.

Reading A–Z. (n.d.). *Leveled books*. Tucson, AZ: Author. Retrieved from *www.readinga-z.com*.

Simon, S. (2005). *Bridges*. San Francisco: Chronicle Books.

Acknowledgments

We give special thanks to Donna Alvermann, Nell Duke, and Amy Wilson-Lopez for helping to organize the preconference research institute at the International Literacy Association.

We would also like to thank Craig Thomas and Anna Nelson at The Guilford Press for guiding us through the publication process.

Contents

CHAPTER 1

Introduction

MELANIE R. KUHN

One of the major differences between successful readers and their less successful peers involves the type of interactions they have with oral and written language (Cunningham & Stanovich, 1998; Hirsch, 2003). In general, successful students experience rich language in their homes (e.g., Sparks, 2015), through media (e.g., *PBS Kids*; Manzo, 2009), and in their broader environment (e.g., going to the library for story time; Neuman & Celano, 2012). It is also the case that the differences in these language encounters begin early and continue throughout a student's schooling (e.g., Stanovich, 1986). However, the good news is that these differences are not insurmountable. Research indicates that effective instruction, beginning in preschool (e.g., Whorrall & Cabell, 2016) and continuing through high school (e.g., Massey & Heafner, 2004), can counter these differences, making it possible to create a more positive classroom environment for all our learners.

In addition, the body of research exploring effective literacy development presents numerous ways to expand students' conceptual knowledge (e.g., Gambrell, Malloy, Marinak, & Mazzoni, 2014). This includes instructional approaches ranging from simply structuring student discussion in ways that ensure active participation to approaches that expose students to complex text in the content areas (Hiebert, 2009). By focusing on these varying areas of instruction, it becomes possible for teachers to concentrate on the unconstrained skills of vocabulary and comprehension development (Paris, 2005), skills that underlie academic success both within and beyond the primary grades. Because vocabulary and comprehension are areas of virtually unlimited growth, they underlie learning from the earliest moments and, depending on an individual's

1

interest, can continue throughout a lifetime; as such, they play a role in successful reading across all subjects and school years. Constrained skills (i.e., phonological awareness, decoding, and fluency), while critical to successful reading, differ insofar as they develop over a relatively brief period of time, can be taught directly, and incorporate a limited set of knowledge. Fortunately, the growth of vocabulary and conceptual knowledge can have a positive effect on the development of constrained skills as well (Stanovich, 1986).

The Need for Focused Attention on Conceptual Development

We consider this volume to be particularly critical at this point in time for two reasons. First, whether the Common Core or various state standards stand the test of time (e.g., Greene, 2018), expanding students' vocabulary and conceptual knowledge in the ways discussed here can make an important contribution to closing the achievement gap (e.g., Cunningham & Stanovich, 1998). Second, we believe that the process of becoming a skilled reader requires multiple approaches to classroom instruction. This does not mean every theory or instructional approach leads to success; in fact, holding on to disproven notions can actually harm rather than help our most vulnerable students (e.g., Ash, Kuhn, & Walpole, 2009). At the same time, if we insist on focusing on only one piece of the literacy puzzle, be it comprehension or decoding or oral language development, we create readers who are likely to be skilled only in one area (students who can comprehend but who are not competent decoders, or decoders who are unable to understand what they are reading; e.g., Jones, Conradi, & Amendum, 2016).

As a field, we know a great deal about oral and written language development (e.g., Alvermann, Unrau, Sailors, & Ruddell, 2019; O'Connor & Vadasy, 2011). Given this knowledge, the overarching question of this book is: How can we apply this knowledge across a range of settings? Our goal for this volume is to contribute to that answer. As editors, we have included multiple perspectives in this collection. As we noted in the previous paragraph, we have done so because we believe our ability to serve learners improves when we think about literacy in multiple ways. We view skilled reading as a complex endeavor—one in which multiple elements are necessary for success, but in which none is sufficient in and of itself. To illustrate this understanding, we use this collection to look at aspects of literacy learning across grade levels, text types, and content areas.

Overview of This Book

We begin by looking at the importance of expanding PreK and kindergarten students' vocabulary knowledge as a basis for later literacy success. In Chapter 2, Claire E. Hamilton and Paula J. Schwanenflugel provide practical approaches for developing oral language interactions with young children. The program focuses on social studies and science words that are intentionally selected and taught through explicit instruction; they are then reinforced as part of the curriculum using storybook reading, extension activities, and conversations with the students. The research was initially undertaken with low-income children attending ethnically and linguistically diverse preschools in the Mississippi Delta. It has since been implemented in multiple sites and identified as research that "meets WWC (What Works Clearinghouse) evidence standards without reservations" (U.S. Department of Education, 2012, p. 1). As such, these practices have a distinct potential to support the language development of all young learners.

Chapter 3 focuses on the interactive reading of informational texts as a means of developing conceptual knowledge in the primary grades. Here, Mariam Jean Dreher and Sharon B. Kletzien look at informational books as a means to build engagement and enjoyment among young learners, while simultaneously increasing their vocabulary and conceptual knowledge. By integrating these texts into classroom practice, teachers can provide a way to build interest in reading for a range of learners: not only those students who prefer nonfiction over fiction and those who enjoy both genres equally, but also those who are likely to develop an interest in these selections once they have been exposed to them as part of the classroom curriculum (Reutzel, Jones, Fawson, & Smith, 2008). The guidelines suggested by Dreher and Kletzien support the integration of interactive reading in ways that increase students' broader interest in and comfort with reading, while expanding vocabulary and conceptual knowledge as well.

In Chapter 4, Pei-Yu Marian Pan, Brian W. Miller, and Richard C. Anderson explore the importance of collaborative reasoning as a further means of developing students' understandings of nonfiction texts. Classroom talk often remains dominated by a format in which teachers initiate interactions by asking their students a question, waiting for an answer, then evaluating that response (initiation–response–evaluation [IRE]; Cazden, 2001). However, the authors show that moving away from teacher-led conversation and toward student, or peer, interaction allows students to both expand their thinking skills and deepen their text comprehension. Not only do Pan, Miller, and Anderson demonstrate a process in which student discussion occurs within a social context, but they also show how it leads to richer thinking. Furthermore, such student engagement allows for talk that is more complex than would otherwise be the case and allows for better transfer of these skills to the comprehension of novel material.

Jeanne Swafford, in Chapter 5, considers the importance of integrating multimodal text sets into the classroom as a way of expanding conceptual knowledge. Today's texts have moved beyond the traditional print format to include a range of features, platforms, and types, from visual to aural, and the amount of material available to individuals in our society has expanded exponentially. Given the range of media with which students interact daily, it is essential that they be introduced to multimodal text sets in the classroom; such integration will help them develop the ability to navigate a variety of text types, both critically and flexibly. Swafford discusses ways to identify texts that are relevant and interesting to learners, and that can be built upon in terms of breadth and depth of a topic. She also explores ways to interact with selections presented in multiple formats and provides resources to assist teachers in the creation and use of text sets that will help to deepen students' conceptual knowledge.

A key component to developing conceptual knowledge in the classroom involves determining which texts to use. Text complexity is one factor that teachers can use to help make their choices, and Heidi Anne E. Mesmer explores this component of text selection in Chapter 6. She begins by clarifying the difference between text difficulty and text complexity, and goes on to discuss the role that word familiarity, text cohesion, and word concreteness play in determining the ease or difficulty of a given text. Although it may seem that these concepts would be consistent across genre, Mesmer looks at the ways in which these factors can vary depending on the content area. For example, she notes how familiar words can take on new meanings depending on the subject or how the repetition of unfamiliar words across a passage can affect the ease of reading. And rather than assume that a single element, such as reading levels or lexiles, provides sufficient information for making an appropriate choice of text, she suggests using multiple factors, along with knowledge of students, to determine which material should be selected in particular instructional situations.

In Chapter 7, Jill Castek and Michael Manderino look at the role that digital literacies can play in expanding disciplinary learning. Digital literacies continue to serve as a general means of motivation and student engagement; however, Castek and Manderino argue that there are three unique aspects of digital texts and tools that make them powerful aids to student learning. To begin with, students may have greater amounts of experience and comfort interacting with technology than do many of their teachers. Because of this, as disciplinary knowledge is developed, students and teachers are likely to have increased interactions (bidirectionality). Second, when digital literacies are carefully and intentionally integrated into the instructional process, it can democratize the classroom, providing all students with the opportunity to contribute to the learning process. Third, given the myriad resources available, the focus of study can expand beyond that which is traditionally undertaken in the classroom. The chapter provides insight into the potentials and problems of these materials.

Next, students' ability to use writing as a means of conceptual development within disciplinary subjects is covered by Estanislado S. Barrera IV and Kim Skinner in Chapter 8. They discuss ways in which content teachers can use the reciprocal nature of reading and writing to support their students' learning across a range of subjects and as a means of building a better understanding of each. Specifically, Barrera and Skinner highlight the importance of creating a central question to encourage disciplinary writing in a meaningful way. They further introduce a multistep procedure (Moje, 2015) designed to assist both teachers and learners in this endeavor. The authors continue by highlighting a range of nonfiction text types, the unique features of differing genre, and the importance of identifying the specific writing strategies for particular types of text. In other words, Barrera and Skinner stress that teaching effective writing strategies is not a one-size-fits-all process; instead, they provide guidance for thinking about the uniqueness of each content area and how doing so can, correspondingly, help to improve students' writing.

Science texts are often a challenge in terms of their vocabulary, structure, and ideas, but they can be particularly problematic for English language learners (ELLs). In Chapter 9, Marco A. Bravo, Saúl I. Maldonado, and Jorge L. Solís focus on these challenges, along with ways to develop ELLs' conceptual knowledge in the sciences. Critically, this means that in addition to their reading and writing on the topic, students must have plentiful opportunities to engage in science-focused conversations. The authors go on to discuss the role both individual factors (i.e., English proficiency, prior knowledge, student personality) and text factors (i.e., figurative language, use of words with general and subject-specific meanings, science-specific text features) can play in student learning, along with ways to address each of these. By applying these suggestions, it becomes possible to create classroom environments that allow for fuller participation and greater science proficiency on the part of ELLs, as well as those who are native speakers.

Creating greater representation, and the engagement that derives from it, are at the center of Chapter 10, by Catherine Lammert, Stacia L. Long, and Jo Worthy. By choosing text sets from a broad range of books written by diverse authors who chronicle diverse lives and experiences, teachers can create learning communities that are more inclusive, as well as pedagogy that is culturally sustaining. One way to ensure all students have access to a given text is through a read-aloud; however, to be successful, this process must incorporate an active role for the students. To achieve this, Lammert et al. suggest making purposeful choices not only when determining a unit but also when contemplating the discussion and the written responses to the texts. In particular, it is essential that students are allowed to be the primary participants. By supporting students in their conversations, they can learn to think critically, and to listen and to respond respectfully to ideas that differ from their own. By creating such a space, teachers provide students with an opportunity to explore an expanded understanding of themselves and others.

Finally, in Chapter 11, Maria Grant, Diane Lapp, and Thomas DeVere Wolsey look at the way writing in school prepares students for the world of work. Although the dominant descriptive and argumentative essays used in schools develop the kind of thinking required to communicate information clearly and concisely, the type of writing required in the workplace is often much broader, incorporating a wide range of content and conceptual knowledge. Grant, Lapp, and Wolsey explored this discrepancy by speaking to 18 professionals across a range of fields to determine what types of writing they use most frequently at work and how well school prepared them for the writing they undertook on the job. The authors then analyzed responses from both the workplace experts and educators to think about refining writing instruction across an array of elements (e.g., purpose, features, precision). They further provide graphic organizers that can be used as a guide for helping learners clarify their written expression. In this way, classrooms can better assist students as they prepare for their future experiences in academics, work, or both.

Conclusion

As we have noted, instructional approaches that support the development of children's conceptual knowledge through oral and written language have a direct impact on their development of both constrained and unconstrained literacy skills. Applying these approaches flexibly across a range of settings, educators can make a positive difference in *all* of their students' literacy development. We consider the multiple threads discussed in this volume as providing useful insight into literacy instruction across both content and grades. However, we also recognize the need to implement these approaches in ways that do not further burden the professionals who have to deliver this content in a classroom. As such, each chapter has been designed to help classroom teachers, literacy specialists, and other school-based educators realize these various ideas in manageable ways. To aid this effort, each chapter also supports the shift from research to practice in closing sections called "Implications for Professional Learning" and "Questions for Discussion" to spur conversations with colleagues. We hope this book is informative in terms of thinking about literacy and useful for making effective changes to literacy instruction within the multidimensional schools that are part of an educator's life today.

REFERENCES

Alvermann, D. E., Unrau, N. J., Sailors, M., & Ruddell, R. B. (Eds.). (2019). *Theoretical models and processes of literacy.* New York: Routledge.

Ash, G. E., Kuhn, M. R., & Walpole, S. (2009). Analyzing "inconsistencies" in practice: Teachers' continued use of Round Robin Reading. *Reading and Writing Quarterly, 25,* 87–103.

Cazden, C. (2001). *Classroom discourse: The language of teaching and learning* (2nd ed.). Portsmouth, NH: Heinemann.

Cunningham, A. E., & Stanovich, K. E. (1998). What reading does for the mind. *American Educator, 22,* 1–8.

Gambrell, L. B., Malloy, J. A., Marinak, B. A., & Mazzoni, S. A. (2014). Evidence-based best practices for comprehensive literacy instruction in the age of the Common Core Standards. In L. B. Gambrell & L. M. Morrow (Eds.), *Best practices in literacy instruction* (5th ed., pp. 3–36). New York: Guilford Press.

Greene, P. (2018, July 12). What ever happened to Common Core? Retrieved from *www.forbes.com/sites/petergreene/2018/07/12/what-ever-happened-to-common-core/#6lc230723270*.

Hiebert, E. H. (Ed.). (2009). *Reading more, reading better: Solving problems in the teaching of literacy.* New York: Guilford Press.

Hirsch, E. D. (2003, Spring). Reading comprehension requires knowledge—of words and the world. *American Educator*, pp. 10–13, 16–22, 28–30.

Jones, J. S., Conradi, K., & Amendum, S. J. (2016). Matching interventions to reading needs: A case for differentiation. *The Reading Teacher, 70*(3), 307–316.

Manzo, K. K. (2009, March 4). Studies support benefits of educational TV for reading. *Education Week, 28*(23), 10.

Massey, D. D., & Heafner, T. L. (2004). Promoting reading comprehension in social studies. *Journal of Adolescent and Adult Literacy, 48*(1), 26–40.

Moje, E. B. (2015). Doing and teaching disciplinary literacy with adolescent learners. *Harvard Educational Review, 85*(2), 254–278.

Neuman, S. B., & Celano, D. C. (2012). *Giving our children a fighting chance: Poverty, literacy, and the development of information capital.* New York: Teachers College Press.

O'Connor, R. E., & Vadasy, P. F. (Eds.). (2011). *Handbook of reading interventions.* New York: Guilford Press.

Paris, S. G. (2005). Reinterpreting the development of reading skills. *Reading Research Quarterly, 40*(2), 184–202.

Reutzel, D. R., Jones, C. D., Fawson, P. C., & Smith, J. A. (2008). Scaffolded silent reading: A complement to guided repeated oral reading that works! *The Reading Teacher, 62*, 194–207.

Sparks, S. D. (2015, April 22). Research on quality of conversation holds deeper clues into word gap. *Education Week, 34*(28), 1, 11.

Stanovich, K. E. (1986). Matthew effects in reading: Some consequences of individual differences in the acquisition of literacy. *Reading Research Quarterly, 21*(4), 360–407.

U.S. Department of Education, Institute of Education Sciences, What Works Clearinghouse. (2012, June). WWC review of the report: The effectiveness of a program to accelerate vocabulary development in kindergarten. Retrieved from *http://whatworks.ed.gov*.

Whorrall, J., & Cabell, S. Q. (2016). Supporting children's oral language development in the preschool classroom. *Early Childhood Education Journal, 44*(4), 335–341.

CHAPTER 2

Developing Vocabulary Skills while Developing Conceptual Knowledge
Strategies from the PAVEd for Success Kindergarten and Prekindergarten Program

CLAIRE E. HAMILTON
PAULA J. SCHWANENFLUGEL

All words are pegs to hang ideas on.
—HENRY WARD BEECHER (1867)

Supporting and enhancing children's vocabulary development broadens their ideas about the world, extends their abilities to communicate their ideas with others, and expands their conceptual development. As noted by the chapter opening Beecher quote, vocabulary is a key to conceptual knowledge and instruction in broad oral language skills, including vocabulary, and can support reading for understanding in the early grades. The guidelines for explicit vocabulary instruction that we present in this chapter are based on the evidence regarding how children acquire new vocabulary words, how adults can scaffold and extend that acquisition and in turn children's conceptual knowledge, and how teachers have applied these strategies in their preschool and kindergarten classrooms. We developed these guidelines, which we call *PAVEd for Success,* based on the belief that effective programs for vocabulary instruction should be appropriate for diverse classroom settings, be taught by early childhood educators themselves, be explicit across multiple strategies designed for intentional planning and teaching, and be flexible enough to adapt to varied curricular approaches.

PAVEd for Success was developed out of research that we conducted with low-income, rural prekindergarten, ethnically and linguistically diverse children (Schwanenflugel et al., 2010); it has since been further evaluated with high-poverty kindergarten students (Goodson, Wolf, Bell, Turner, & Finney, 2010), and adapted and implemented in both urban Head Start programs and in intervention programs for deaf preschool children (Shirin, Creamer, Rivera, & Catalano, 2015). Our continued experiences watching teachers implement these practices has further enriched our understanding of how PAVEd for Success can be used in the varied early childhood settings that serve young children.

PAVEd for Success focuses on three major components for teachers to use in their classrooms: (1) strategies to engage children intentionally in conversations that extend their vocabulary, what we call *Building Bridges*; (2) an organized system for explicitly introducing and reinforcing targeted vocabulary words, referred to as *New V(ocabulary) E(nhancement)hicles* (New VEhicles); and (3) guidelines teachers use to reinforce and extend children's understanding of new vocabulary words through interactive reading, *CAR Quest* (Hamilton & Schwanenflugel, 2011).

Why Focus on Vocabulary?

Children who enter school with oral language issues and limited vocabulary often have reading problems later (DeThorne, Petrill, Schatschneider, & Cutting, 2010). By the time children are 2½ years of age, vocabulary size estimates indicate that those in the top quartile may have twice the number of words as those in the bottom (Mayor & Plunket, 2011). Standardized assessments of vocabulary show that children growing up in low-income, African American homes may have vocabulary levels as much as a full standard deviation below their peers raised in middle-class households (Campbell, Bell, & Keith, 2001; Champion, Hyter, McCabe, & Bland-Stewart, 2003). To put this in context, children with these vocabulary levels would fall decidedly in the "low-average" range and would benefit from intervention directly targeting vocabulary.

To be fair, there have been findings of bias in standardized vocabulary assessments, putting the meaning of these class and race differences in question (Restrepo et al., 2006; Webb, Cohen, & Schwanenflugel, 2008). Class differences in vocabulary knowledge are greatly ameliorated when considering only root words (peeling off any suffixes and prefixes; Biemiller & Slonim, 2001). Race differences disappear when children are asked to narrate a wordless storybook (a task more familiar to young children) and the diversity of words actually deployed during narration is determined (Lai & Schwanenflugel, 2016). Nor is the low vocabulary problem (if it is not a measurement artifact) relegated to children from low-income or African American families. As a result, early childhood teachers need to be alert to potential issues regarding students' overall level of vocabulary and oral language skills.

Building Bridges

The way caregivers talk to children may be partly responsible for the smaller vocabularies displayed by some children. In their much-cited study of caregiver language, Hart and Risley (1995) concluded that conversations between children and parents were the most influential contributors to vocabulary size at age 3. Simple linguistic features such as quantity of words, density of rare words, and diversity of words addressed to children by their caregivers are all related to vocabulary development (Pan, Rowe, Singer, & Snow, 2005; Weizman & Snow, 2001). Children whose parents often initiate conversations tend to have good vocabulary growth (Huttenlocher, Vasilyeva, Cymerman, & Levine, 2002). Parents who use a significant amount of decontextualized language (i.e., "language used in ways that eschew reliance on shared social and physical context in favor of reliance created through the language itself"; Snow, Cancino, De Temple, & Schley, 1991, p. 90), similar to the different features parents may use in structuring conversations when talking with their children on a telephone (decontextualized) versus those used when the family is sitting together for dinner (contextualized), also have children with greater expressive language (Curenton, Craig, & Flanigan, 2008).

Conversational Opportunities

Developing opportunities for conversations is a potentially powerful tool that teachers have for encouraging vocabulary. Early childhood educators too often overlook the practice of intentionally engaging young children in linguistically rich conversations in favor of reading books and direct instruction of vocabulary. In fact, even when they receive professional development explicitly targeting the practice, teachers may find that changing the way they engage in conversations with children can be difficult (Goodson et al., 2010; Piasta, Justice, Cabell, Wiggins, Turnbull, & Curenton, 2012). However, interventions focused solely on changing the quality and quantity of these conversations have had a dramatic impact on the development of children's vocabulary (Cabell, Justice, McGinty, & DeCoster, 2015; Ruston & Schwanenflugel, 2010).

Research suggests that preschool teachers seldom hold conversations with individual children in their classrooms, and students with poor language skills are particularly likely to be ignored (Kontos & Wilcox-Herzog, 1997). One observational study found that although preschool teachers spend a great deal of the school day talking to the whole class, only 10% of their time is spent conversing with individual children (Layzer, Goodson, & Moss, 1993) and the individual conversations that do occur are very brief and of low quality (Cabell et al., 2015). Furthermore, verbally savvy children are more likely to capture their teacher's attention during these spontaneous moments. Generally, when teachers hold these conversations, it does not appear to be intentional or planned. In our own work, we carried out substantial professional development addressing the issue of intentionally scheduling conversations with children, but only slightly over half the teachers carried it out, even when they were supported in this practice, and only approximately one-third sustained the practice over time (Schwanenflugel et al., 2010).

Good, vocabulary-rich conversations often occur during mealtime and free play (Cote, 20011). We have urged teachers to follow children into the play areas and elaborate on what children are seeing and doing through the Building Bridges component of our curriculum. We also suggested that teachers create structured play situations in which children have the opportunity to practice new vocabulary. We recall one kindergarten teacher who used her experiences as an international flight attendant in her teaching as a way to encourage language growth in her classroom in a high-poverty school. She created a *patisserie* in a corner of her classroom with some key kitchen-type items (*whisks, mixing bowls, measuring spoons,* etc.). The children were asked to help *cater* a wedding *reception.* She mentioned that the children had to *measure* the (pretend) *ingredients,* so that their *croissants* would be *light* and *flaky.* They were urged to *knead* the *dough,* so that their *baguettes* would rise. Needless to say, the children had many questions about the catering business, and it provided the teacher with many opportunities to use rich vocabulary. Indeed, research has shown that language growth is one of the consistent impacts of such experiences on children's development (Lillard et al., 2013).

The reality is that teacher participation during meals and free play is diminishing in prekindergarten and, to an even greater extent, in kindergarten these days. When such opportunities do occur, teachers often use them to undertake administrative tasks rather than to converse with children. In her informal Internet sampling of kindergarten daily schedules, Strauss (2014) noted that free play or structured play was hardly ever explicitly scheduled into the school day. Larger surveys paint a similar picture regarding the diminishing role of play in kindergarten (Miller & Almon, 2009). Without free play, opportunities for spontaneous acquisition of vocabulary might disappear also.

Conversational Impact

How do conversations impact vocabulary? While participating in conversations, children capitalize on what's available in the immediate world around them; that is, if they hear an unknown word, children tend to connect it to an unknown item in the nearby context, a process that has been called *Novel Name–Nameless Category*, or N3C (Mervis & Bertrand, 1994). They also use information about the speaker's focus. If children and adults are jointly focusing on something, an unknown word mentioned during the conversation enables the children to connect this new word to something around them. Children can make use of various linguistic cues to learn new words (Hirsh-Pasek, Golinkoff, Hennon, & Maguire, 2004); whether the unknown word is the right part of speech (e.g., "the _____"), in the sentence final position (e.g., as in "This ramp goes way up—yup, it is very *steep*") or merely emphasized (Clark, 2010), children can draw important inferences as to the word's meaning.

Often within a turn or two, children even attempt to use the new word (Clark, 2010). In one of our studies, we captured this moment between two prekindergartners and an adult conversation buddy trained to incorporate vocabulary into conversation (Ruston & Schwanenflugel, 2010):

> BUDDY: Larger? Hmm, what's another word for large? (*to himself*) How about now? (*Blows up a balloon.*) Should it be more *humongous*?
>
> CHILD 1: Yeah!
>
> BUDDY: (*Blows some more.*) Even more *humongous*! Even more *humongous*?
>
> CHILD 2: Make mine '*mungous*!

Research further promotes the idea that these conversational interactions should occur over multiple turns. Teachers should not monopolize the conversation, as they are often wont to do. Instead, they should encourage children to make contributions to the conversation. For example, teachers can ask open-ended questions as part of the conversation and prompt children to offer extended responses. They can encourage children to address other children's points, until this becomes routine. Justice, Jiang, and Strasser (2018) considered these communication-facilitating elements of teacher talk to be particularly important for vocabulary growth in preschool. Indeed, Dickinson and Porche (2011) found that when preschool teachers helped children extend conversations during free play (and elsewhere during the school day), children not only had larger vocabularies a year later but also better reading skills in fourth grade.

Key Components of Building Bridges

Conducting Conversations That Yield Benefits

The basics of Building Bridges are undertaken by the teacher during conversations with children. The specifics follow:

- The children should lead the conversation on topics that interest them to the extent possible, but teachers should encourage children to talk by asking open-ended questions, such as "Why X?," "How X?," "Tell me more about that." These kinds of prompts cannot be answered with a single word or by saying "yes" or "no." Teachers also need to wait for children to answer the questions posed—young children need more time to formulate a complex response.

- Teachers should model complex language along with linguistic recasting of students' statements. For example, if Jamaal says, "I Spider-man!" his teacher can respond by saying, "I can see that you are pretending to be Spiderman!" and essentially fill in all the words that were "missing" in Jamaal's sentence. The goal here is to be conversational, not corrective.

- Teachers should introduce words that are not part of the students' typical working vocabulary into the conversation. We call these "dime" words and use them to supplement children's conversations. In the example in the previous section, the vocabulary buddy used the word *humongous*, when he could have just said *big*. We urge teachers to use their intuition about this and point out that adults are usually quite good judges about whether children know a given word. Teachers should not let any perceived weaknesses in their own vocabulary hinder their attempts at introducing words into the conversation either—the simple fact that they are adults means they know more words than the average 4- or 5-year-old!

There are several domains in which preschool children's vocabularies tend to be rather sparse. Two of these areas are general category terms and category-specific terms. So, if a child says, "I want that chair," the teacher can respond by saying, "That's fine, they're all part of the classroom's *furniture* [a category term]. I guess you like *stools* [a category-specific term]." Another area is emotion and cognitive terms. If a child says, "I feel sad. I can't do this," the teacher can elaborate on this by saying, "Do you feel *glum* today? Do you *understand* why you feel that way? You just haven't *learned* how to do it quite yet. Don't *worry*. You will *master* it."

* Teachers should try to model good conversational skills and encourage students to use conversational practices. For example, teachers should not interrupt the child midturn. They should demonstrate interest and maintain children's topics, unless the topic has dried up. They should try to bring everyone in the group into the conversation.

Carrying Out Frequent Teacher–Student Conversations

Teachers should find times throughout the day when conversations with small groups of children can continue for at least 5 minutes. We have found that teachers who successfully implemented Building Bridges were those who intentionally scheduled the conversations directly into their school day.

Teachers scheduled Building Bridges conversations into their days in a variety of ways. Some teachers scheduled conversations as follow-up to activities that had unequal timing across small groups—perhaps following up on a mathematics activity they knew would not last that long. They knew that some children were early arrivers and others left late, and they held conversations during these classroom transitions. The children would look forward to these special one-on-one times with their teachers. Teachers also carried out conversations with groups of children during play times and art projects. They scheduled *Eat with the Teacher* days and *Walk with Me Recess* days. Some teachers even had an explicit Talking Center, where they parked their assistant or a volunteer. They created a group that comprised their quiet students by themselves, cycling these children into it and allowing them to undertake their own discussions. As any teacher knows, the talkers can monopolize the conversation, and this meant that the quiet students did not have to contend with their more talkative peers when grouped with one another.

For Building Bridges to be effective, each child should have at least three opportunities to engage in conversation with an adult every week, either alone or as part of a small group. The aim should be a total of 15 minutes of conversations per week for each child. To make use of all the adults in the classroom, teachers can provide other grown-ups with a quick training on the key components of the approach (noted earlier) and model how these conversations should go. In our work, we provided professional development to these additional adults ourselves. However, we found one of the dangers of using untrained adults is that their conversations can become extended versions of the vocabulary activities that occur in other parts of the curriculum, where the focus is merely on the topics of the week. If the children bring those topics up, that is fine, but the conversation about them should be natural rather than directly instructional. Those teachers who were able to schedule the Building Bridges conversations successfully within their curriculum were also able to make effective use of all the adults in the room (the teacher, the assistants, and volunteers).

Given the language input that children receive at home, is this kind of classroom practice really worth it? Research on this instruction says "yes." For example, Ruston and Schwanenflugel (2010) found that an intervention using only the Building Bridges component of the program had a tremendous impact on children's vocabularies. In that study, pre-kindergarten children received approximately 500 minutes of intentional conversations with an adult (called a Talking Buddy), distributed over 10 weeks rather than an entire school year as it was for PAVEd for Success. Not only did the program improve the standardized vocabulary assessment scores of the intervention children when compared to control children, but the children who initially began the intervention with lowest levels of vocabulary benefited more than their peers with more extensive word knowledge. So, these conversations are particularly valuable for enhancing the verbal skills of low-verbal children.

Explicit Vocabulary Enhancement Practices for Young Children: New VEhicles and CAR Quest

The language-rich conversations of Building Bridges are a way to expand children's conceptual and vocabulary knowledge implicitly by addressing children's interests and experiences. The PAVEd for Success approach also includes explicit and intentional means for teaching vocabulary. These explicit approaches, incorporated into vocabulary units designed around themes or topics, also support young learners' building of conceptual knowledge. Vocabulary programs that combine explicit (i.e., specific strategies that teach target vocabulary words) and implicit practices (e.g., shared book reading, complex conversations) for expanding vocabulary growth are more successful in supporting children's word learning (Gonzalez et al., 2014; Marulis & Neuman, 2010). Additionally, these more complex programs improve children's abilities to infer the meanings of new unknown words (Coyne et al., 2010) and their overall conceptual knowledge (Neuman, Newman, & Dwyer, 2011).

Themes, Topics, or Units

The choice of units or topics to best support vocabulary learning and conceptual knowledge is one that we believe is best made by teachers themselves, based on the context of their program and their individual classroom. They can use their knowledge of the diversity of the children served, the community in which they are located, the overall curricular approach (including district or program standards), as well as the evolving interests of the children themselves as a source for constructing thematic units. Topics drawn from science and social studies content areas are especially well suited to vocabulary instruction, because they offer a range of content-specific and typically unfamiliar vocabulary words already organized within a conceptual framework (Gonzalez et al., 2014; Hamilton & Schwanenflugel, 2011; Leung, 2008; Neuman, Kaefer, & Pinkam, 2014). The key to choosing a theme for a vocabulary-boosting unit is identifying topics that are highly likely to promote vocabulary learning. There are many areas worth exploring in early childhood classrooms that may not be ideal for vocabulary instruction. For example, many of the early childhood programs in Claire E. Hamilton's community, located near the Springfield, Massachusetts, home of Dr. Seuss, have units that focus on the many wonderful books written by him.

These units are useful for teaching many early literacy skills, including those related to decoding print, or narrative structure; however, a unit based on these books is less likely to support vocabulary learning because of the author's use of words, many of which are made up. In contrast, apple production (a major local crop) is another typical focus of units in this community, and a good one around which to construct a vocabulary unit. These units typically focus on science topics related to seasons and plant growth or social studies themes centered on farms and food production, topics that are more likely to include vocabulary words that are unfamiliar to the students.

Unit-based vocabulary teaching is easily integrated into the approaches most commonly used in early childhood curricula; that is, once a content area or topic is identified, children's picture books related to the topic or theme are selected for shared reading sessions, and several classroom lessons or activities are planned to provide children with extended exploration of the concepts and ideas that are the focus of their study. Designing vocabulary units differs from other instructional approaches, because teaching vocabulary is the central goal—and the theme or topic is chosen with an eye toward the vocabulary opportunities it affords. Activities that teach these new and unfamiliar words are intentionally embedded in the structure of the unit. Vocabulary instruction guides the storybook choices teachers make, as well as identification of the specific vocabulary words on which to focus. Even the classroom activities and lessons are designed with the goal of providing multiple opportunities for children to learn and use their new words.

Choosing Theme-Related Books and Identifying Target Vocabulary Words

Picture books have long been an avenue for children to access the more sophisticated but less familiar words that are the basis, or "new vehicles," for building their vocabulary. Since picture books offer a rich source of unfamiliar vocabulary (Chamberlain & Leal, 1999), they are unlike early reader books with predictable text. As a result, teachers are likely to engage in more linguistically complex conversations with children as they read picture books (Dickinson, Hofer, Barnes, & Grifenhagen, 2014). Picture books that directly relate to the unit theme and ones that represent a variety of genres, including expository (informational) texts and fictional narratives, are particularly good vocabulary-building options. Even informational alphabet or counting books can be relevant choices. For example, the book *Firefighters A to Z* (Demarest, 2001) contains great theme-related words, such as *helmet, hydrant, nozzle,* and *pickax,* that can easily be incorporated into a community helper theme. By including different genres of books, teachers not only expose students to different styles of narrative but also increase the chances of identifying good vocabulary (Baker et al., 2013). Expository texts often offer more content-based options for vocabulary learning, while storybooks afford a narrative context that is useful for organizing new information.

When designing a vocabulary unit, teachers should choose two picture books that, between them, provide 10 unfamiliar vocabulary words and are the focus for identifying target words. Teachers should also include other books that relate to the unit, so that children can see their new vocabulary words in varied contexts. For example, for a unit based on winter, a teacher could include Jan Brett's *The Mitten* (1989), a classic folktale about a boy losing and then finding his mitten in the winter snow, and *Winter,* a wildlife seasons book (Hirschi, 1990), as the two focal vocabulary books, plus *The Big Snow* (Hader & Hader, 1948) and *Snowy Day* (Keats, 1962) as supplemental storybooks. These books represent different genres and include a range of potentially unfamiliar theme-related vocabulary words.

Identifying 10 Weekly Target Vocabulary Words

What words make good target vocabulary words for children to learn? There are no definitive rules for selecting individual words or even lists of the specific vocabulary words children should be taught (Wasik, Hindman, & Snell, 2016). We think that teachers should identify "dime" words (as discussed earlier); these words are found infrequently in books or conversations, are useful across a variety of situations or domains (Beck, McKeown, & Kucan, 2013), and expand children's understanding of the topic or theme. We have sometimes been initially bewildered by teachers' choices of a target vocabulary word because, to us, a word such as *triangle* seems too simple for prekindergarten children. Our observations and discussions with teachers, however, continue to reinforce the idea that teachers have a good sense as to what words are likely to be unfamiliar for their students (Vuattoux, Japel, Dion, & Dupere, 2014).

The words teachers select as unfamiliar should be introduced to the children using picture cards, so it is important to choose target words that represent concrete objects that can be easily depicted. When referring back to the unit on winter we discussed earlier, for example, we recognize that there are well over 10 potential vocabulary words in the theme books, *The Mitten* and *Winter*. However, only some of these words would be good target vocabulary. For example, *den, burrow,* and *cocoon* are nouns and therefore concrete; furthermore, they relate to the theme and can be easily depicted. And while *glisten* and *crunching* are equally likely to be unfamiliar, they are difficult to depict. On the other hand, the word *ptarmigan* is an easy-to-depict noun that is unfamiliar even to some adults; however, it is not a word that is likely to be useful across a variety of domains and would therefore be less useful for children to learn.

Providing Student-Friendly Quick Definitions and Creating Picture Cards

One of the challenges teachers face when introducing vocabulary words involves presenting a clear definition of the words as they are introduced or read (Dickinson & Porche, 2011). It helps if teachers write a child-friendly, simple explanation or definition for each target vocabulary word to which they can refer when talking to their students: "A *den* is the place where a bear sleeps in the winter"; or "An *icicle* is ice that hangs down from trees or houses." Note that these definitions are unlike real dictionary definitions in some respects. For example, we have avoided using difficult vocabulary within the definition itself. Nor do the definitions capture every instance of the word; they are instead designed to serve as an initial "hook" into the word, one that will be built upon incrementally over children's lives. Planning ahead will make the task of presenting a child-friendly definition easier when it is implemented later in the classroom. As a result, when a word is first introduced, teachers can just refer to these definitions as the initial explanation of the word's meaning.

Providing picture cards or props as part of either interactive reading or explicit vocabulary instruction is an effective general practice in helping children gain an initial understanding of an unfamiliar vocabulary word (Marulis & Neuman, 2010; Wasik & Bond, 2001) and is specifically recommended for dual-language learners (Baker et al., 2014). In the PAVEd for Success program, we also include picture cards to serve as useful points of reference throughout the unit; however, we introduce each target vocabulary word paired with pictures of familiar objects and words (this is explained below). Teachers should create or find pictures that depict each of the 10 unfamiliar words, as well as a set of 20 picture cards that depict known or familiar words (e.g., *sock, cat, ball, house*).

Thankfully, given the available Web-based teacher resources, this is not a daunting task. Teachers can easily find images through Creative Commons (*https://creativecommons.org*) or a vast array of online teacher resources (see also Hamilton & Schwanenflugel, 2011, for picture card resources). Writing the simple, kid-friendly definitions on the picture cards is also a very useful way to help all the adults who participate in the classroom activities remember and use these definitions.

New VEhicles

With the vocabulary unit designed, the theme or topic chosen, the target vocabulary words identified, and picture cards and definitions in place, we can now see what New VEhicles looks like in practice.

In presenting words for the first time, the PAVEd for Success program takes advantage of a strategy that children have for word learning, because children tend to use their knowledge of familiar words to quickly identify the referent of an unfamiliar word (i.e., the N3C strategy); in this case, the teacher essentially plays a guessing game with the picture cards and presents to children pictures of two objects represented by known words and a picture of an object represented by a target vocabulary word.

Following the example of the winter unit, the teacher could hold up three picture cards—a card with picture of an *icicle,* a card with a picture of a *ball,* and a third card with a picture of a *sock.* The teacher then asks the children, "Which one is an *icicle?*" Words like *ball* and *sock* are familiar, and most children are likely to be immediately successful at this task; even the children who may not respond verbally are likely to make the connection between the picture of the unknown object and the new vocabulary word—the word *icicle* is associated with the new picture. This is *fast mapping,* or the ability of young children to use linguistic and physical context to quickly narrow down the likely meaning of a new word. We have seen teachers introduce the words by selecting three children to serve as "picture card holders," who stand in the front of the room, each holding a card (one holding *icicle,* another *sock,* and another *ball*). Then, when she merely asks the class to guess the one that is the picture of the *icicle,* virtually all the children will be great guessers. Children also need to understand the basic meaning of the vocabulary word, so once the N3C presentation for the word is completed, the teacher reads the quick definition she has created for it. Teachers introduce each of the new target vocabulary words in this way as they begin each unit.

On subsequent days, the focus should probably be on the vocabulary cards alone. Teachers simply display the vocabulary cards, reinforcing the word meaning by supplying a quick definition again. Alternatively, they can just ask children to provide the word labels for the vocabulary cards. Teachers will find many uses for these picture cards. We have observed some teachers displaying the cards on an easel or bulletin board throughout the unit. Some teachers include the cards as sorting or matching games for small-group activities. Others provide copies of the picture cards for children to use in creating word books; the children copy down the words from the vocabulary cards. Teachers have also placed picture cards, along with the unit's picture books, in the book corner, so children can look at them during their independent time.

We have found New VEhicles to be the best strategy for introducing the target vocabulary words. This way of explicitly teaching vocabulary lets children quickly learn the new words by capitalizing on the fast mapping strategies they already possess. However, New VEhicles, by itself, is only the beginning. For children to truly own these new words as "pegs to hang ideas on," they will need more extensive experience with the contexts in which these words are used and multiple opportunities to practice using these new words themselves.

Interactive Book Reading and CAR Quest

Interactive reading is a standard practice in early childhood classrooms that embeds vocabulary in meaningful contexts. Shared book reading, as typically practiced by teachers, yields the richest mixture of academic language elements and talk about vocabulary used naturally by teachers and children across the day in their conversations (Dickinson et al., 2014). Furthermore, incorporating elements of interactive book reading, such as teacher prompts and questions (Whitehurst & Lonigan, 1988), encourages children to be more engaged in this process. When interactive reading around a theme is paired with deliberate planning for vocabulary instruction, it is likely to support even deeper conceptual understanding for children (Baker et al., 2013). This intentional focus means thinking about how books are read, for example, whether book reading occurs in large- or small-group contexts, and the frequency of book reading sessions.

Research on shared book reading provides evidence that interaction around book reading alone provides modest gains in children's literacy skills. However, interactive reading in combination with explicit teaching of new vocabulary provides even more benefits (Marulis & Neuman, 2010). Read-alouds that prompt children to actively engage with the text, that require them to go beyond the immediate information presented in the text, and that ask children to make connections between the text and their own experiences are recommended practice for young learners, especially those who are dual-language learners (Baker et al., 2014; Foorman et al., 2016). Although there are various approaches to interactive book reading, we have found that teachers can easily organize book reading prompts using CAR (*Competence, Abstract,* and *Relate*), a simple acronym that represents different types of questions.

Competence questions are literal questions that relate directly to the text (e.g., "Where is the baby bear sleeping?") and can elicit a verbal answer or a simple pointing gesture. Competence questions allow children to be successful and may engage reluctant participants to join in a book conversation. Those who have language disorders, dual-language learners, as well as children who are somewhat shy socially, may feel more comfortable responding to questions for which there is a clear answer. Competence questions also provide children with much needed practice in *school talk,* or the common discourse patterns teachers adopt in classroom settings, and in building the literal understanding of the text needed to engage in more inferential thinking (van Kleeck, 2008).

Abstract questions are more challenging and prompt children to think more deeply about the text, make inferences, and support their conceptual knowledge; again, thinking about our winter unit, questions such as "Why are the squirrels lining their nests with sticks and leaves?" or "Do you think all the animals could really fit in Baba's mitten?" would provide specific examples for the books *Winter* (Hirschi, 1990) and *The Mitten* (Brett, 1989).

Relate questions are intended to motivate children to make connections between the events and ideas in the text and their own lives and experiences. These questions encourage children to use their prior knowledge about the world around them as a foundation for understanding new concepts and ideas. Questions such as "How do we keep our pets warm in the winter?" or "Do you have any mittens at home?" can lead to very animated classroom discussions.

Teachers have sometimes expressed concerns to us that too many questions interrupt the story narrative and may be distracting. We have found that incorporating six questions (two each of competence, abstract, and relate prompts) strikes a good balance in maintaining the narrative flow of the text and encouraging interaction. Teachers also find it helpful to review the books and prepare their prompts in advance of the book reading sessions. Writing the prompts on sticky notes ahead of time and inserting them into the book is an easy way to keep track of what questions to ask as the book is read. (It is also worth noting that not all read-alouds need to follow this format; there can be time to simply listen to some of the additional books that connect to the unit or other books that are simply chosen for enjoyment.)

As teachers and parents know, children love to hear stories read over and over and over again. The frequency of book reading is associated with children's increased understanding of unfamiliar vocabulary words across repeated book reading sessions and in overall gains in their general vocabulary skills (Sénéchal, 1997). We recommend reading each book three times: twice as a large-group activity and once as a small-group activity. The affordances of large-group instruction, such as opportunities for more academic language use and discourse (Marulis & Neuman, 2010), may be tempered by the fact that instruction in larger groups also features more teacher talk focusing on behavior management (Dickinson & Porche, 2011). For younger learners, especially those who may begin with lower vocabulary levels or fewer oral language skills, those who may be dual-language learners, or those who have difficulty focusing in larger settings, the benefits of reading aloud are amplified by small-group settings (Whitehurst et al., 1994).

Extension Activities

Converging lines of research suggest that vocabulary learning is dependent on providing multiple opportunities for children to use their new vocabulary words across many settings. Children benefit most when teachers find ways to encourage the use of new and unfamiliar vocabulary words in lots of different situations. Extension activities undertaken as part of small-group work periods, learning centers, science and social studies blocks, or free play allow this to occur. Extension activities should be planned in ways that relate to the overall unit's theme and provide opportunities for children to practice their new words. And prekindergarten and kindergarten teachers who adapt their units directly from social studies or science standards may be able to draw on activities included as part of science kits or social studies curricula.

The New VEhicle picture cards we discussed earlier in the chapter can be incorporated into extension activities as well. Examples include vocabulary Bingo games using the same pictures, vocabulary centers in which children illustrate words and make their own vocabulary books, or matching games during independent work time. Early childhood educators working in classrooms with 3- and 4-year-olds may also incorporate extension activities into their learning centers and outside play times. book centers may include target books, picture cards, and prop baskets. Playground walks may include a search in nature for related, new vocabulary words. A vocabulary show-and-tell table can be developed around materials children bring from home and include items that represent target vocabulary words. Sensory tables may also include manipulatives that relate to individual words (e.g., *mittens*) and the theme or unit.

Though not a classroom extension activity, we also suggest that teachers think of ways that families can be involved in vocabulary learning. In our studies, teachers have shared the target vocabulary with families and have suggested activities that may be done at home as a way of supplementing classroom activities. The teachers have further posted examples of classroom activities on the school website as a way of communicating their emphasis on vocabulary. The more opportunities a child has to use and make connections with new vocabulary words, the more the child will own those new vocabulary words.

We have found that vocabulary units work well when they are implemented over a 5-day thematic period. The sample schedule in Figure 2.1 illustrates how teachers can put together all the components of the program—Building Bridges, New VEhicles, and CAR Quest activities—into a unit that can be carried out within a 1-week time frame. On a given day, teachers easily can include both New VEhicles and the large-group CAR Quest book reading as part of morning meetings or circle time. We have seen that teachers typically schedule Building Bridges and small-group CAR Quest as part of small-group work time; this can occur either during or before the vocabulary extension activities, as a transition to other small-group activity times, on the playground, during lunchtime, or as part of the class's arrival and departure transitions. The teachers we see who are most successful are those who carefully plan how and when they will implement each practice both across the unit as a whole and within the daily schedule.

PAVEd for Success in Practice

Let's take a look at two classrooms (all names are pseudonyms) in action—first Ms. Sanchez's kindergarten classroom, then Mr. Josh's preschool class of 3- and 4-year-olds.

Days 1–2
• Introduce target vocabulary words using N3C (novel name–nameless category) picture cards, and child-friendly definitions each day. • Read book 1 using CAR Quest, comprehension question strategies, a minimum of three times in large and small groups. • Provide daily extension activity incorporating the use of the target vocabulary words. • Conduct Building Bridges, teacher–child conversation strategies, sessions with small groups of children.

Days 3–4
• Query target vocabulary using picture cards each day. • Read book 2 using CAR Quest a minimum of three times in large and small groups. • Provide daily extension activity incorporating the use of the target vocabulary words. • Conduct Building Bridges sessions with small groups of children.

Day 5
• Query target vocabulary using picture cards each day. • Read an additional theme-related picture book using CAR Quest. • Provide daily extension activity that incorporates the use of the target vocabulary words. • Conduct Building Bridges sessions with small groups of children.

FIGURE 2.1. Sample schedule for a 5-day vocabulary unit for a typical classroom.

Example 1: Ms. Sanchez's Kindergarten Classroom

Ms. Sanchez teaches in a rural school district serving a high proportion of dual-language learners. All of the elementary teachers, including those teaching kindergarten, are expected to follow a structured curriculum for both science and social studies.

Preparation for Kindergarten PAVEd for Success

This week, Ms. Sanchez has decided to integrate the vocabulary unit into her science curriculum and has designed a unit around the theme of winter animal habitats. Because it is already part of the district's science curriculum, she can draw on the science kits, trade books, and teacher resources her district provides as resources for these content areas. She has chosen two books with vocabulary in mind, *The Mitten* (Brett, 1989), and *Winter* (Hirschi, 1990), and has identified 10 target vocabulary words within these books that relate to the science theme (e.g., *den, burrow, cocoon*). These will serve as her New VEhicles targets. She has used Internet resources to find pictures for these words, and a set of additional picture cards for words that children already know for the N3C activity. She has created quick definitions she can use when introducing vocabulary. She will conclude the unit by reading *The Big Snow* (Hader & Hader, 1948) for Friday's longer cozy story time. She writes down CAR Quest questions on sticky notes and inserts them into the books.

Ms. Sanchez has adapted three activities included in the science kits as vocabulary-boosting extension activities to be carried out during the afternoon small-group science block. These extension activities include a matching game in which children pair an animal with its winter habitat, vocabulary Bingo based on the target vocabulary words, and a worksheet from the science kit. She also schedules the small-group book-reading times for her sixth-grade reading buddies and the vocabulary extension activities.

Ms. Sanchez decides to schedule the Building Bridges conversations as part of the small-group literacy lessons to even out the timing of her small-group activities. Her assistant will carry out these conversations. On her school's class website, Ms. Sanchez posts the target vocabulary words and quick definitions, along with the activities students will be doing in math, reading, and social studies as a way to make home–school connections.

Kindergarten PAVEd for Success in Action

Children begin trickling into the classroom; some come directly after arriving on the bus, others a bit later, after eating school breakfast. During this time, Ms. Sanchez conducts Building Bridges conversations with a small group of children, while others individually complete their math work. When the morning bell rings, Ms. Sanchez calls her students to the morning meeting. She takes attendance, completes the lunch count, and calls the vocabulary helpers to the front of the room. She hands Lia, Alejandra, and Alang the picture cards, which they hold up as she does a review of the target vocabulary words using the N3C New VEhicles strategy.

The vocabulary helpers line the whiteboard with the vocabulary picture cards. Ms. Sanchez reminds everyone to listen carefully as she reads *Winter* and do a thumbs up if they hear one of the week's target words. As she reads, she pauses to ask the CAR Quest prompts she has written on sticky notes and placed in the book. When she reaches the prompt "Can you find the *owl* in the tree?" she calls on Lena, one of her quiet students. Lena often seems less confident about participating in class discussions, but this is a task she can do, and Lena cautiously points her finger and says quietly "There." When Ms. Sanchez asks, "How do we keep our pets warm in winter?" hands shoot up. When she finishes reading, she reviews the daily schedule, reminding the children that after lunch, the sixth-grade reading buddies will be coming during small-group work time. During small-group time, Ms. Sanchez will begin her small-group literacy skills sessions with a Building Bridge session. To combine these activities with literacy, she includes the weekly vocabulary as words that children will need to recognize when written and spelled. The science buddies will reread *Winter* with two or three children, using the CAR Quest prompts posted in the book, then they will all play a game of vocabulary Bingo.

Example 2: Mr. Josh's Preschool Classroom

Mr. Josh, as he prefers to be called, is the teacher of a preschool class that is part of a large early childhood program in an urban area. The teachers in Mr. Josh's program use a more child-centered approach to planning, one modeled on the project approach (Katz & Chard, 2000). Note that his extension activities capture the developmental status of the preschoolers.

Preparation for Preschool Unit PAVEd for Success

Mr. Josh has decided to focus on the topic *Dental Health*, sparked by the fact that his high-poverty school would soon be visited by the mobile dental health van. He chose two books, *Make Way for Tooth Decay* (Katz, 2002) and *Just Going to the Dentist* (Mayer, 2001), as his shared reading books and identified target vocabulary words with which children might be unfamiliar, including *dental floss, X-ray, hygienist, cavity, saliva,* and *patient*, among others. He has put these books in the book area and included *Sugarbug Doug* (Magleby, 2008), which he will read on the last day of the unit. The preschool teachers in his school collaborate on and share project resources, which makes it easier to prepare for the vocabulary units. There is already a stock of picture cards with known words in the teacher resources library. He created the target vocabulary word cards for the *Dentist* unit using images he had found on the Internet. He made several copies of the picture cards, along with the printed child-friendly definitions, to display in the various centers in his classroom and to serve a reference for the children, himself, and the assistant teacher.

Mr. Josh also writes CAR Quest questions on sticky notes that both he and his assistant will use in large- and small-group readings. He creates a Dentist Corner in his room and prints out Google images of teeth X-rays. As an activity, he will have the children draw cavities on them in brown marker. He will let children pretend to be the dentist, the hygienist, and the patient. He will equip the corner with dental floss, mouthwash (colored water), and the X-rays. For the sensory area, he cuts off the bottoms of soda bottles to serve as teeth when placed upside down. Children can practice brushing soap suds (soap crayons) off with toothbrushes and floss (white yarn) to prevent cavities. His assistant will carry out Building Bridges conversations in this center, and he will read the books to children in small groups. Additional times for Building Bridges are scheduled for morning and afternoon snack times. Mr. Josh has also posted the project website and a list of the target vocabulary words by the children's cubbies. During the week, he will add photos of the children taking part in the various extension activities, so that parents can see what their children are doing.

Conclusion

In this chapter, we have presented specific strategies and techniques that early childhood educators can adopt to support children's vocabulary development intentionally and explicitly; in turn, this expands children's conceptual understanding of the world around them. Unfortunately, the research evidence is clear that although well-designed opportunities for talk are priceless for developing young minds, an explicit focus on vocabulary and oral language skills is not a common practice in most early childhood programs (Neuman & Dwyer, 2009; Neuman & Roskos, 2005) and remains a serious challenge for early childhood educators (Snow & Matthews, 2016).

In PAVEd for Success, we have tackled this challenge by developing guidelines for explicit vocabulary instruction based on the research about how children learn, and have also built on the implicit practices valued by early childhood educators—talking with children, reading books, and thinking about ideas. We have had the opportunity to develop and replicate the program in prekindergarten classrooms in high-poverty settings in northeastern Georgia and have worked with others to implement the program in kindergarten classrooms in the Mississippi Delta. The findings in both these studies indicate that the PAVEd for Success program improves the vocabulary skills of the participating children when compared to children who receive their typical classroom curriculum (Goodson et al., 2010; Schwanenflugel et al., 2010). Critically, the approach also improves children's academic knowledge (Goodson et al., 2010). Furthermore, in each study, we see that teachers have been able to implement the program successfully in classrooms for young children. Taken together, these studies provide the empirical base that is desirable when deciding to implement a particular approach for improving language and vocabulary skills. Doing so can assist all the children in the classroom in developing the type of word and conceptual knowledge that may serve as a base for their later academic understanding.

● IMPLICATIONS FOR PROFESSIONAL LEARNING ●

- Both implicit and explicit instructional techniques can be used in preschool and kindergarten classrooms to teach vocabulary and build conceptual knowledge.

- Placing an emphasis on vocabulary in preschool and kindergarten classrooms leads to noticeable improvements in children's vocabularies. This is particularly important for children who arrive at school with vocabularies that do not match academic requirements.

- Creating opportunities for child-focused conversations with small groups of children throughout the week is beneficial for vocabulary growth. Conversations should include teacher turns that are rich in vocabulary and linguistic complexity, and that encourage the same in children.

- Including vocabulary-rich, child-centered topics encourages vocabulary learning in children. These topics should be elaborated on through the use of vocabulary-rich books in teacher read-alouds and hands-on extension activities that allow practice of new words and build children's conceptual knowledge.

QUESTIONS FOR DISCUSSION

1. Where in your classroom schedule can you find several 5-minute blocks in which you can hold small-group teacher–child conversations?

2. Which topics in your curriculum might make good ones for targeting vocabulary?

3. Find a favorite informational text you currently use during classroom read-alouds. Which words might serve as good vocabulary words to target (i.e., they are depictable, lend themselves to hands-on activities, and relate to the topic or theme)? Can you find another informational text or an expository text on the same topic that also has difficult vocabulary?

4. How can you schedule several interactive, small-group read-aloud sessions during the school day?

REFERENCES

Baker, S., Lesaux, N., Jayanthi, M., Dimino, J., Proctor, C. P., Morris, J., et al. (2014). *Teaching academic content and literacy to English learners in elementary and middle school* (NCEE 2014-4012). Washington, DC: National Center for Education Evaluation and Regional Assistance, Institute of Education Sciences, U.S. Department of Education. Retrieved from *http://ies.ed.gov/ncee/wwc/publications_reviews.aspx.*

Baker, S. K., Santoro, L. E., Chard, D. J., Fien, H., Park, Y., & Otterstedt, J. (2013). An evaluation of an explicit read aloud intervention taught in whole-classroom formats in first grade. *Elementary School Journal, 113*(3), 331–358.

Beck, I. L., McKeown, M. G., & Kucan, L. (2013). *Bring words to life: Robust vocabulary instruction.* New York: Guilford Press.

Beecher, H. W. (1867). *Prayers from Plymouth pulpit.* New York: A. C. Armstrong & Son. Online digitized version available from the Princeton Theological Seminary Library at *https://archive.org/details/prayersfromplymo00beec.*

Biemiller, A., & Slonim, N. (2001). Estimating root word vocabulary growth in normative and advantaged populations: Evidence for a common sequence of vocabulary acquisition. *Journal of Educational Psychology, 93*(3), 498–520.

Brett, J. (1989). *The mitten.* New York: G. P. Putnam's Sons. (Anniversary edition 2009)

Cabell, S. Q., Justice, L. M., McGinty, A. S., DeCoster, J., & Forston, L. D. (2015). Teacher–child conversations in preschool classrooms: Contributions to children's vocabulary development. *Early Childhood Research Quarterly, 30*(Pt. A), 80–92.

Campbell, J. M., Bell, S. K., & Keith, L. K. (2001) Concurrent validity of the Peabody Picture Vocabulary Test–Third Edition as an intelligence and achievement screener for low SES African American children. *Assessment, 8*(1), 85–94.

Chamberlain, J., & Leal, D. (1999). Caldecott Medal books and readability levels: Not just "picture" books. *The Reading Teacher, 52*(8), 898–902.

Champion, T. B., Hyter, Y. D., McCabe, A., & Bland-Stewart, L. M. (2003). "A matter of vocabulary": Performances of low-income African American Head Start children on the Peabody Picture Vocabulary Test–III. *Communication Disorders Quarterly, 24*(3), 121–127.

Clark, E. V. (2010). Adult offer, word-class, and child uptake in early lexical acquisition. *First Language, 30*(3–4), 250–269.

Cote, L. R. (2011). Language opportunities during mealtimes in preschool classrooms. In D. K. Dickinson & P. O. Tabors (Eds.), *Beginning literacy with language: Young children learning at home and school* (pp. 205–222). Baltimore: Brookes.

Coyne, M. D., McCoach, D. B., Loftus, S., Zipoli, R., Ruby, M., Crevecoeur, Y., et al. (2010). Direct and extended vocabulary instruction in kindergarten: Investigating transfer effects. *Journal of Research on Educational Effectiveness, 3*(2), 93–120.

Curenton, S. M., Craig, M. J., & Flanigan, N. (2008). Use of decontextualized talk across story contexts: How oral storytelling and emergent reading can scaffold children's development. *Early Education and Development, 19,* 161–187.

De Thorne, L. S., Petrill, S. A., Schatschneider, C., & Cutting, L. (2010). Conversational language use as a predictor of early reading development: Language history as a moderating variable. *Journal of Speech, Language, and Hearing Research, 53*(1), 209–223.

Demarest, C. L. (2001). *Firefighters A to Z.* New York: Scholastic.

Dickinson, D. K., Hofer, K. G., Barnes, E. M., & Grifenhagen, J. F. (2014) Examining teachers' language in Head Start classrooms from a system linguistics approach. *Early Childhood Research Quarterly, 29,* 231–244.

Dickinson, D. K., & Porche, M. V. (2011). Relation between language experiences in preschool classrooms and children's kindergarten and fourth-grade language and reading abilities. *Child Development, 82*(3), 870–886.

Foorman, B., Beyler, N., Borradaile, K., Coyne, M., Denton, C. A., Dimino, J., et al. (2016). *Foundational skills to support reading for understanding in kindergarten through 3rd grade* (NCEE 2016-4008). Washington, DC: National Center for Education Evaluation and Regional Assistance, Institute of Education Sciences, U.S. Department of Education. Retrieved from *http://whatworks.ed.gov.*

Gonzalez, J. E., Pollard-Durodola, S., Simmons, D. C., Taylor, A. B., Davis, M. J., Fogarty, M., et al. (2014). Enhancing preschool children's vocabulary: Effects of teacher talk before, during, and after shared reading. *Early Childhood Research Quarterly, 29,* 214–226.

Goodson, B., Wolf, A., Bell, S., Turner, H., & Finney, P. B. (2010). *The effectiveness of a Program to Accelerate Vocabulary Development in Kindergarten (VOCAB): Kindergarten Final Evaluation Report* (NCEE 2010-4014). Washington, DC: National Center for Education Evaluation and Regional Assistance.

Hader, B., & Hader, E. (1948). *The big snow.* New York: Macmillan.

Hamilton, C. E., & Schwanenflugel, P. J. (2011). *PAVEd for Success: Building vocabulary and language development in young learners.* Baltimore: Brookes.

Hart, B., & Risley, T. R. (1995). *Meaningful differences in the everyday experience of young American children.* Baltimore: Brookes.

Hirschi, R., with photographs by Mangelsen, T. D. (1990). *Winter.* New York: Cobblehill Books.

Hirsh-Pasek, K., Golinkoff, R., Hennon, E. A., & Maguire, M. J. (2004). Hybrid theories at the frontier of developmental psychology: The emergenist coalition of word learning as a case in point. In D. G. Hall & S. R. Waxman (Eds.), *Weaving a lexicon* (pp. 173–204). Cambridge, MA: MIT Press.

Huttenlocher, J., Vasilyeva, M., Cymerman, E., & Levine, S. (2002). Language input and child syntax. *Cognitive Psychology, 45*(3), 337–374.

Justice, L. M., Jiang, H., & Strasser, K. (2018). Linguistic environment of preschool classrooms: What dimensions support children's growth? *Early Childhood Research Quarterly, 42,* 79–82.

Katz, B. (2002). *Make way for tooth decay*. New York: Scholastic.

Katz, L. G., & Chard, S. C. (2000). *Engaging children's minds: The project approach* (2nd ed.). Stamford, CT: Ablex.

Keats, E. J. (1962). *The snowy day*. New York: Penguin Books.

Kontos, S., & Wilcox-Herzog, A. (1997). Teachers' interactions with children: Why are they so important? Research in review. *Young Children, 52*(2), 4–12.

Lai, S. A., & Schwanenflugel, P. J. (2016). Validating the use of D for measuring lexical diversity in low-income kindergarten children. *Language, Speech, and Hearing Services in Schools, 47*(3), 225–235.

Layzer, J., Goodson, B. D., & Moss, M. (1993). *Life in preschool: Final report of the Observational Study of Early Childhood Programs*. Cambridge, MA: Abt Associates.

Leung, C. B. (2008). Preschoolers' acquisition of scientific vocabulary through repeated read-aloud events, retellings, and hands-on science activities. *Reading Psychology, 29*, 165–193.

Lillard, A. S., Lerner, M. D., Hopkins, E. J., Dore, R. A., Smith, E. D., & Palmquist, C. M. (2013). The impact of pretend play on children's development: A review of the evidence. *Psychological Bulletin, 139*(1), 1–34.

Magleby, B. (2008). *Sugarbug Doug*. North Charleston, SC: Booksurge.

Marulis, L. M., & Neuman, S. B. (2010). The effects of vocabulary intervention on young children's word learning: A meta-analysis. *Review of Educational Research, 80*(3), 300–335.

Mayer, M. (2001). *Just going to the dentist*. New York: Random House.

Mayor, J., & Plunkett, K. (2011). A statistical estimate of infant and toddler vocabulary size from CDI analysis. *Developmental Science, 14*(4), 769–785.

Mervis, C. B., & Bertrand, J. (1994). Acquisition of the novel name–nameless category (N3C) principle. *Child Development, 65*(6), 1646–1662.

Miller, E., & Almon, J. (2009). *Crisis in the kindergarten: Why children need to play in school*. College Park, MD: Alliance for Childhood.

Neuman, S. B., & Dwyer, J. (2009). Missing in action: Vocabulary instruction in Pre-K. *The Reading Teacher, 62*(5), 384–392.

Neuman, S. B., Kaefer, T., & Pinkham, A. M. (2014). Improving low-income preschoolers' word and world knowledge: The effects of content-rich instruction. *The Elementary School Journal, 116*(4), 652–674.

Neuman, S. B., Newman, E., & Dwyer, J. (2011). Educational effectiveness of a vocabulary intervention on preschoolers' word knowledge and conceptual development: A cluster randomized trial. *Reading Research Quarterly, 46*, 246–272.

Neuman, S. B., & Roskos, K. A. (2005). The state of prekindergarten standards. *Early Childhood Research Quarterly, 20*(2), 125–145.

Pan, B. A., Rowe, M. L., Singer, J. D., & Snow, C. E. (2005). Maternal correlates of growth in toddler vocabulary production in low-income families. *Child Development, 76*(4), 763–782.

Piasta, S. B., Justice, L. M., Cabell, S. Q., Wiggins, A. K., Turnbull, K. P., & Curenton, S. M. (2012). Impact of professional development on preschool teachers' conversational responsivity and children's linguistic productivity and complexity. *Early Childhood Research Quarterly, 27*, 387–400.

Restrepo, L. A., Schwanenflugel, P. J., Blake, J., Neuharth-Pritchett, S., Cramer, S. E., & Ruston, H. P. (2006). Performance on the PPVT-III and the EVT: Applicability of the measures with African American and European American preschool children. *Language, Speech, and Hearing Services in Schools, 37*(1), 17–27.

Ruston, H. P., & Schwanenflugel, P. J. (2010). Effects of a conversation intervention on expressive vocabulary development of prekindergarten children. *Language, Speech, and Hearing Services in Schools, 41*, 303–310.

Schwanenflugel, P. J., Hamilton, C. E., Neuharth-Pritchett, S., Restrepo, M. A., Bradley, B. A., & Webb, M.-Y. (2010). PAVEd for Success: An evaluation of a comprehensive literacy program for 4-year-old children. *Journal of Literacy Research, 42*, 227–275.

Sénéchal, M. (1997). The differential effect of storybook reading on preschoolers' acquisition of expressive and receptive vocabulary. *Journal of Child Language, 24*, 123–138.

Shirin, A., Creamer, M., Rivera, M. C., & Catalano, J. (2015). Vocabulary for Success. Retrieved from *http://clad.education.gsu.edu/curriculum/vocabulary.*

Snow, C. E., Cancino, H., De Temple, J., & Schley, S. (1991). Giving formal definitions: A linguistic or metalinguistic skill. In E. Bialystok (Ed.), *Language processing in bilingual children* (pp. 90–112). New York: Cambridge University Press.

Snow, C. E., & Matthews, T. J. (2016). Reading and language in the early grades. *The Future of Children, 26*(2), 55–74.

Strauss, V. (2014, June 2). You won't believe these kindergarten schedules. Retrieved from *www.washingtonpost.com/news/answer-sheet/wp/2014/06/02/you-wont-believe-these-kindergarten-schedules/?utm_term=.d48d1173b5ab.*

Van Kleeck, A. (2008). Providing preschool foundations for later reading comprehension: The importance of and ideas for targeting inference in storybook-sharing interventions. *Psychology in the Schools, 45*(7), 627–643.

Vuattox, D., Japel, C., Dion, E., & Dupere, V. (2014). Targeting the specific vocabulary needs of at-risk preschoolers: A randomized study of the effectiveness of an educator-implemented intervention. *Prevention Science, 15*(2), 156–164.

Wasik, B. A., & Bond, M. A. (2001). Beyond the pages of a book: Interactive book reading and language development in preschool classrooms. *Journal of Educational Psychology, 93*, 243–250.

Wasik, B. A., Hindman, A. H., & Snell, E. K. (2016). Book reading and vocabulary development: A systematic review. *Early Childhood Research Quarterly, 37*, 39–57.

Webb, M. L., Cohen, A. S., & Schwanenflugel, P. J. (2008). Latent class analysis of differential item functioning on the Peabody Picture Vocabulary Test–III. *Educational and Psychological Measurement, 68*(2), 335–351.

Weizman, Z. O., & Snow, C. E. (2001). Lexical input as related to children's vocabulary acquisition: Effects of sophisticated exposure and support for meaning. *Developmental Psychology, 37*(2), 265–279.

Whitehurst, G., Arnold, D. S., Epstein, J. N., Angell, A. L., Smith, M., & Fischel, J. E. (1994). A picture book reading intervention in day care and home for children from low-income families. *Developmental Psychology, 30*(5), 679–689.

Whitehurst, G. J., & Lonigan, C. J. (1998). Child development and emergent literacy. *Child Development, 69*(3), 848–872.

CHAPTER 3

"I Don't Just Want to Read, I Want to Learn Something"

Best Practices for Using Informational Texts to Build Young Children's Conceptual Knowledge

MARIAM JEAN DREHER
SHARON B. KLETZIEN

Our chapter title comes from a kindergartner whom we call Sarah. During a parent conference, Sarah's teacher informed her mother that she was worried because Sarah did not seem to like reading. Dislike of reading didn't match what Sarah's mother saw at home or in their many trips to the library, where Sarah eagerly checked out a wide variety of books. When her mother talked with Sarah, it became apparent that reading at school was all stories. But, as Sarah said, "I don't just want to read, I want to learn something."

Sarah's comment underscores two very important features of information books and other informational texts. First, although stories are important, information books are an equally important part of balanced reading, offering powerful resources for motivating children to read (Dreher, 2003). Informational texts appeal to children's curiosity, and curiosity is a strong motivator for reading (Baker & Wigfield, 1999; Schiefele, Schaffner, Möller, & Wigfield, 2012). Studies of preferences show that young children are just as likely to choose information books as storybooks (Cervetti, Bravo, Hiebert, Pearson, & Jaynes, 2009; Kletzien & DeRenzi, 2001; Mohr, 2006; Repaskey, Schumm, & Johnson, 2017). There is also considerable research establishing that young children enjoy and learn from information books (e.g., Maloch & Horsey, 2013; Pappas, 1993; Pappas & Barry, 1997; Varelas & Pappas, 2006). Second, information books can contribute to building children's conceptual knowledge (Neuman, Kaefer, & Pinkham, 2016) and can play an important role in increasing children's vocabulary (Kletzien & Dreher, 2016). In this chapter, we offer evidenced-based practices about how teachers can use the motivating appeal of informational texts for children's conceptual development and vocabulary acquisition.

We use the term *informational text* as the equivalent to nonfiction, similar to the Common Core State Standards' use of the term (National Governors Association Center for Best Practices, Council of Chief State School Officers [NGA & CCSSO], 2010) (Dreher & Kletzien, 2015). Within that broader term, we identify three types of text: expository, narrative–informational, and mixed text. Authors writing *expository text* use timeless verbs (*jump* vs. *jumped*) and generic nouns (*frogs* vs. *Papa Frog*), with the intent of providing accurate information about the subject. Often, expository text is written in compare–contrast, cause–effect, description, generalization–example, or sequence structures. Examples of expository text include reports, essays, procedures, descriptions, persuasive arguments, explanations, and chronological accounts. Although authors writing *narrative–informational* text also intend to provide information about a topic, they use a typical narrative structure to do so. As a result, a narrative–informational text includes characters, setting, plot, and solution. Science texts of this type often use an individual to represent a group, as in *Hip-Pocket Papa*, which explains the lives of hip-pocket frogs via the story of Papa Frog (Markle, 2010). Many believe that it is easier for young children to relate to narratives and choose to present information in this fashion. However, researchers have documented problems with this approach (Brabham, Boyd, & Edgington, 2000; Gill, 2009; Jetton, 1994). The final category, *mixed texts*, include elements of both narrative–informational and expository texts. For example, the main text in *Snowflake Bentley* (Martin, 1998) is an accurate narrative about the man whose interest in snow led to amazing discoveries about snowflakes. But this book also includes frequent expository sidebars with additional information on the man and the science of snow.

Unfortunately, even in an age of heightened awareness of the importance of attention to informational text as evidenced by the Common Core State Standards (NGA & CCSSO, 2010), research documents that there is still too little attention to these texts in many classrooms. This situation is particularly true when it comes to expository text. More recent studies continue to find patterns of underuse of informational text (e.g., Jeong, Gaffney, & Choi, 2010; Ness, 2011; Wright, 2013; Yopp & Yopp, 2012), similar to earlier work (e.g., Duke, 2000; Pappas, 1993). In our graduate classes, current inservice teachers—in school systems that emphasize informational text in their curricula—report being uncomfortable using informational text unless it is narrative–informational. Thus, in this chapter, we focus on expository texts and evidence-based practices relevant to their use in developing young children's conceptual knowledge and vocabulary knowledge. We first define concepts and how they are related to vocabulary. Then we describe research examples of contributions of informational text to conceptual knowledge and vocabulary. Finally, we offer examples of how information books might be used for conceptual development/vocabulary acquisition.

What Are Concepts, and How Are Concepts and Vocabulary Related?

Fitzgerald, Elmore, Kung, and Jackson Stenner (2017) have offered a concise definition of *concept* in relation to vocabulary words:

> The basic definition of concept . . . [is] the commonly agreed-upon definition used by concept theorists and concept researchers across the decades: a mental representation (a class or category) of an object, process, or idea. . . . Importantly, across several decades, concept researchers and theorists from the fields of psychology, linguistics, and education have widely agreed that every spoken or printed word is a label for a concept. (pp. 417–418)

In this chapter, we follow Fitzgerald et al.'s (2017) definition, as well as their reasoning that "because words are labels for concepts . . . , individuals' concept acquisition and growth are manifested in their vocabulary repertoire, and that acquisition and growth can be related to vocabulary exposure in printed text" (p. 418). Indeed, print exposure is a well-documented predictor of vocabulary knowledge (Mol & Bus, 2011). In particular, we argue that informational texts offer an important context for developing conceptual knowledge and vocabulary, specifically, academic vocabulary.

Although definitions of *academic vocabulary* vary (Baumann & Graves, 2010), most researchers would accept the idea that "academic vocabulary represents terms that are not commonly used in conversational language but occur often in written texts" (Dreher & Kletzien, 2015, p. 100). Beck, McKeown, and Kucan's (2002) discussion of three tiers of words helps to clarify the concept of academic vocabulary. At

Tier One, they described basic, everyday, familiar words. Tier Two consists of more sophisticated words that are of use across a wide spectrum of content, similar to what others have called academic vocabulary. Tier Three words are rare or are specific to particular domains. As Dreher and Kletzien (2015) pointed out:

> Children learn Tier One words from everyday interactions with others and with the popular media. Tier Two and Tier Three words are important for academic success but are not often found in conversation or other forms of popular oral communication. This academic vocabulary, however, is abundant in informational texts especially in the disciplines such as science and social studies. (p. 100)

How Might Informational Texts Contribute to Conceptual Knowledge and Vocabulary?

Exposure to Academic Vocabulary

Researchers have concluded that "informational text typically carries a heavier vocabulary load than does literary text" (Pearson, Hiebert, & Kamil, 2007, p. 294). Among the challenges in informational texts is that vocabulary is often more conceptually difficulty than in narrative texts (Armbruster & Nagy, 1992; Hiebert & Cervetti, 2011). For example, Wright (2013) has explained:

> In storybooks, sophisticated words often represent new or more nuanced words for concepts that children already know. . . . For example, children might need to learn that hilarious means "very funny." . . . In contrast, new vocabulary words in informational texts often represent completely new concepts for children. . . . For example, when a young child encounters the new word photosynthesis in an informational text about plants, the child needs to learn lots of new information about the complex process of photosynthesis—what it is, how it works, why it is important for plant growth and development. (pp. 360–361)

Hence, informational texts can be a meaty source for developing conceptual knowledge and the labels for those concepts.

Our findings in a recent study support this argument. We (Kletzien & Dreher, 2016) examined the type of vocabulary experience offered to young children by books recommended on various trade book lists, with a focus on the expository books in comparison to fiction. Specifically, we examined books on the National Science Teachers Association (NSTA) list of Outstanding Science Trade Books for Students K–12, the National Council for the Social Studies (NCSS) list of Notable Social Studies Trade Books for Young People, and the International Literacy Association (ILA) list of Teachers' Choices. We started by identifying all the books recommended for K–2 students (the earliest recommended grade range) on these three lists for both 2011 and 2012. We then examined all the expository books for those years ($N = 13$), as well as a random sample of the recommended fiction books (there were 22 fiction titles, so we randomly selected 13 in order to match the number of expository books), for a total of 26 texts.

We checked the words in all 26 books against the Dale–Chall list of the 3,000 most common words (and all linguistic forms of the base words) known by fourth graders (Chall & Dale, 1995). We assumed that if a word is not known by fourth graders, it is likely to be an uncommon word for K–2 students. In other words, we considered words (and their variants) not on the Dale–Chall as proxies for academic vocabulary for K–2 students. Although the words fourth graders know have changed somewhat since it was created, the Dale–Chall list remains an important resource, with current researchers still drawing on it (e.g., Dickinson & Porche, 2011; Weizman & Snow, 2001). Moreover, when vocabulary for young children is considered, Wright and Neuman (2013) have pointed out that words not on the Dale–Chall list are likely choices for vocabulary instruction.

We found that the expository books recommended for K–2 students had many more uncommon words (average of 67) than the recommended fiction titles (average of 27). So exposure to the expository titles on these recommended book lists would afford children more opportunity to encounter uncommon words than would the fiction titles. As noted, print exposure is a well-documented predictor of vocabulary knowledge, and these findings along with other work (e.g., Hiebert & Cervetti, 2011) suggest that expository titles are likely to contribute more academic words to developing children's knowledge.

Semantic Relatedness

Researchers have also suggested that the vocabulary in informational texts differs from the vocabulary in narrative texts, because the words are likely to be more related semantically in informational texts (Armbruster

& Nagy, 1992; Hiebert & Cervetti, 2011). In her study of kindergarten teachers' read-alouds, Wright (2013) found support for this assertion:

> The words that teachers discussed during informational text read-alouds . . . often tended to cluster together conceptually. . . . In contrast, the words teachers explained during storybook read-alouds were related to the story in the book, but not to one another. Teachers taught some wonderful words during read-alouds of fiction, but outside of the context of the book, these words look as though they were randomly selected. (p. 362)

In our study of the vocabulary in expository versus fiction books on recommended books for young children (Kletzien & Dreher, 2016), we examined not only the number of uncommon words, as described earlier, but also the semantic relatedness of the words in each book. To do so, we drew on earlier research that grouped words into related categories called *superclusters* and *megaclusters*. Superclusters come from Marzano and Marzano's (1988) work, which involved developing semantic categories for 7,000 words taken from *Basic Elementary Reading Vocabulary, The American Heritage Word Frequency Book,* and *Word Frequency of Spoken American English.* Marzano and Marzano categorized these words into 61 superclusters of words that are semantically related. Then Hiebert (2011) took Marzano and Marzano's (1988) superclusters and combined similar ones into 13 megaclusters of semantically related words, as shown in Table 3.1.

We used the supercluster/megacluster approach to categorize the uncommon words in our sample of recommended expository and fiction books for young children. For words not listed in Marzano and Marzano's (1988) work, we identified likely synonyms (e.g., *debris* was not categorized by Marzano and Marzano, but it is similar to *rubbish,* which is categorized), establishing high interrater reliability for those decisions. We then calculated the mean number of megaclusters by genre, as well as the mean word-to-megacluster ratio by genre. We were particularly interested in the word-to-megacluster ratio, because a text with more words per megacluster indicates vocabulary that is more closely related than a text with fewer words per megacluster. We found that both fiction and expository books had an average of eight megaclusters. But the ratio of words to megaclusters differed greatly. Fiction titles had a ratio of 25:8, indicating an average 25 words to eight (of the 13 possible) megaclusters, while expository selections averaged 66 words over eight megaclusters.

TABLE 3.1. Vocabulary Megaclusters and Superclusters

Megacluster	Superclusters included in each megacluster
1. Emotions and attitudes	Feelings/emotion; attitudinals
2. Communication, sounds, thinking, perceiving	Communication; mental actions; senses/perceptions; facial expressions/actions, noises, sounds
3. Physical and nonemotional traits	Nonemotional traits, physical traits of people
4. Relationships	Ownership/possession, popularity/knownness, life/survival, conformity/complexity
5. Occupations, types of groups	Occupations, types of people, types of groups
6. Action and motion	Action, motion, touching/grabbing, actions involving legs, helpful/destructive actions
7. Body, clothing, health/disease	Human body, clothing, health/disease
8. Features of events/things/people	Value/correctness, similarity/dissimilarity. Cleanliness/uncleanliness, difficulty/danger, causality
9. Places, shelter, events	Places where people live, dwellings/shelter, rooms, furnishings, events
10. Physical attributes of things/events/experience	Size/quantity, time, location/direction, shapes/dimensions, texture/durability, color
11. Natural environment, animals, chemicals	Animals, foods, water/liquids, land/terrain, vegetation, soil/metal/rock, light, weather, mathematics, temperature/fire, chemicals, electricity
12. Machines, transportation, materials	Machines/engines/tools, transportation, materials
13. Culture and social systems	Literature/writing, money/finance, sports/recreation, language, entertainment/arts

Note. Adapted from Hiebert (2011, Table 3). Copyright © 2011 TextProject, Inc.

These results show that the uncommon words from the expository books are more clearly semantically related than those in the fiction books.

If words are semantically related, they can be grouped together for teaching. For example, Table 3.2 shows the uncommon words we identified in *About Habitats: Grasslands* (Sill, 2011) categorized according semantic relatedness (Kletzien & Dreher, 2016). As can be seen, *About Habitats: Grasslands*—one of the expository books on the recommended

TABLE 3.2. Vocabulary Analysis of Sill's (2011) *About Habitats: Grasslands*

Word	Megacluster	Supercluster
common	4	42
provide	6	2
regal	8	26
approximate	8	27
habitat	9	21
periods	10	7
boundaries	10	14
bison	11	4
rhinoceros	11	4
impala	11	4
giraffe	11	4
pronghorn	11	4
budgerigar	11	4
wildebeest	11	4
zebra	11	4
ostrich	11	4
skylark	11	4
prairie	11	20
savanna	11	20
steppe	11	20
taiga	11	20
hummock	11	20
pampas	11	20
area	11	20
ebony	11	24
shrubs	11	24
illustrated	13	15

books for young children we examined—has 27 uncommon words in seven megaclusters. However, most of these words (19 of 27, or 70%) fall into the same megacluster, number 11 (natural environment, animals, chemicals). Within that megacluster, most words are either in the animal supercluster (no. 4 in the last column) or the land/terrain (no. 20). Teachers can take advantage of this semantic relatedness in their instruction.

Our analysis of semantic relatedness in uncommon words in expository versus fiction books (Kletzien & Dreher, 2016) showed similar results to those in a study by Hiebert and Cervetti (2011). In their research, Hiebert and Cervetti compared the words suggested for teaching in an English Language Arts (ELA) program and a science program from the same publisher for fourth grade. Words suggested for instruction in the science text were more semantically related than those in the ELA text. In our study (Kletzien & Dreher, 2016), we looked at all the uncommon words in trade books, while Hiebert and Cervetti (2011) looked at words chosen by the publisher for instruction in ELA versus science. But the results in both analyses show greater semantic relatedness in the informational texts than in the fiction.

As Hiebert (2011, p. 6) has argued, instead of teaching several isolated words for a text, teachers can teach words "clustered according to conceptual connections," making it more likely that students will remember them. In fact, Neuman, Newman, and Dwyer (2011) found that when Head Start teachers taught content-area words in related categories, children were better able to learn new vocabulary and build networks of concepts. Given that the words in informational texts tend to be more semantically related, these texts may be particularly useful in extending children's vocabulary by building conceptual networks.

How Might Information Books Be Used for Conceptual Development/Vocabulary Acquisition?

Facilitate Conceptual Development by Grouping Related Words for Instruction

As we have described, informational texts tend to have a heavier vocabulary load than narrative texts, affording children more exposure to uncommon words. Of course, more uncommon words can make texts harder, but uncommon words in informational texts are typically more semantically related than those in fiction texts. Teachers can use this semantic relatedness to ease the load for children by teaching the needed vocabulary grouped into categories. As shown in the example in Table 3.2, the vocabulary in expository titles for young children often falls into a small number of clusters. In the case of *About Habitats: Grasslands* (Sill, 2011), the overwhelming majority of uncommon words are in the same megacluster and fall into either the animal supercluster or the land/terrain supercluster.

Other expository titles for young children follow similar patterns that teachers can use to their advantage. For example, one of the recommended books that we examined, *Time for a Bath* (Jenkins & Page, 2011), has 37 uncommon words in eight megaclusters. But 49% of these words are in megacluster 11 (natural environment, animals, chemicals), and of those words, almost all are in the subcategory of animals. Likewise, the recommended book *How Did That Get in My Lunchbox?* (Butterworth, 2011) has 39 uncommon words across nine megaclusters, with 41% of the words in megacluster 11 (natural environment, animals, chemicals). But with this book, many of the megacluster 11 words are in the subcategory of foods/meals.

On average, 45% of the uncommon words in the expository books that we examined in our analysis of recommended books were from megacluster 11 (natural environment, animals, chemicals). This was by far the most common megacluster in the expository books we examined—and the percentage of megacluster 11 words in the expository books was more than double that for fiction titles we examined. Accordingly, teachers can screen expository books for related vocabulary with a particular focus on megacluster 11 and the superclusters it includes, as summarized in Table 3.1.

Some books also have features that facilitate grouping vocabulary words for instruction. For example, Susan Neuman created a series of book for prereaders specifically to aid vocabulary and concept development. Each book offers a vocabulary tree at the beginning. In *Swing, Sloth!* (Neuman, 2013), the vocabulary tree features three main branches, each with terms underneath: rain forest—*rain, tall, tree, hot, sun*; animals— *sloth, snake, macaw, butterfly, monkey*; and activities—*swing, slither, call, flutter, climb, lie*. There are numerous titles in this series, including *Sleep, Bear!* (Alinsky, 2015) and *Hop, Bunny!* (Neuman, 2014), as well as versions in Spanish (e.g., *¡Salta, Cachorrito!*, Neuman, 2016). These vocabulary trees help teachers illustrate the connections among key words for children.

These vocabulary trees can also help teachers generate vocabulary activities. For example, for *Swing, Sloth!*, teachers can have children act out the *activities* category from the vocabulary tree. Students can pretend to *flutter, slither, climb,* and so forth. Putting these words into action will help develop the students' understanding of them. Teachers can encourage students to notice these words as they read the book together to learn which animals match each activity ("Listen for these words as we read the book. We can learn more about each activity. Which animal swings? Which animal slithers?," etc.).

There are lots of possibilities for conceptual development, especially with multiple readings of a book. For *Swing, Sloth!,* teachers might give each pair of students a set of word cards with the animal names on them, and instruct students to hold up the animal name when they see the picture. Children can point out the picture labels in the book as a way to identify information for the types of animals. As children look at the photograph of macaws perched on a branch, they can describe what they see and begin to develop an understanding of characteristics of a macaw ("They are birds, they sit on branches, they are brightly colored," etc.).

Not all books have vocabulary trees, but teachers can help children create representations that show how things link conceptually. Paquette, Fello, and Jalongo (2007) adapted an existing approach, *talking drawings* (McConnell, 1993), to help young children see the relations among words on a particular topic by making pre- and postreading diagrams with labels. In creating these diagrams, children integrate what they already know with what they have learned from an expository text. With this technique, teachers pick a descriptive informational text on a focused topic, such as jellyfish. Before reading the text, teachers show children examples of diagrams of other topics labeled with appropriate terms. Children then work individually or in pairs to produce a diagram of what they already know about the topic they will be learning. These prereading diagrams will likely be sparse and may contain incorrect information. After children listen to or read the text, they revisit their diagrams in pairs to discuss what they have learned, correct any misconceptions, and add labels. This kind of experience makes children aware of what they don't know, and it uses visual images to reinforce vocabulary, showing the connections among related words.

However, it is important to note that just because several words are related, it is not necessary or advisable to teach all of them (Dreher & Kletzien, 2015). It is essential to choose which words to spend valuable class time discussing, because there is not enough time in the school year to teach all the words with which children may be unfamiliar. Teachers should choose words carefully based on several criteria:

- How important the word is in understanding or writing about the text.
- How useful the word is likely to be in future work.
- How the word fits within the network of concepts on which the teacher is focusing.

For example, the 27 uncommon vocabulary words from *About Habitats: Grasslands* (see Table 3.2) represent seven megaclusters, but 70% of these words are in megacluster 11 (natural environment, animals, chemicals). Further analysis shows that many of the words are animals, whereas many others represent land or terrain. Some of these words may not be very important for young children to learn, whereas others may be encountered again in different disciplinary contexts.

By grouping the few words that teachers want children to learn, conceptual networks can be developed. For *About Habitats: Grasslands,* teachers might connect terrain with the animals associated with it, in order to create a network of knowledge for students. For example, teachers might group animals that would be found in a specific geographic area, such as a savanna, where giraffes, zebra, and wildebeests roam. Depending on curricular goals, a teacher might decide that *budgerigar* wouldn't be a particularly useful word to spend much time on, or that students are less likely to be able to use the word *taiga* in the future.

Support Conceptual Development with Interactive Read-Alouds of Information Books

Regularly reading aloud to children has long-standing support (International Reading Association & National Association for the Education of Young Children [IRA/NAEYC], 1998; Snow, Burns, & Griffin, 1998; Shanahan et al., 2010). Research demonstrates that reading aloud increases reading achievement, strengthens vocabulary, promotes independent reading, and provides scaffolding that makes a book easier to approach for struggling readers (Dreher & Kletzien, 2015). But despite these positive outcomes, information books are often neglected when it comes to read-alouds (Jacobs, Morrison, & Swinyard, 2000; Kraemer, McCabe, & Sinatra, 2012; Stead, 2014; Yopp & Yopp, 2006; Wright, 2013).

The continued neglect of information books in read-alouds needs to be remedied. As argued in the Common Core State Standards, "Having students listen to informational read-alouds in the early grades helps lay the necessary foundation for students' reading and understanding of increasingly complex texts on their own in subsequent grades" (NGA & CCSSO, 2010, p. 33). Moreover, when vocabulary and conceptual development are considered, it is important to recall Wright's (2013) finding that information book read-alouds were stronger contexts for vocabulary development than stories. Unfortunately, Wright also found that information book read-alouds did not occur very often. Across 55 kindergarten teachers, on average, only 17% of read-aloud time involved informational text, "with most teachers (58.5%) never reading aloud from informational text at all" (p. 361).

Because information books read-alouds are such powerful venues for enhancing vocabulary and conceptual development, it is important to greatly raise the frequency with which they occur. In addition, it is important to make them *interactive read-alouds*. Smolkin and Donovan (2003, p. 28) "use the term *interactive* to describe a context in which a teacher genuinely shares, not abandons, authority with the children during the reading of the book." As Varelas, Pieper, Arsenault, Pappas, and Keblawe-Shamah (2014) explained,

> In interactive read-alouds of science texts, teachers do not wait till the end of the read-aloud to invite children, often by posing questions, to share their thinking about the ideas presented in the book. Instead, opportunities for children to reveal and communicate their interpretation, inference, and comprehension occur throughout, with many initiated by the students themselves. Such opportunities are created in a variety of ways including the teacher pausing to offer children time to think and share, asking children questions, allowing and supporting further discussion on a student comment, or modeling her/his own thinking about the ideas presented in the book. (pp. 1248–1249)

Although Varelas et al. (2014) referred to science texts, this kind of approach has been shown to enhance vocabulary growth in a variety of informational texts. Not only is there much research to support the value of informational texts in read-alouds, but there are also many accounts of the successful use of expository text in read-alouds with young children. For example, Heller (2006) described using 10 expository books by noted author Seymour Simon in 12 read-aloud sessions with a group of first-grade girls who varied widely in their reading levels. Similarly, using the example of *Face to Face with Lions* (Joubert, & Joubert, 2008), McClure and Fullerton (2017) detailed how a third-grade teacher regularly engaged her students in whole-class expository read-alouds.

It is worth highlighting how much of the research that demonstrates the effectiveness of using informational texts as interactive read-alouds has been done in urban, high-poverty schools, including those with children who are English language learners (e.g., Blachowicz & Obrochta, 2005; Pappas & Barry, 1997; Pappas, Varelas, Patton, Ye, & Ortiz, 2012; Varelas & Pappas, 2006; Varelas et al., 2014). These efforts have been highly successful. Pappas et al. (2012), for example, showed how a second-grade teacher used read-alouds of science books in English in her bilingual classroom "to strengthen both language/literacy and science instruction" (p. 263). As they explained,

> [She] scaffold[ed] knowledge-building and language use. . . . She often made many intertextual links to ideas already shared in the classroom discourse. She also extended student ideas, asking them to further explain or to answer their own questions. Moreover, she prompted students to examine new concepts using book illustrations. In addition, she highlighted and reinforced vocabulary in various ways, a key element in the learning of science discourse . . . and second language acquisition. (p. 270)

Similarly, Blachowicz and Obrochta (2005) studied the efforts of first-grade teachers and the reading specialist at an urban school, where one teacher observed, "Our students are smart, but they need more concept and vocabulary development. Every time we take a field trip they learn a lot. I wish we could take more field trips!" (p. 262). Since they couldn't afford more field trips, the teachers decided to turn interactive read-alouds into virtual field trips "using scaffolded book read-alouds, active learning with visuals, and other activities that appeal to the senses while developing new concepts and vocabulary" (p. 263).

In addition to engaging their students in informational text read-alouds at school, teachers can also involve parents. Gibson and Dreher (2007) studied parents and first graders who participated in a *nonfiction book club* that involved interactive parent–child read-alouds. Parents attended an information session to overview the project. This session included showing a brief video of a parent engaged in very informal interactive reading with a first-grade child. Children then had access to a lending library of over 500 nonfiction books. The collection contained 10 target books with selected target vocabulary of which the children and parents were unaware. The targeted vocabulary words were selected as words that were likely to be unfamiliar to the children based on the judgment of the first-grade teacher and confirmed by an age-leveled vocabulary list. In addition, these words needed to be presented in the books in a way that supported comprehension; that is, a word was defined by being restated in simpler language, explained with an example, or shown in an illustration or graphic. For example, the target word *expand* in *Hot and Cold* (Fowler, 1994), is supported in all three ways. The text states, "A high, or warm, temperature causes many things to *expand*, or grow bigger. On bridges, a little space is left between the steel beams. This gives the beams room to *expand* on hot days" (p. 18). Furthermore, a photograph of a bridge includes an inset close-up of the spaces between steel beams on the bridge's road surface. These target books were cycled to children's homes twice over 11 weeks, along with other nonfiction books that were self-selected by the students. Even though parents received minimal guidance on how to engage in interactive read-alouds, their children grew more in expressive vocabulary from pretest to posttest than did their peers who were in a randomly assigned comparison group.

Use Information Books as Part of Content-Rich Instruction

Content-rich instruction plays a critical role in developing young children's conceptual knowledge, and information books are important in such instruction. Neuman et al. (2016) created a content-rich environment for preschoolers from low-income families, with information books in a key role. This approach involved integrating literacy and science with the goal of expanding children's vocabulary and world knowledge. Drawing on life science topics, Neuman et al. created a multimedia curriculum in which "vocabulary words are introduced first through video clips, then through information books and picture cards, allowing children to develop an understanding of these words in multiple contexts" (2016, p. 658). To support word learning, Neuman et al. grouped words for instruction in related categories. Moreover, they also grouped information books, so that children got multiple exposure to the words and concepts in each science/literacy unit. Throughout the units, children experienced shared reading of information *big books* (oversized books with print and illustrations large enough for children to see from their seats). Shared book sessions are characterized by interactive reading in which children contribute to the reading of a book with the support of a teacher who models proficient reading and demonstrates reading strategies. Neuman et al. found that this form of shared book reading in an integrated context resulted in more growth in vocabulary and science concepts for students than was the case for children who did not experience the intervention.

Other researchers have developed content-rich instruction by integrating literacy and science; this has also resulted in young children's conceptual growth and improved literacy performance. Guthrie, Anderson, Alao, and Rinehart (1999) studied the effectiveness of an integrated approach, concept-oriented reading instruction (CORI), which involves hands-on science activities, inquiry, peer collaboration, and information books. Compared to traditional instruction, CORI enhanced reading comprehension and science conceptual learning for third and fifth graders in multicultural, high-poverty schools.

Similarly, Varelas et al. (2014) studied third graders' meaning making during informational read-alouds as part of hands-on science explorations, while Varelas and Pappas (2006) focused first and second graders' intertextuality in read-alouds during such units. In both these studies, children in urban, high-poverty schools benefited from interactive science read-alouds and related hands-on activities. Such experiences contribute to conceptual knowledge. For example, as Varelas and Pappas explained,

> The multiple texts, along with the multiple hands-on explorations, and the dialogically oriented extensive discussions around them, offered children and their teachers numerous opportunities for intertextuality and hybrid discourse. These two resources, in turn, allowed children to use both their own ideas and language and that of science to make sense and talk science, to refer to empirical evidence, and to theorize about how the world works. (p. 254)

Despite the successes demonstrated in these studies, there is still much to do to clear up assumptions about what young children are capable of doing. For example, Adair, Colegrove, and McManus (2017) were surprised to discover that even after educators viewed a film of mostly Latino/a first graders engaged in what they termed *agentic* learning experiences, or experiences in which the learners demonstrate their agency, these "caring, experienced educators explained that Latinx immigrant students could not handle dynamic, agentic learning experiences because they lacked vocabulary" (p. 309). Yet there are numerous studies that show otherwise. Indeed, Varelas and Pappas (2006) specifically noted that their study "debunks deficit theories for urban children by highlighting funds of knowledge that these children bring to the classroom" (p. 211). Evidence indicates that content-rich instruction can help build conceptual knowledge for all children.

Choose Information Books That Are Worth the Time Spent on Them

To help children learn new vocabulary and related concepts, teachers need to choose quality information books. Critical factors in selecting information books include accurate content, appealing design and format, engaging style, appropriate text complexity, and good organization. Because we have addressed these selection factors in detail elsewhere (Dreher & Kletzien, 2015), we focus here on sources that may be helpful in locating quality information books.

Recommended book lists and award lists can be good starting sources. Earlier, we mentioned three sources that can be valuable: the NSTA's Outstanding Science Trade Books for Students K–12 (*www.nsta.org/publications/ostb*), the NCSS's Notable Social Studies Trade Books for Young People (*www.socialstudies.org/publications/notables*), and the ILA's Teachers' Choices (*www.literacyworldwide.org/get-resources/reading-lists/teachers-choices-reading-list*). In addition, the ILA also offers Children's Choices (*www.literacyworldwide.org/get-resources/reading-lists/childrens-choices-reading-list*). These lists include both fiction and nonfiction, along with brief descriptions of the books and recommended grade levels.

Teachers can also access lists of books that have won Caldecott and Newbery Medals at the websites of the American Library Association (*www.ala.org*) and the Children's Book Council website (*www.cbcbooks.org*). These websites include each year's winners and honor books, with both fiction and nonfiction books eligible for the awards. In addition, two awards single out information books. Teachers can find the winners and honor books for the Orbis Pictus Award for Outstanding Nonfiction for Children at the National Council of Teachers of English website (*www2.ncte.org/awards/orbis-pictus-award-nonfiction-for-children*), while the winners of the Robert F. Sibert Information Book Award for the most outstanding information book are listed at its Association for Library Services to Children website (*www.ala.org/alsc/awardsgrants/bookmedia/sibertmedal*).

Such lists are helpful in identifying quality titles, given that the books on these lists are screened by committees of professionals. However, since most lists include both fiction and nonfiction, teachers first need to identify the nonfiction titles, then, within those titles, look carefully to be sure they also identify expository books. Depending on the list, recommended informational books are often narrative–informational. In the study we conducted, we found that nonfiction books on the NSTA's Outstanding Science Trade Books list were more likely to be expository than narrative–informational. But nonfiction titles on the NCSS's Notable Social Studies Trade Books and the ILA's Teachers' Choices lists had a higher percentage of narrative–informational books than expository books (Dreher & Kletzien, 2016). If teachers choose mostly narrative–informational books, then students are not exposed to expository text features. Furthermore, as we noted earlier, expository books are likely to offer more academic words to contribute to developing children's knowledge than do narrative titles. Therefore, when using these lists, it is important to look for expository books, not just narrative–informational books.

Just like other quality children's books, expository books can rate highly on features such as accuracy, appealing design and format, engaging style, appropriate text complexity, and good organization (Dreher & Kletzien, 2015). Children's author Melissa Stewart (2017a, 2017b) has referred to the term *expository literature*. She credited the term to Terrell Young at Brigham Young University and used it "to differentiate finely crafted expository writing from the traditional expository writing often found in series books" (2017a). This notion highlights the issue of quality, making clear that well-chosen expository books will not only appeal to children but support conceptual development.

Conclusion

By tapping into children's natural curiosity, well-chosen information books can be wonderful contexts for building children's conceptual knowledge and academic vocabulary. Although information books are still scarce in read-alouds and shared reading in many young children's classrooms, evidence indicates that the opportunity to experience informational books can contribute to young children's motivation to read, as well as their learning. We have described evidenced-based practices that can help teachers promote children's conceptual development and vocabulary acquisition using information books, with a particular focus on using expository books effectively with young children. We hope these ideas will be useful in your classroom and serve to inspire more ideas.

● IMPLICATIONS FOR PROFESSIONAL LEARNING ●

- Information books are motivational; children like and learn from them.
- Information books can help develop conceptual knowledge and vocabulary.
- Information books have more academic vocabulary that is semantically related than do stories.
- Teachers can take advantage of the rich potential of information books by
  - Teaching words in related categories to help children to build networks of concepts.
  - Using interactive read-alouds to support conceptual learning.
  - Including information books as part of content-rich instruction.
  - Choosing quality information books, with an eye to selecting expository books.

QUESTIONS FOR DISCUSSION

1. With your colleagues, discuss the type of books children in your classes are experiencing during read-alouds. We noted studies indicating that teachers of young children tend to use stories in read-alouds. Is this the case for you and your colleagues? If you are incorporating information books into your read-alouds, examine your choices. Are they mostly narrative–informational or are you using expository titles? Discuss whether changes need to be made and, if so, what steps you can take to make these changes and to reduce any potential discomfort with expository book read-alouds. For example, to start, can you identify appealing expository titles?

2. We pointed out the benefits of interactive read-alouds. Discuss whether your and your colleagues' read-alouds are interactive. Try recording a read-aloud session. Discuss what you see in terms of characteristics of interactive read-alouds. If needed, discuss what steps you can take to help yourself and your colleagues make things more interactive.

3. Discuss the issue of semantic relatedness with your colleagues. Select an information book appropriate for your students, and

consider how you might implement the suggestions for identifying and teaching related words. Which words would you choose? How would you group the words? How would you teach the words to involve physical and visual stimuli?

REFERENCES

Adair, J. K., Colegrove, K. S.-S., & McManus, M. E. (2017). How the word gap argument negatively impacts young children of Latinx immigrants' conceptualizations of learning. *Harvard Educational Review, 87,* 309–334.

Alinsky, S. B. (2015). *Sleep, bear!* Washington, DC: National Geographic Society.

Armbruster, B. B., & Nagy, W. E. (1992). Vocabulary in content area lessons. *The Reading Teacher, 45,* 550–551.

Baker, L., & Wigfield, A. (1999). Dimensions of children's motivation for reading and their relations to reading activity and reading achievement. *Reading Research Quarterly, 34,* 452–477.

Baumann, J. F., & Graves, M. F. (2010), What is academic vocabulary? *Journal of Adolescent and Adult Literacy, 54,* 4–12.

Beck, I. L., McKeown, M. G., & Kucan, L. (2002). *Bringing words to life: Robust vocabulary instruction.* New York: Guilford Press.

Blachowicz, C. L. Z., & Obrochta, C. (2005). Vocabulary visits: Virtual field trips for content vocabulary development. *The Reading Teacher, 59,* 262–268.

Brabham, E., Boyd, P., & Edgington, W. D. (2000). Sorting it out: Students' responses to fact and fiction in informational storybooks as read-alouds for science and social studies. *Reading Research and Instruction, 39,* 265–290.

Butterworth, C. (2011). *How did that get in my lunchbox?* Somerville, MA: Candlewick Press.

Cervetti, G. N., Bravo, M. A., Hiebert, E. H., Pearson, P. D., & Jaynes, C. A. (2009). Text genre and science content: Ease of reading, comprehension, and reader preference. *Reading Psychology, 30,* 487–511.

Chall, J., & Dale, E. (1995). *Readability revisited and the new Dale–Chall readability formula.* Cambridge, MA: Brookline Books.

Dickinson, D. K., & Porche, M. V. (2011). Relation between language experiences in preschool classrooms and children's kindergarten and fourth-grade language and reading abilities. *Child Development, 82,* 870–886.

Dreher, M. J. (2003). Motivating struggling readers by tapping the potential of information books. *Reading and Writing Quarterly, 19,* 25–38.

Dreher, M. J., & Kletzien, S. B. (2015). *Teaching informational text in K–3 classrooms: Best practices to help children read, write, and learn from nonfiction.* New York: Guilford Press.

Dreher, M. J., & Kletzien, S. B. (2016). Have recommended book lists changed to reflect current expectations for informational text in K–3 classrooms? *Reading Psychology, 37,* 371–391.

Duke, N. K. (2000). 3.6 minutes per day: The scarcity of informational texts in first grade. *Reading Research Quarterly, 35,* 202–224.

Fitzgerald, W. J., Elmore, J., Kung, M., & Jackson Stenner, A. (2017). The conceptual complexity of vocabulary in elementary-grades core science program textbooks. *Reading Research Quarterly, 52,* 417–442.

Fowler, A. (1994). *Hot and cold.* New York: Children's Press.

Gibson, R., & Dreher, M. J. (2007, December). *The effects of parent-led read-alouds of nonfiction books on first-graders' vocabulary acquisition and motivation to read.* Paper presented at the National Reading Conference No. 57, Austin, TX.

Gill, S. R. (2009). What teachers need to know about the "new" nonfiction. *The Reading Teacher, 63,* 260–267.

Guthrie, J. T., Anderson, E., Alao, S., & Rinehart, J. (1999). Influences of concept-oriented reading instruction on strategy use and conceptual learning from text. *Elementary School Journal, 99,* 343–366.

Heller, M. F. (2006). Telling stories and talking facts: First graders' engagements in a nonfiction book club. *The Reading Teacher, 60,* 358–369.

Hiebert, E. H. (2011). *Growing capacity with the vocabulary of English language arts programs* (Reading Research Report No. 11.02). Santa Cruz, CA: TextProject.

Hiebert, E. H., & Cervetti, G. N. (2011). *What differences in narrative and informational texts mean for the learning and instruction of vocabulary* (Reading Research Report No. 11.01). Santa Cruz, CA: TextProject.

International Reading Association & National Association for the Education of Young Children. (1998). Learning to read and write: Developmentally appropriate practices for young children. *The Reading Teacher, 52,* 193–216.

Jacobs, J. S., Morrison, T. G., & Swinyard, W. R. (2000). Reading aloud to students: A national probability study of classroom reading practices of elementary school teachers. *Reading Psychology, 21,* 171–193.

Jenkins, S., & Page, R. (2011). *Time for a bath.* New York: Houghton Mifflin.

Jeong, J., Gaffney, J. S., & Choi, J. O. (2010). Availability and use of informational texts in second-, third-, and fourth-grade classrooms. *Research in the Teaching of English, 44,* 435–456.

Jetton, T. (1994). Information-driven versus story-driven: What children remember when they are read informational stories. *Reading Psychology, 15,* 109–130.

Joubert, B., & Joubert, D. (2008). *Face to face with lions.* Washington, DC: National Geographic Society.

Kletzien, S. B., & DeRenzi, A. (2001, December). *"I like real books": Children's genre preferences.* Paper presented at the National Reading Conference, San Antonio, TX.

Kletzien, S. B., & Dreher, M. J. (2016, December). *Vocabulary demands in recommended books: A comparison of fiction and expository books.* Paper presented at the Literacy Research Association, Nashville, TN.

Kraemer, L., McCabe, P., & Sinatra, R. (2012). The effects of read-alouds of expository text on first graders' listening comprehension and book choice. *Literacy Research and Instruction, 51,* 165–178.

Maloch, B., & Horsey, M. (2013). Living inquiry: Learning from and about informational texts in a second-grade classroom. *The Reading Teacher, 66,* 475–485.

Markle, S. (2010). *Hip-pocket papa* (A. Marks, Illus.). Watertown, MA: Charlesbridge.

Martin, J. B. (1998). *Snowflake Bentley* (M. Azarian, Illus.). Boston: Houghton Mifflin.

Marzano, R. J., & Marzano, J. S. (1988). *A cluster approach to elementary vocabulary instruction.* Newark, DE: International Reading Association.

McClure, E. L., & Fullerton, S. K. (2017). Instructional interactions: Supporting students' reading development through interactive read-alouds of informational texts. *The Reading Teacher, 71*, 51–59.

McConnell, S. (1993). Talking drawings: A strategy for assisting learners. *Journal of Reading, 36*, 260–269.

Mohr, K. A. J. (2006). Children's choices for recreational reading: A three-part investigation of selection preferences, rationales, and processes. *Journal of Literacy Research, 38*, 81–104.

Mol, S. E., & Bus, A. G. (2011). To read or not to read: A meta-analysis of print exposure from infancy to early adulthood. *Psychological Bulletin, 137*, 267–296.

National Governors Association Center for Best Practices, Council of Chief State School Officers. (2010). *Common Core State Standards for English language arts and literacy in history/social studies, science, and technical subjects.* Washington, DC: Authors.

Ness, M. (2011). Teachers' use of and attitudes toward informational text in K–5 classrooms. *Reading Psychology, 32*, 28–53.

Neuman, S. B. (2013). *Swing, sloth!* Washington, DC: National Geographic Society.

Neuman, S. B. (2014). *Hop, bunny!* Washington, DC: National Geographic Society.

Neuman, S. B. (2016). *¡Salta, cachorrito!* Washington, DC: National Geographic Society.

Neuman, S. B., Kaefer, T., & Pinkham, A. M. (2016). Improving low-income preschoolers' word and world knowledge: The effects of content-rich instruction. *Elementary School Journal, 116*, 652–674.

Neuman, S. B., Newman, E. H., & Dwyer, J. (2011). Educational effects of a vocabulary intervention on preschoolers' word knowledge and conceptual development: A cluster-randomized trial. *Reading Research Quarterly, 46*, 249–272.

Pappas, C. C. (1993). Is narrative "primary"?: Some insights from kindergartners' pretend readings of stories and information books. *Journal of Reading Behavior, 25*, 97–129.

Pappas, C. C., & Barry, A. (1997). Scaffolding urban students' initiations: Transactions in reading information books in the read-aloud curriculum genre. In N. J. Karolides (Ed.), *Reader response in elementary classrooms: Quest and discovery* (pp. 215–236). Mahwah, NJ: Erlbaum.

Pappas, C. C., Varelas, M., Patton, S. K., Ye, L., & Ortiz, I. (2012). Dialogic strategies in read-alouds of English-language information books in a second-grade bilingual classroom. *Theory Into Practice, 51*, 263–272.

Paquette, K. R., Fello, S. E., & Jalongo, M. R. (2007). The talking drawings strategy: Using primary children's illustrations and oral language to improve comprehension of expository text. *Early Childhood Education Journal, 35*, 65–73.

Pearson, P. D., Hiebert, E. H., & Kamil, M. L. (2007). Vocabulary assessment: What we know and what we need to learn. *Reading Research Quarterly, 42*, 282–296.

Repaskey, L. L., Schumm, J., & Johnson, J. (2017) First and fourth grade boys' and girls' preferences for and perceptions about narrative and expository text. *Reading Psychology, 38*, 808–847.

Schiefele, U., Schaffner, E., Möller, J., & Wigfield, A. (2012). Dimensions of reading motivation and their relation to reading behavior and competence. *Reading Research Quarterly, 47*, 427–463.

Shanahan, T., Callison, K., Carriere, C., Duke, N. K., Pearson, P. D., Schatschneider, C., et al. (2010). *Improving reading comprehension in kindergarten through 3rd grade: A practice guide* (NCEE 2010-4038). Washington, DC: National Center for Education Evaluation and Regional Assistance, Institute of Education Sciences, U.S. Department of Education.

Sill, C. (2011). *About habitats: Grasslands* (J. Sill, Illus.). Atlanta, GA: Peachtree.

Smolkin, L., & Donovan, C. (2003). Supporting comprehension acquisition for emerging and struggling readers: The interactive information book read-aloud. *Exceptionality, 11*, 25–38.

Snow, C. E., Burns, M. S., & Griffin, P. (Eds.). (1998). *Preventing reading difficulties in young children*. Washington, DC: National Academies Press.

Stead, T. (2014). Nurturing the inquiring mind through the nonfiction read-aloud. *The Reading Teacher, 67*, 488–495.

Stewart, M. (2017a). A look at expository literature. Retrieved from *http://blogs.slj.com/afuse8production/2017/09/21/guest-post-melissa-stewart-a-look-at-expository-literature/#_.*

Stewart, M. (2017b). What the heck is expository literature? Retrieved from *http://celebratescience.blogspot.com/2017/02/behind-books-what-heck-is-expository.html.*

Varelas, M., & Pappas, C. C. (2006). Intertextuality in read-alouds of integrated science–literacy units in urban primary classrooms: Opportunities for the development of thought and language. *Cognition and Instruction, 24*, 211–259.

Varelas, M., Pieper, L. Arsenault, A., Pappas, C. C., & Keblawe-Shamah, N. (2014). How science texts and hands-on explorations facilitate meaning making: Learning from Latina/o third graders. *Journal of Research in Science Teaching, 51*, 1246–1274.

Weizman, Z. O., & Snow, C. E. (2001). Lexical input as related to children's vocabulary acquisition: Effects of sophisticated exposure and support for meaning. *Developmental Psychology, 37*, 265–279.

Wright, T. S. (2013). From potential to reality: Content-rich vocabulary and informational text. *The Reading Teacher, 67*, 359–367.

Wright, T. S., & Neuman, S. B. (2013). Vocabulary instruction in commonly used kindergarten core reading curricula. *Elementary School Journal, 113*, 386–408.

Yopp, R. H., & Yopp, H. K. (2006). Informational texts as read-alouds at school and home. *Journal of Literacy Research, 38*, 37–51.

Yopp, R. H., & Yopp, H. K. (2012). Children's limited and narrow exposure to informational text. *The Reading Teacher, 65*, 480–490.

CHAPTER 4

What Does Discussion Add to Reading for Conceptual Learning?

PEI-YU MARIAN PAN
BRIAN W. MILLER
RICHARD C. ANDERSON

Reading appears to be a solitary endeavor: a child under the covers with a flashlight, a student huddled in a cozy corner of the library, a scholar staring into a computer's pale glow. However, we argue that reading is, and should be, anything but solitary. As Mark Haddon (2004) wrote, "Reading is a conversation. All books talk, but a good book listens as well." In this chapter, we claim that reading is, ideally, a conversation, and that reading to learn concepts is especially dialogic, or an interaction between the reader and the text. As such, we urge educators to embed reading comprehension instruction in a social context, because doing so helps students learn the thinking skills needed to read effectively and to think through conceptual topics in a deep way. We further urge theorists to embrace this approach to ensure that innovations in social approaches to reading continue to flourish.

The idea that reading comprehension should be taught in a social context is not new, nor is it restricted to educational theorists. Teachers display a belief in this principle when they use the phrases "Let's struggle with the text," "You need to engage with the text," and "We should be challenging the text." This language reveals an intuitive understanding that the process of reading should be akin to a conversation between the reader and the author, and that the classroom is the proper place to begin that conversation. Teachers often make reading a social event by reading aloud to children, having children read to each other, and talking about texts.

However, it is not at all clear that teachers understand the critical distinction between talking as a way to understand a particular text and talking as a way to gain the skills of reading comprehension. As repeated research has demonstrated, teachers tend to dominate classroom discourse. Teachers mostly use a pattern of speaking in which they present a question, pick a student to respond, then evaluate that response, followed quickly by another question—a pattern called the IRE, which stands for initiation–response–evaluation (Cazden, 2001). This pattern of talk is well structured for certain tasks, such as reviewing the details of a story, or checking whether students have read the story. However, it requires mostly surface-level comprehension, and it does not model reading comprehension strategies. For this reason, it is unlikely to lead to better reading comprehension of new conceptual texts. Quality discussion, on the other hand, can improve reading comprehension skills that can then be applied to future texts.

A number of studies have shown that quality classroom discussion does indeed improve students' reading comprehension. In a meta-analysis of 42 empirical studies, Murphy, Wilkinson, Soter, Hennessey, and Alexander (2009) calculated the effect sizes of nine major approaches to classroom discussions on reading comprehension measures. The authors grouped these approaches by the stance they took toward the text. Approaches that took an *efferent* stance focused on gaining knowledge from the texts; these included questioning the author (Beck & McKeown, 2006), instructional conversations (Goldenberg, 1993), and shared inquiry (Great Books Foundation, 1987). Approaches that took an *aesthetic* stance focused on encouraging children to make a personal response to texts; these included literature circles (Short & Pierce, 1990), grand conversations (Eeds & Wells, 1989), and book club (Raphael & McMahon, 1994). Finally, the approaches that took a *critical–analytic* stance were focused on questioning the claims and issues raised by the text and included collaborative reasoning (Anderson, Chinn, Waggoner, & Nguyen, 1998), paideia seminar (Billings & Fitzgerald, 2002), and philosophy for children (Sharp, 1995). Results from the analysis indicate that efferent discussion approaches led to improved literal and inferential reading comprehension, whereas critical–analytic discussion approaches led to improved critical thinking, reasoning, and argumentation. There is also evidence that shared inquiry, questioning the author, and collaborative reasoning showed that the gains made in reading comprehension are transferable to new texts.

Why Do Discussions Lead to Improved Reading Comprehension?

The sociocultural perspective provides a plausible explanation for why discussions might lead to improved comprehension. The sociocultural perspective is most closely associated with the developmental psychologist Lev Vygotsky (1978), who wrote:

> Every function in the child's cultural development appears twice: first, on the social level, and later, on the individual level; first, between people (interpsychological) and then inside the child (intrapsychological). This applies equally to voluntary attention, to logical memory, and to the formation of concepts. All the higher functions originate as actual relationships between individuals. (p. 57)

In Vygotsky's vision, the interlocutor with which we converse in the process of learning is the internalized voices of our parents, teachers, friends, and community. When we talk back to the text, we are responding to the internalized voice of the imagined author. Logically following from this vision, Vygotsky promoted children talking with other children, talking with parents and the teacher, and talking to themselves as a means of developing individual thinking (Au & Kawakami, 1983). Discussion helps us create an inner dialogue. As Morris and his colleagues (2018) suggest, discussion can give children the understanding of "the self as agent and others as audience" (p. 245).

Reznitskya and colleagues (2001) extended the idea of internalization by combining it with schema theory (Anderson & Pearson, 1984). A *schema* is a generalized type of knowledge. It is a flexible outline that allows people to more easily understand specific ideas. For example, everyone has ideas about how to make an argument, which is called an argument schema. A well-developed argument schema guides a person to make a claim and to provide convincing evidence. It can also help a person quickly understand and evaluate new arguments. Reznitskya and her colleagues proposed the *argument schema theory* to explain how people develop argument schemas as they talk with each other; they internalize the norms, expectations, and skills that constitute the ability to present or understand an argument.

To better understand the social nature of argument schema theory, let us compare this theory with some of the most influential models of reading comprehension today. These models are built on the metaphor of the mind as a machine or computer. In this metaphor, individual pieces of knowledge are like light bulbs on a vast board, and each light bulb is connected to many other bulbs. Most of the time, any particular bulb is off, but when one bulb lights up, then the bulbs connected to it also light up. When we read, each word and phrase causes ideas to light up, which in turn causes many other ideas to light up. For example, when the word *wolf* is read, the mind may also be reminded of the words *dog, Little Red Riding Hood,* and *the dark forest.*

One example of such a theory specifically designed to account for conceptual reading is the knowledge revision components (KReC) framework recently proposed by Kendeou, Walsh, Smith, and O'Brien (2014). In the KReC framework, each piece of information that is read brings to mind all the other information associated with it. The theory suggests that these thoughts are brought to mind automatically, whether the reader wants this to happen or not. When the incoming information conflicts with existing information, the reader attempts to integrate both pieces of information and make a coherent understanding from them. The newly formed and coherent conception will coexist with the original conception in memory. Over time, if the reader keeps receiving information consistent with the new conception, it will be reinforced and become better rooted in the knowledge network. Eventually, the new conception will come to mind more readily, and the original one will fade away.

The KReC gives one plausible explanation regarding why reading so-called "refutational texts"—texts that present both scientific conceptions and common misconceptions—are more effective than traditional texts that only present the scientific understanding (Sinatra & Broughton, 2011; Tippett, 2010). However, theories such as KReC are designed from the perspective of one individual; they do not directly address other people. Furthermore, they envision the text as simply an inert source of information—not as a thing with which you can converse. Theories such as KReC suggest that fostering conceptual learning is primarily a matter of properly exposing students to more information. Readers are perceived as individual agents who independently construct accurate conceptual understanding from a text when presented with the right information.

Argument schema theory is different (Reznitskaya et al., 2001, 2009). The dialogical approach requires readers to go beyond their own understanding of the text. In theories based on the Vygotskian idea of internalization, readers change the way they read as a result of their interactions with other people. They are exposed to novel ideas from

other discussants that might elaborate or conflict with their own understanding. Through the dynamic reasoning process, they are stimulated
to evaluate critically and refine their own thoughts regarding the text.
The final comprehension outcome is stretched beyond textual meaning
construction at the individual level. Yet there is a caveat: Not all types
of discussion stretch thinking; therefore, it is important to examine the
kind of discussion that can add to reading for conceptual learning.

What Kind of Discussion?

In our exploration of reading within the context of discussion, it is
important to make a distinction between the many types of discussion
that exist. Discussion is already a widely practiced activity in classrooms.
However, there are various definitions regarding what constitutes a discussion.

One teacher might ask students a question such as "Why did Jack
and Jill go up the hill?" These questions are intended to help reinforce
the details of the story or to determine who has actually read the story.
Students participating in these discussions learn to ask themselves factual questions as they read to monitor how well they are comprehending
the story at the most basic level. These discussions are usually conducted
in the familiar IRE format described earlier.

Another teacher might say, "This week we are reading a nonfiction
text about erosion. Has anyone here been to the Grand Canyon? What
did you see there?" These questions are intended to help students make
personal connections with the text. Any answer to these questions is
acceptable, because all answers help students to learn the skill of conversing with the text by responding with their own memories, thoughts,
and feelings.

However, to learn concepts, neither of these types of discussion is
ideal, because concepts are not simple facts or personal experiences.
Concepts are complex and multifaceted. Concepts are embedded in
larger belief systems. Concepts can be true in one way and not another.
To understand concepts within a text is to engage with the text in an
argumentative way. By *argumentative*, we do not mean combative, but
rather the kind of discussion in which all participants seek to achieve a
better understanding by proposing, analyzing, and challenging claims.

Let's take the concept of keystone species as an example. Here is a
short text we wrote to explain this concept:

"A keystone species is a critical species in an ecosystem. If the key-stone species disappeared, an ecosystem would change dramatically. If other species disappeared there would be smaller changes. A key-stone species is often a large predator, like a wolf, because these species regulate the population size of many other prey, scavenger, and competitor species. The reintroduction of wolves to Yellowstone National Park is a documented example of the keystone species con-cept. When wolves were reintroduced to Yellowstone, the popula-tions of many species changed. The number of elk changed, because the wolves ate them. Wolves do not eat beavers, but the number of beavers also changed. Since the elk were hunted by wolves, the elk spent less time near water, which allowed willow trees to grow, which allowed beavers to survive winter, which led to more beavers being born in spring."

Even within this abbreviated explanation of the keystone species concept, there are several features intended to make the reader under-stand and believe the concept. Even the name supports understanding of the concept. The name *keystone* is an analogy to the keystone of an arch that allows all of the other stones to remain in place. To fully understand the concept, readers need to understand and evaluate this analogy.

Understanding the keystone concept also depends on relational and causal thinking. *Relational thinking* is the type of thinking that analyzes the connections, or relationships, between things. In the case of beavers, there is a complex relationship involving a cascade of effects. It is easy to understand direct connections, but it is more difficult to understand a long causal chain, like the one that describes the relationships between wolves, elk, willow trees, and beavers.

As the example of the keystone species concept illustrates, learn-ing concepts from text requires a host of thinking skills. Sociocultural perspectives describe how people acquire these thinking skills by talking with other people.

The Collaborative Reasoning Approach to Classroom Discussion

We developed an approach to discussion called collaborative reasoning (CR), which can serve as a model for discussions designed to support the learning of those thinking skills needed for conceptual reading. CR is an approach to peer collaboration in which students argue about a controversy (Anderson et al., 1998). The controversy is raised by a text students have read, then presented to them as a single big question. Students take positions on the big question and support their positions with evidence-based reasoning. They are expected to listen carefully to what others say and evaluate their colleagues' statements and evidence. They are also encouraged to challenge views different from their own with counterarguments.

Students control the flow of discussion, interacting with one another freely, without raising their hands. Teachers are present, but they play a supporting role and only provide scaffolding when needed. No hierarchy is imposed on the group, such as assigning a discussion moderator, although student leaders usually emerge spontaneously (Sun, Anderson, Perry, & Lin, 2017).

The CR discussion structure endorses a minimal role for teachers and a maximal role for students. This is beneficial for two reasons. First, minimal teacher input (e.g., ask for clarification, prompt for reasoning) is sufficient to keep the student discussions going (Jadallah et al., 2011) and still promote cognitive gains (e.g., Chi & Wiley, 2014; Reznitskaya et al., 2009). Second, peer communication can be more effective than teacher–student communication due to the correspondence in peers' speech (Noddings, 1985); that is, students can better understand each other's thoughts than those of adults, and can provide explanations accordingly (Vedder, 1985). For instance, student modeling throughout a discussion is more effective than teacher modeling in promoting relational thinking (Lin, Jadallah, et al., 2015). Teacher models of relational thinking may be too complicated for students to understand. In contrast, peer models are often much easier to comprehend and therefore more appropriate for use in the discussion.

How Do CR Discussions Help Children Understand and Evaluate Concepts in Texts?

Careful observation of CR discussions has shown that when a student uses a particularly useful stratagem, other students copy that same technique. For example, if one student challenges another student by saying, "Some people might say [counterargument]," it is likely that another student will use a similar phrase to accomplish the same goal, because this approach allows the speaker to challenge an argument in an indirect nonthreatening way. As time goes by, more and more students use these successful stratagems with increasing frequency—a process Anderson et al. (2001) called *snowballing*. Stratagems are often introduced in the discussion by social leaders in the group, then picked up by other students (Lin, Anderson, et al., 2015). In addition to argument stratagems (Dong, Anderson, Kim, & Li, 2008), some of the many skills we have documented as snowballing include analogical thinking (Lin et al., 2012) and causal reasoning (Ma et al., 2017).

Using the Vygotskian vocabulary (Vygotsky, 1978), students' snowballing of argument moves is an indication of *partial internalization*—an early stage of learning in which students can accomplish a process in a social context but are not yet able to perform it on their own. Fully internalized argument moves will occur when the different roles performed by multiple people in the social context all occur in the student's own mind. It is like an internal dialogue between a student and the rest of the class. For instance, as a student is formulating an argument in his or her mind, he or she will also be aware of other disagreeing "voices" with potentially plausible evidence to counter his or her argument. To make her claim stand, the student will need to address those possible counterarguments.

We investigated whether the process of internalization had occurred by asking students to read a new story, *Pine Wood Derby*. It presented an ethical dilemma that involved weighing the relative importance of many competing ethical challenges, including cheating, keeping secrets, being kind to people less fortunate, and obeying authority (e.g., Reznitskaya et al., 2001). Participants then individually wrote essays explaining their opinions. Students who had previously participated in CR discussions used the text to generate more satisfactory arguments, counterarguments, and rebuttals than similar students who had not participated in CR discussions. This result has been replicated in several different educational settings, including online discussions, and in face-to-face discussions in large and small American cities, urban and rural areas of China, as well as Korean and Malaysian communities (Dong et al., 2008; Kim, Anderson, Miller, Jeong, & Swim, 2011; Kim, Anderson, Nguyen-Jahiel, & Archodidiou, 2007; Ma'rof, 2014; Morris et al., 2018; Reznitskaya et al., 2001).

The repeated finding that students can use ways of thinking they have acquired in their discussions in a new and different individual task is a demonstration of the Vygotskian idea of internalization (Vygotsky, 1978). The tools of reasoning begin as ways of communicating with others, to help each other clarify ideas, and to improve argumentation quality; they gradually become internalized for students to use freely. The once external voices have become one's own voice.

Multilink Causal Reasoning for Conceptual Learning

CR improves students' ability to engage in multilink causal reasoning (Ma et al., 2017). Reading about concepts often requires students to consider claims about a series of relationships. The effect of wolves on beavers, described earlier, is an example of a multilink causal chain. Table 4.1 presents another example of a causal chain. Students needed to decide whether a pack of wolves should be kept or eradicated because they are a potential threat to community safety. They then wrote an individual policy letter explaining their own opinion on the issue. CR students produced significantly longer causal chains than other students. Multilink causal reasoning pushes students to consider different aspects of the issue, including ecology (i.e., the imbalance between elks and plants) and economy (i.e., hunters and timber companies), then ponder the relationship among potential factors, as well as how they can influence one another. With this skill, students can better evaluate the relationships in a previously unread text.

Analogical Reasoning for Empathy

Analogical reasoning is an important form of higher-order cognition that can be developed through CR discussions (Dong et al., 2008; Lin et al., 2012). Through analogical reasoning, one can identify possibly important elements of a novel target domain (e.g., electrons), and the relationship among these elements (e.g., how electrons flow along a wire); this can occur through a comparison of the novel target domain (e.g., electrons) to a familiar source domain (e.g., water flowing in a ditch) (Gentner, 1983; Hummel & Holyoak, 1997).

Lin et al. (2012) found that when children first participated in CR discussions, they began to repeat or elaborate on analogies that were presented by previous speakers. Over time, students learned to generate new analogies and did so at an increasing rate. The construction of new analogies, such as those discussed earlier, suggests that students learned to analyze situations in terms of deeper relationships; in other words, they were able to perceive the situations from a new angle. Indeed, analogical reasoning is a vital skill, because it enables students to critically examine and compare the overall significant components and relational features in each information source, especially when they encounter information inconsistent with their prior knowledge. An example is the keystone

TABLE 4.1. An Example of a Multilink Causal Chain in Collaborative Discussion

KAYLA: I think that wolves help:: [clears throat] I think that wolves help balance the um::like balance the food web and balance the food chain of how things go, because if there was too many elk then the number of producers would go down. If you know:: If it, too:: If there was too less elk, the number of producers will go up too bad. And I think that:: I know:: I wouldn't want to go outside, keep on cutting, cutting, cutting down trees, but that's:: does:: for the timber company to do, right? That's why I think:: That's why um the elk is eating the trees up and that the wolves are kill the elk. So the trees are growing more. That's why the wolf:: um the timber company is making more. And then:: But, second, I'm now thinking about the hunters, because the hunters aren't getting that much money, because the wolves are already killing all the food, and they can't take roadkill. I wouldn't eat roadkill.

JOHN: Uh-uh. Yeah, like you said, if the elk get over popular [populated], they will eat all the grass and stuff. Then there will be other animals that eat grass, they won't have anything to eat. So they might starve you know.

MARCELO: Yeah, and like we in my activity booklet, we made a pie chart, like on Jaylen's box, box B. Well, half:: Timber makes half the money, right? And if the wolves, if they kill the wolves, there is no more wolves in Winona, the elk population will go up and they'll eat most of the trees that the timber has to cut. Now think of this, if the timber has to shut down, we'll only have these three major businesses left to carry the city.

JOHN: And timber makes most money.

MARCELO: Yeah. Four million dollars a year. That's [1] half of the money. [1]

KAYLA: [1] If that happened, [1] if that may happen, I think that the timber company wouldn't technically shut down, but have to cut down some of our trees that we actually use and stuff. And like [2] our apple trees and [2] stuff like that. 'Cause you know how we have them apple thingies when we go [3] [3] yeah, and stuff like that. And I think they'll end up cutting those down and then after they cut those down they have to cut:: they have to stop making houses, stop making tables and chairs, we have to sit on the floor.

Note. [1], [2], [3] indicate segments of interjected and overlapped speech. :: denotes sentence fragments.

described earlier, a specially shaped piece of stone, which holds the other pieces together so that the structure stays intact. In an ecosystem, the wolf is one of the keystone species, which means that major changes to the species has the potential to significantly alter the ecosystem. If someone claims that relocation of a wolf pack is beneficial to the ecosystem, students who understand the keystone analogy will immediately raise a red flag about this statement.

Analogical reasoning enables students to transfer social values from one setting to another. In the dialogue excerpted in Table 4.2, Bruce puts himself in the position of the wolves. Then, he draws an analogy between people living in their own houses and wolves living in their natural habitat. He claims that eradicating the wolves from their territory is just like

TABLE 4.2. Illustration of the Use of Analogy to Instill Empathy

BRUCE: I would:: My main idea is I just wouldn't want to kill the wolves, 'cause if you are a wolf living in your own territory, not bother no elks, [Dan] Exactly. [Dan] you would not:: You wouldn't want to be messed with or getting chased down by hunters or cars or anything. You just want to live in your natural habitat, like what:: [Avril] Right [Avril] we lived in our:: we lived in our houses.

AVRIL: It's like:: it's like:: it's like:: it's like:: it's like nature killing:: it's like:: it's like you're killing yourself, because you:: you don't want any:: you don't want any big animal killing you, right?

SALLY: Or it's like saying:: You know how animals, they get killed, or we could get, like:: We could get shot, we can go to jail. It's the same thing like they get caged. Feels like we are getting in jail. [Bruce] Exactly. [Bruce] Or they are getting hunt, like we getting killed by someone else.

AVRIL: Like:: like:: like if we kill them a:: another animal could kill us for killing someone, for killing an animal that they might rely on. So you know::

BRUCE: Or:: And it's like if:: if you li*:: You're living in your house peacefully, not bother nobody, and some people just:: [Avril] And somebody:: somebody just come in and try to kill you, or whatever. [Avril] Yeah, and people just:: and people just come in without even knock on your door or telling you that they are coming. And they just broke in, right in your door [Avril] Right, just bust in the door. [Avril] And tell you to get out of your house. That's probably was what the wolves feel like. If they got killed:: so I wouldn't want to kill them, because we would feel the same:: feel the same way.

Note. [Name] [Name] indicates segment of overlapped or interjected speech. :: denotes sentence fragments.

someone breaking into someone's house to kill the people. Bruce's analogy is revoiced and elaborated by others in the discussion.

Seeing the relevance of social values in new and different situations is a source of empathy toward others, which is crucial for social understanding and prosocial behavior (Findlay, Girardi, & Coplan, 2006). Analogical reasoning is particularly observed when students discuss texts in social sciences and the humanities, such as history, political science, and ethnic studies that bear on public policy. Public policy always involves social values and is not necessarily straightforward or black and white. Analogical reasoning can enable transfer of social norms, and consequently, empathy, from one situation to another; thus, it can help students better understand different voices and consider the emotional implications of possible courses of action.

Metacognition for Conceptual Learning

CR appears to improve students' metacognition as well (Latawiec et al., 2016). *Metacognition* is the ability to reflect on and evaluate one's own thoughts; for example, did my claim make sense to my audience, did my evidence support my point? Based on such an evaluation, you can deliberately adjust your performance to achieve a goal (Winne & Azevedo, 2014). Metacognition is important in reading for conceptual learning, because it is often necessary for students to accommodate their existing concepts in light of new concepts. When reading is difficult or confusing because you have beliefs that conflict with what you are supposed to learn, reading slows down; to succeed, readers have to exercise control over what is ordinarily a largely automatic process (Dole, 2000). Rather than just accepting thoughts that bubble up, it may take some self-conscious work to come to a resolution.

Without skill and the disposition to reflect on what they are reading, students may fail to realize that there are discrepancies between their prior beliefs and the information in a text (Chi, 2008). Sustained engagement in the type of metacognition required to resolve conflicting ideas is difficult for individual readers (Thiede, Griffin, Wiley, & Reford, 2009), because it can create a heavy cognitive load. Juggling alternative interpretations requires readers to keep in mind more information than is normally needed for reading. A collaborative discussion can help students cope with a large amount of possibly conflicting information, enabling students to think critically and analytically about a conceptual text despite the obstacles (Dole & Sinatra, 1998).

Through the group process, peers' challenges, or requests for clarification, students become aware of inadequacies in their own ideas and are introduced to new possibilities. To play their part in a discussion, students must strive to make their contributions complete and cogent. Then, peers provide further feedback and students once again try to improve their ideas until all are satisfied. Continuous feedback from peers alleviates the cognitive demands of self-evaluation. Students learn to form their thoughts through a more reflective and critical lens.

Table 4.3 presents an excerpt from a discussion of *Amy's Goose* (Holmes, 1977) to illustrate how students endeavor to refine an argument

TABLE 4.3. Illustration of Argument Development in Response to Peer Feedback

AURETHA:	But the//
KEVIN:	Yeah, but the bar-, barn door's closed.
TIMOTHY:	// Yeah, but if they knock it down.
SYLVIA:	What kind of fox : could do that?
AURETHA:	: How, how could the fox knock out the door? [children giggle]
TIMOTHY:	Jump on it?
KEVIN:	: Yeah, right.
SYLVIA:	: No, he's not strong enough.
MARCEL:	I don't :: that's gonna?
AURETHA:	:: OK, jump down the door, knock out the door, if, the door's rusty, and wiggly.
TIMOTHY:	::: Yeah, but if it won't,
KEVIN:	::: And if it is very old, too.
TIMOTHY:	But people open the door, to get in there, the fox can sneak in, so while they're gone//
SYLVIA:	// Yeah, but they could see the fox sneak in.

Note. : denotes the first occurrence of overlapping speech. :: and ::: denote the second and third occurrences, respectively. The first // indicates where the speech is interrupted, whereas the adjacent // denotes the interjecting speech.

in response to peer feedback. In the excerpt, Auretha, Kevin, and Timothy argue that a fox could knock down a door to enter the barn. However, Sylvia is not convinced by their claim and continues to point out flaws in their argument. Because of Sylvia's immediate and continuous feedback, the other students were able to realize the inadequacies in their argument and further improve it. Such a collaborative context enables students to develop and exercise metacognition. Research has found that CR students are able to internalize this skill and employ it when writing an individual essay. In their essays, students entertain the pros and cons of multiple possibilities as if they were responding to an imaginary challenger (Reznitskaya et al., 2009).

Conclusion

To understand a conceptual text, readers need to reason actively with the ideas it contains, ideas that possibly conflict with readers' existing beliefs. The necessary reasoning skills can include drawing causal relationships, comparing similar concepts, synthesizing different sources of information, evaluating peers' and one's own conceptual understanding, and reconciling conflicting ideas. Such thinking is fostered in a dialogical context, such as CR, an open, student-managed approach to classroom discussion. CR has been shown to be effective in developing causal reasoning (Ma et al., 2017), analogical thinking (Lin et al., 2012), decision making (Zhang et al., 2016), stratagems for arguing (Anderson et al., 2001), and facility in metacognition (Latawiec et al., 2016). Students who participate in CR develop a more complete argument schema, including the knowledge that a sound argument incorporates evidence and considers both sides of the issue (Anderson et al., 2001; Reznitskaya et al., 2009).

Social interaction exposes students to novel reasoning skills. In collaborative discussion, socially and cognitively advanced peers serve as models of good thinking; the skills they display are picked up and internalized by other students. Later, students are able to use the thinking skills for individual tasks, such as essay writing. The discussion brings forth various perspectives as students help one another evaluate the cogency and comprehensiveness of ideas. Through collaboration, students can co-construct ideas about complex and difficult concepts; the co-construction process refines their conceptual understanding.

Besides the cognitive benefits, CR fosters positive social and affective dispositions foundational for conceptual learning. Student leadership of discussions emerges and in turn improves learning outcomes (Li et al., 2007; Sun et al., 2017). CR facilitates engagement and positive feelings (e.g., enjoyment, curiosity, interest, excitement) toward thinking about difficult issues, especially in students who were previously less engaged in school. Positive feelings are associated with increased engagement, and both engagement and positive feelings are significantly related to learning outcomes (Sun et al., 2018). Increased engagement, interest, and curiosity promote the kind of deep reading of texts necessary for conceptual growth (Miller et al., 2014).

In summary, intellectually and socially stimulating dialogue, such as that in CR discussions, can elevate students' reading experience. In discussions, children encounter ideas that may not occur to an individual child. The need to communicate presses children to express ideas that they would leave vague or incomplete if they were working alone. In collaborative discussions, thinking skills emerge that support learning from conceptual texts. Collaborative discussions inspire the disposition to look at the other side, to spontaneously consider counterarguments invoked, we may suppose, by a little voice, distilled from the many voices of classmates and others with whom one has argued, that whispers, "Wait, what's wrong with that idea? What would someone who disagrees say?" Talking with peers about controversial issues is fun for children and socially fulfilling. Positive feelings and social stimulation fuel students' motivation to read texts deeply and further enhance learning outcomes. Supported by research evidence, CR is a viable discussion approach that can be integrated into reading instruction to optimize conceptual learning.

● IMPLICATIONS FOR PROFESSIONAL LEARNING ●

- Student-centered discussions can extend concepts introduced in reading as students strive to explain themselves to their classmates and respond to criticisms.
- During discussions, students can learn academic vocabulary and begin to acquire higher-order thinking skills by observing peers.
- Students as early as grade 3 can collaboratively conduct an argumentative discussion. Minimal teacher support, such as prompts for evidence or clarification, is sufficient to maintain the discussion flow.

QUESTIONS FOR DISCUSSION

1. How would you formulate a big question for discussion?
2. What are the expectations and norms you intend for students to follow during discussions?
3. What is a suitable size for a discussion group? How would you decide which children to put in each group?

REFERENCES

Anderson, R. C., Chinn, C., Waggoner, M., & Nguyen, K. T. (1998). Intellectually stimulating story discussions. In J. Osborn & F. Lehr (Eds.), *Literacy for all* (pp. 170–196). New York: Guilford Press.

Anderson, R. C., Nguyen-Jahiel, K., McNurlen, B., Archodidou, A., Kim, S.-Y., Reznitskaya, A., et al. (2001). The snowball phenomenon: Spread of ways of talking and ways of thinking across groups of children. *Cognition and Instruction, 19*, 1–46.

Anderson, R. C., & Pearson, D. (1984). A schema-theoretic view of basic processes in reading comprehension. In P. D. Pearson, R. Barr, M. L. Kamil, & P. Mosenthal (Eds.), *Handbook of reading research* (pp. 255–291). New York: Longman.

Au, K. H.-P., & Kawakami, A. J. (1983). Vygotskian perspectives on discussion processes in small-group reading lessons. In P. Peterson (Ed.), *The social context of instruction: Group organization and group processes* (pp. 209–225). New York: Academic Press.

Beck, I. L., & McKeown, M. G. (2006). *Improving comprehension with questioning the author: A fresh and expanded view of a powerful approach.* New York: Scholastic.

Billings, L., & Fitzgerald, J. (2002). Dialogic discussion and the Paideia Seminar. *American Educational Research Journal, 39*(4), 907–941.

Cazden, C. (2001). *Classroom discourse: The language of teaching and learning* (2nd ed.). Portsmouth, NH: Heinemann.

Chi, M. T. H. (2008). Three types of conceptual change: Belief revision, mental model transformation, and categorical shift. In S. Vosniadou (Ed.), *International handbook of research on conceptual change* (pp. 61–82). New York: Routledge.

Chi, M. T. H., & Wiley, R. (2014). The ICAP framework: Linking cognitive engagement to active learning outcomes. *Educational Psychologist, 49*(4), 219–243.

Dole, J. A. (2000). Readers, texts and conceptual change learning. *Reading and Writing Quarterly, 16*, 99–118.

Dole, J. A., & Sinatra, G. M. (1998). Reconceptualizing change in the cognitive construction of knowledge. *Educational Psychologist, 33*(2), 109–128.

Dong, T., Anderson, R. C., Kim, I., & Li, Y. (2008). Collaborative reasoning in China and Korea. *Reading Research Quarterly, 43*, 400–424.

Eeds, M., & Wells, D. (1989). Grand conversations: An exploration of meaning construction in literature study groups. *Research in the Teaching of English, 23*(1), 4–29.

Findlay, L. C., Girardi, A. B., & Coplan, R. J. (2006). Links between empathy, social behavior, and social understanding in early childhood. *Early Childhood Research Quarterly, 21*, 347–359.

Gentner, D. (1983). Structure-mapping: A theoretical framework for analogy. *Cognitive Science, 7,* 155–170.

Goldenberg, C. (1993). Instructional conversations: Promoting comprehension through discussion. *The Reading Teacher, 46*(4), 316–326.

Great Books Foundation. (1987). *An introduction to shared inquiry.* Chicago: Great Books Foundation.

Haddon, M. (2004). B is for bestseller. Retrieved from *www.theguardian.com/books/2004/apr/11/booksforchildrenandteenagers.features3.*

Holmes, E. T. (1977). *Amy's goose.* New York: Crowell.

Hummel, J. E., & Holyoak, K. J. (1997). Distributed representations of structure: A theory of analogical access and mapping. *Psychological Review, 104,* 427–466.

Jadallah, M., Anderson, R. C., Nguyen-Jahiel, K., Miller, B. W., Kim, I., Kuo, L., et al. (2011). Influence of a teacher's scaffolding moves during child-led small-group discussions. *American Educational Research Journal, 48*(1), 194–230.

Kendeou, P., Walsh, E. K., Smith, E. R., & O'Brien, E. J. (2014). Knowledge revision processes in refutation texts. *Discourse Processes, 51,* 374–397.

Kim, I.-H., Anderson, R. C., Miller, B. W., Jeong, J., & Swim, T. (2011). Influence of cultural norms and collaborative discussions on children's reflective essays. *Discourse Processes, 48,* 501–528.

Kim, I.-H., Anderson, R. C., Nguyen-Jahiel, K., & Archodidiou, A. (2007). Discourse patterns in children's collaborative online discussions. *Journal of the Learning Sciences, 16,* 333–370.

Latawiec, B. M., Anderson, R. C., Nguyen-Jahiel, K., Ma, S., Kim, I.-H., Kuo, L.-J., et al. (2016). Influence of oral discussion on metadiscourse in children's essays. *Text and Talk, 36,* 23–46.

Li, Y., Anderson, R. C., Nguyen-Jahiel, K., Dong, T., Archodidou, A., Kim, I., et al. (2007). Emergent leadership in children's discussion groups. *Cognition and Instruction, 25*(1), 75–111.

Lin, T.-J., Anderson, R. C., Hummel, J. E., Jadallah, M., Miller, B. W., Nguyen-Jahiel, K., et al. (2012). Children's use of analogy during collaborative reasoning. *Child Development, 83,* 1429–1443.

Lin, T.-J., Anderson, R. C., Jadallah, M., Nguyen-Jahiel, K., Kim, I.-H., Kuo, L.-J., et al. (2015). Social influences on the development of relational thinking during small-group discussions. *Contemporary Educational Psychology, 41,* 83–97.

Lin, T.-J., Jadallah, M., Anderson, R. C., Baker, A. R., Nguyen-Jahiel, K., Kim, I.-H., et al. (2015). Less is more: Teachers' influence on peer collaboration. *Journal of Educational Psychology, 107,* 609–629.

Ma, S., Anderson, R. C., Lin, T.-J., Zhang, J., Morris, J. A., Nguyen-Jahiel, K., et al. (2017). Instructional influences on English language learners' storytelling. *Learning and Instruction, 49,* 64–80.

Ma'rof, A. M. (2014). *Think, talk, read, and write better English: Improving L2 literacy skills of Malaysian school children through collaborative reasoning.* Unpublished doctoral dissertation, University of Illinois at Urbana–Champaign, Champaign, IL.

Miller, B. W., Anderson, R. C., & Morris, J., Lin, T.-J., Jadallah, M., & Sun, J. (2014). Effects of anticipating an argumentative discussion on text reading and conceptual change. *Learning and Instruction, 33,* 67–80.

Morris, J. A., Miller, B. W., Anderson, R. C., Nguyen-Jahiel, K. T., Lin, T.-J., Scott, T., et al. (2018). Instructional discourse and argumentative writing. *International Journal of Educational Research, 90*(1), 234–247.

Murphy, P. K., Wilkinson, I. A. G., Soter, A. O., Hennessey, M. N., & Alexander, J. F. (2009). Examining the effects of classroom discussion on students' comprehension of text: A meta-analysis. *Journal of Educational Psychology, 101*(3), 740–764.

Noddings, N. (1985). Small groups as a setting for research on mathematical problem solving. In E. A. Silver (Ed.), *Teaching and learning mathematical problem solving* (pp. 345–360). Hillsdale, NJ: Erlbaum.

Raphael, T. E., & McMahon, S. I. (1994). Book club: An alternative framework for reading instruction. *The Reading Teacher, 48*(2), 102–116.

Reznitskaya, A., Anderson, R. C., McNurlen, B., Nguyen-Jahiel, K., Archodidou, A., & Kim, S. (2001). Influence of oral discussion on written argument. *Discourse Processes, 32,* 155–175.

Reznitskaya, A., Kuo, L.-J., Clark, A.-M., Miller, B., Jadallah, M., Anderson, R. C., et al. (2009). Collaborative reasoning: A dialogic approach to group discussions. *Cambridge Journal of Education, 39,* 29–48.

Sharp, A. M. (1995). Philosophy for children and the development of ethical values. *Early Child Development and Care, 107*(1), 45–55.

Short, K., & Pierce, K. M. (1990). *Talking about books: Creating literate communities.* Portsmouth, NH: Heinemann.

Sinatra, G. M., & Broughton, S. H. (2011). Bridging reading comprehension and conceptual change in science education: The promise of refutation text. *Reading Research Quarterly, 46*(4), 374–393.

Sun, J., Anderson, R. C., Morris, J. A., Lin, T.-J., Miller, B. W., Ma, S., et al. (2018). *Children's engagement and affect during collaborative learning and direct instruction.* Unpublished manuscript, Center for the Study of Reading, Champaign, IL.

Sun, J., Anderson, R. C., Perry, M., & Lin, T.-J. (2017). Emergent leadership in children's cooperative problem solving groups. *Cognition and Instruction, 35*(3), 212–235.

Thiede, K. W., Griffin, T. D., Wiley, J., & Redford, J. S. (2009). Metacognitive monitoring during and after reading. In D. J. Hacker, J. Dunlosky, & A. C. Graesser (Eds.), *Handbook of metacognition and self-regulated learning* (pp. 85–106). Mahwah, NJ: Erlbaum.

Tippett, C. D. (2010). Refutation text in science education: A review of two decades of research. *International Journal of Science and Mathematics Education, 8*(6), 951–970.

Vedder, P. (1985). *Cooperative learning: A study on processes and effects of cooperation between primary school children.* Groningen, the Netherlands: Rijkuniversiteit Groningen.

Vygotsky, L. S. (1978). *Mind in society: The development of higher psychological processes.* Cambridge, MA: Harvard University Press.

Winne, P. H., & Azevedo, R. (2014). Metacognition. In R. K. Sawyer (Ed.), *The Cambridge handbook of the learning sciences* (2nd ed., pp. 63–87). Cambridge, UK: Cambridge University Press.

Zhang, X., Anderson, R. C., Morris, J. A., Miller, B. W., Nguyen-Jahiel, K., Lin, T.-J., et al. (2016). Improving children's competence as decision makers: Contrasting effects of collaborative interaction and direct instruction. *American Educational Research Journal, 53,* 194–223.

CHAPTER 5

Using Multimodal Text Sets to Support Conceptual Understandings

JEANNE SWAFFORD

Today, the kinds of texts that literate individuals must read critically are much different than in the past. No longer are texts made up of only printed words. Now, texts typically comprise print and visuals, such as illustrations, diagrams, photographs, moving pictures, spoken text, movement, and music. With the increasing demands of multimodal text and the sheer volume of text that is created and published each day, being literate takes on a whole different meaning (Serafini, 2011). To adequately educate the U.S. citizenry for the demands of the 21st century, it is essential that reading instruction focus on more than simply the literal and inferential meaning of printed text and locating the correct answer on a high-stakes test. To be literate today, individuals must be able to "navigate, interpret, design and interrogate the written, visual and design elements of multi-modal texts" (Serafini, 2012, p. 152).

Because it is important that students are taught to read multimodal texts, it is vital that the texts used in school reflect those used in the world outside of school. No longer will instruction with a single textbook or class novel adequately prepare students to live productive lives. However, simply incorporating different kinds of texts into classrooms is not enough to persuade students to read.

Many factors related to academic reading influence whether young people choose to read, including self-efficacy, self-confidence in reading ability, attitudes toward reading in general, and attitudes toward a particular content area or type of text. Also, young people are involved in many activities outside school, and reading tends to be the last priority for many. Furthermore, students may not see the value of reading to learn, often because school studies seem to be irrelevant to their lives outside school (Jang, Conradi, McKenna, & Jones, 2015). In direct contrast to students' resistance to reading school-related texts, outside the academic arena, young people read and write constantly on their electronic devices (e.g., cell phones).

To ensure that students engage with school activities, it is important to craft instruction so that content is viewed as relevant and interesting today, not simply as preparation for the future. Research indicates that focusing on issues or concepts relevant to students, as well as supporting student inquiry and choice of reading materials (including multimodal texts), can foster student engagement in reading; such instruction contributes to "reading in which motivational processes (such as interest) and cognitive strategies (such as self-monitoring) are simultaneously occurring" (Guthrie, McRae, & Klauda, 2007, p. 238)

It is crucial that instruction is designed around concepts that can be approached from perspectives that are not only important but also relevant and interesting to students. The instructional materials teachers choose to incorporate into the classroom play a large role in how engaged students will be in learning. One way to choose and organize instructional material that supports the use of multimodal texts, student inquiry, and the development of conceptual knowledge is to construct and use multimodal text sets.

The focus of this chapter is on text sets and how they can be developed to support concept-based instruction that will engage students. I begin by describing texts and text sets. Then, based on the professional literature, I explain important considerations for developing text sets. Next, I discuss different ways to organize and scaffold instruction with text sets. Embedded in these discussions are examples of how text sets have been used by teachers. Finally, I suggest resources for locating print and nonprint texts and recommend resources for teaching students to analyze multimodal texts and primary sources.

What Are Text Sets?

To explain what text sets are, first it is important to understand how text is defined. In the context of this chapter, *text* includes print, nonprint, and multimodal texts. Hartman and Hartman (1993) suggested that texts fall on a continuum from linguistic texts at one end to nonlinguistic texts on the other end. Linguistic texts include, but are not limited to, books, journal articles, newspapers, digital texts, song lyrics, and primary sources (e.g., written documents, letters), as well as aural (i.e., nonprint) texts such as podcasts, recorded interviews, or speeches. Nonlinguistic texts include musical recordings (without lyrics), and visual texts such as photographs, artwork (e.g., paintings, sculpture), movement (e.g., dance). Multimodal texts are represented by film, advertisements, cultural artifacts (e.g., objects made or used by individuals during a particular time period), and picture books.

Most texts fall somewhere in the middle of the continuum, because they include a combination of print and nonprint text; that is, they are multimodal texts. For example, picture books, texts commonly found in schools, are considered multimodal texts. Ideas are communicated with printed words, their typography, and the illustrations (visuals); the reader must consider all of these when constructing meaning with the text (Serafini & Clausen, 2016; Sipe, 1998). The illustrations and the print, together, tell the story. Nonfiction texts rely heavily on the use of visuals to further explain and/or extend print text (Kiefer & Tyson, 2014). The publication of graphic novels that represent a variety of genres (e.g., historical fiction, fantasy, nonfiction) have proliferated as well. Likewise, illustrated novels are increasing, particularly those written for middle grade students (Short, 2018).

Some books fall closer to the ends of the linguistic and nonlinguistic continuum. For example, traditionally written novels tend to fall close to the linguistic end. However, even novels include cover art, which provides a glimpse into the story a novel tells. Wordless picture books fall toward the nonlinguistic end of the continuum. Nonetheless, they include a print title, information on the book flap, and other peritextual elements that precede or follow the main text (Short, 2018). As you can see, multimodal texts are all around us. To summarize, *text* as defined in this chapter, includes all forms of texts that communicate meaning and support concept development (Swafford & McNulty, 2010).

Now let's consider what text sets are. *Texts sets* are differentiated collections of print, nonprint, and multimodal texts focused on a common topic, theme, concept, essential question, or anchor text (Cappiello & Dawes, 2013; Elish-Piper, Wold, & Schwingendorf, 2014; Wright & Gotwals, 2017). In this chapter, the focus is on text sets developed around a common concept or theme. Although some may argue that concepts and themes are not the same, for the purposes of this chapter, I use the words interchangeably as "abstract representations of events, motives, interactions, and causes" (Guthrie, 2013) and that can be transferred across different situations (Lanning, 2013).

Text Sets: A New Name for an Old Idea?

One might wonder whether a *text set* is simply a new name for instructional units many teachers developed in the past. This was my first impression. In fact, text sets can be developed in much the same way as thematic units; they use multiple texts to guide instruction. However, text sets for developing concepts differ in two important ways. First, text sets are made up of more diverse texts than thematic units of the past. Today, we have easy access to many different kinds of texts, such as primary sources, videos, and visual images. Second, materials for text sets are purposefully chosen to (1) support and deepen students' understanding of concepts, (2) scaffold reading of increasingly complex texts, (3) teach strategies for reading multiple texts, and (4) provide different perspectives on a concept. This is not to say that units of the past were not developed in similar ways. However, the previously mentioned purposes for deliberately selecting texts need to be kept in mind to avoid collecting every available book; accumulating too many texts can be overwhelming when planning their use for scaffolding concepts and reading development.

Finally, although there is no "right" way to decide the focus of a text set, text sets as described in this chapter are designed around concepts that are relevant to students, broad enough to encourage in-depth inquiry, and support students as they develop generalizations that may be applied in other contexts. This focus contrasts with units that concentrate on familiar topics, such as apples, community helpers, or the rain forest, in which the goal is to help students develop factual knowledge about a chosen topic, but not necessarily deeper conceptual understandings. (See "Designing Text Sets for Concept Development" below for more details.)

Transitioning Topical Units to Concepts-Based Text Sets

Thankfully, teachers do not need to abandon topical units they developed in the past. There is no doubt that a study of topics such as the Holocaust, Japanese internment, or harsh treatment of African Americans in the United States is engaging to many students. However, if you want to focus on concept-based text sets, it is useful to consider how these topics could be viewed through a broader, conceptual lens. In this example, a text set could be developed to focus on the concept of fear and how it fuels injustice. Another way to expand a study beyond a topic is to focus on an essential question that will help students understand commonalities among historical events. For example, an essential question related to these topics could be: Who protects the rights of the vulnerable?

Designing Texts Sets for Concept Development

To develop conceptual knowledge, researchers (Erikson, 2007; Swan, 2003) have described necessary conditions to consider when creating text sets. First, texts should be relevant to students, activate students' existing knowledge, and provide new information and experiences that allow students to make connections (Gelzheiser, Hallgren-Flynn, Connors, & Scanlon, 2014). To further develop a concept, students need to discover patterns and connections among ideas, think critically (i.e., evaluate the truth of these understandings based on the supporting evidence provided in the texts; Boyd & Ikpeze, 2007), and transfer the new understandings across time or situations (Cervetti, Wright, & Hwang, 2016).

When designing a text set, the first step is to determine the focus of instruction (i.e., the concept) and plan how that concept may be best developed. This involves breaking down a broad concept or theme into "generalizations and enduring understandings" (Erikson, 2007, p. 15), then dividing it further into topics or attributes of concepts to help make planning more manageable (Erikson, 2008). Breaking down concepts helps teachers better understand which kinds of texts will best connect with students' experiences. When developed intentionally and in relationship to concepts relevant to students (i.e., not simply bringing in every text available about a concept or theme), text sets can motivate students to read and foster inquiry (Coombs & Bellingham, 2015), conditions that are necessary for concept development (Swan, 2003).

An instructional approach that incorporates a variety of texts and strategic instruction to assist students in developing concepts is concept-oriented reading instruction (CORI; e.g., Guthrie, Anderson, Alao, & Rinehart, 1999; Guthrie et al., 1996; Guthrie, Klauda, & Ho, 2013). Research has demonstrated CORI's effectiveness for engaging readers and developing concepts. The use of texts sets is supported across the four phases of CORI: (1) engaging students and creating interest in content using a variety of experiences and texts, (2) teaching students strategies for accessing information from different kinds of texts, (3) teaching students how to construct meaning from information they gather and as they learn to synthesize information across sources to develop conceptual understandings, and (4) teaching students various ways to communicate to authentic audiences (Guthrie et al., 1996; Swan, 2003), for example, through the use of mentor texts to organize information and communicate effectively (Coombs & Bellingham, 2015).

Text Selection

As noted earlier, text sets should include selections that represent monomodal and multimodal texts to give students access to information in different forms and from various perspectives (Swan, 2003). It is important to realize that when beginning to track down texts related to a concept, your initial search will undoubtedly reveal many more resources than you will use. Ultimately, however, using the suggestions below, you can select texts that best support the development of a concept and encourage student engagement.

Variety of Texts

It is important that texts represent multiple genres, formats, text structures, and difficulty levels (Coombs & Bellingham, 2015; Gelzheiser et al., 2014). Because text sets represent texts of varying difficulty, they provide all readers with access to diverse selections related to a theme or concept (Ogle & Correa-Kovtun, 2010). Reading accessible texts that vary in complexity builds students' background knowledge and vocabulary, supports their understanding of increasingly complex texts, and increases their reading self-efficacy. Just as important, however, a variety of texts allows teachers to more easily scaffold instruction so students can read progressively more complex texts of all kinds and develop deeper and/or broader understandings of a concept.

Different Perspectives

Selecting texts representing different perspectives on an issue or concept is also important to consider when creating text sets. Providing meaningful contexts in which teachers can teach students to read with a skeptical eye is crucial (Boyd & Ikpeze, 2007; Coombs & Bellingham, 2015; Dunkerly-Bean & Bean, 2015; Erikson, 2007; Tracy, Menickelli,

& Scales, 2017). Students need to understand that authors' writing is often biased and reflects their particular perspectives. Thus, it is important to challenge students to break the cycle of deferring to authors and accepting their ideas or perspectives as truth (Serafini, 2012; Wineberg, 2016), teaching students how to interrogate or talk back to the author instead (Leland, Ociepka, Kuonen, & Bangert, 2018). Teaching students to weigh the evidence, question whose voices are heard, whose are being silenced, and to recognize authors' purposes will help them become more critically aware and informed citizens (Leland et al., 2018).

Reading texts that offer different perspectives also provides opportunities for creating cognitive dissonance (Cooper & Carlsmith, 2001). Confronting cognitive dissonance and determining how (or whether) understandings fit into a conceptual framework are important for concept development. This is not easy, but teachers can introduce a variety of methods to help students address misconceptions.

An example of a text set that provides students with different perspectives on a theme or concept was described by Coombs and Bellingham (2015). Seventh-grade students explored an essential question that was truly relevant to them: "What makes a true friend, and how can I develop the characteristics of a good friend?" (p. 91). They engaged in reading, discussing, and writing during this study. Students reported that because they read texts that expressed different viewpoints, they were better able to empathize with characters' struggles they had not experienced themselves. The concept, which was important to students, also helped motivate them. Moreover, providing students with a variety of perspectives on a single concept helped them confront the myths of a single story rather than simply accept the perspective of a single author (Adichie, 2009; Elish-Piper et al., 2014; Lupo, Strong, Lewis, Walpole, & McKenna, 2017; Tracy et al., 2017; Tschida, Ryan, & Ticknor, 2014).

Scaffolding Concept-Based Instruction

Text sets are identified by many names, such as *linked text sets* (Elish-Piper et al., 2014), *quad text sets* (Lupo et al., 2017), and *thematic text sets* (Bersh, 2013; Gelzheiser et al., 2014). What texts sets have in common is that they focus on providing students with opportunities to become engaged in relevant content, examine multiple texts, and develop general and conceptual knowledge (Lupo et al., 2017). Text sets also provide contexts in which teachers can provide instructional support, so students can experience success.

It is important to note that identifying the focus and selecting texts for a text set is only the beginning of planning instruction. Teaching students how to navigate these texts is critical. But even before instruction begins, students need to be convinced that reading is worth their time and learning academic content can be interesting. Guthrie and colleagues (1996) developed an instructional framework to investigate how literacy engagement changed when the CORI program was implemented. They defined *reading engagement* as "a construct that fuses motivational, cognitive and behavioral attributes of students" (Guthrie et al., 2007, p. 238). In other words, engaged readers are motivated to read, use strategies to construct meaning, and put forth the effort to persist when they encounter difficult tasks. The CORI framework focuses on five motivational practices: (1) relevance of concepts to students' lives, (2) student choice to support autonomy, (3) student success to promote reading self-efficacy, (4) collaboration with peers to support social motivation, and (5) thematic units, which provide a context for coherent instruction that integrates strategic reading instruction with science or history concepts (Guthrie, et al., 2007). Research using the CORI framework with elementary and middle school students has shown positive results in terms of concept development, motivation, and engagement (Guthrie et al., 1999, 2013; Guthrie & Klauda, 2014). Building these practices into instruction using text sets paves the way for engaging students and supports concept development.

Hierarchical Scaffolding

When implementing CORI, the first stage is to engage students and create interest in content using a variety of experiences and texts. What kinds of activities or texts are most suitable for the first phase? Generally speaking, texts can be organized somewhat hierarchically, starting with the most concrete or authentic experience (Swan, 2003). Real-world experiences in which students actually observe and participate are the most powerful for generating interest. However, when this is not possible, video or film is the next best experience. Concrete objects that represent cultural artifacts and photographs, which provide a glimpse into a particular context or single moment in time, are the next in line, followed by diagrams, drawings, and other kinds of visuals that represent an object, person, or event. Books with print and accompanying visuals, such as photographs and/or painterly illustrations, would be the next most powerful experience. Finally, a written description without accompanying visuals would be the least authentic experience. This is not to say that a written description or account cannot be engaging; however, other, less abstract experiences are more likely to create initial interest and intrigue in students (Swan, 2003). In the following section, I describe different ways teachers develop instruction using text sets.

Quad Text Sets

Lewis and Walpole (2016) and Lupo, McKenna, and Walpole (2015) recommend the use of quad text sets: four kinds of digital and verbal texts used to scaffold students' concept learning and prepare them to read more complex texts. Lupo et al. (2015) found that the order in which the texts are introduced is important. They suggest beginning with a digital or visual text to engage students and build their background knowledge. Next, they recommend using a variety of short, informational texts to continue building the background knowledge that students need to understand the third, and more complex, target text. Finally, the fourth text should be a contemporary text that students will enjoy and that will help them synthesize ideas and extend their understandings of the broader concept under study.

Linked Text Sets

Elish-Piper et al. (2014) suggest that linked text sets can be used as a way to scaffold students' reading to prepare them for reading a more complex text. They described a text set developed by a 10th-grade English teacher that focused on the theme of prejudice and was used to scaffold the reading and study of the canonical text *To Kill a Mockingbird* (Lee, 1960). Initially, he engaged students by introducing the essential question: "Why is growing up so difficult?" (p. 568). To answer the question, students explored topics such as unfairness, abuse, bullying, and peer pressure.

To further explore the theme, the class read the young adult novel *Staying Fat for Sarah Byrnes* (Crutcher, 1993). This book was interesting to students and reasonably accessible for the majority of them. Moreover, students could easily relate this book to the essential question. This book also provided a contemporary context for reading *To Kill a Mockingbird*. However, to help students understand the context of the story, they needed to expand their knowledge about the segregated South under the control of Jim Crow laws. The teacher brought in texts such as a YouTube video *Jim Crow Laws 1930's Intro* (t bro, 2010) and the chapter "Jim Crow and the Detested Number Ten" from Hoose's (2009) biography about Claudette Colvin, to build their background knowledge and provide students with a better sense of the context of the story. To assess students' understanding of the concept at the end of the study, the teacher provided students with choices of culminating projects, which they related back to the essential question and the theme of prejudice. An example of a project follows:

> Compare *To Kill a Mockingbird* and *Staying Fat for Sarah Brynes* regarding issues of prejudice and unfairness. Write a paper or create a media text . . . that examines how the theme of prejudice is revealed in these two books. Identify and discuss the role models or heroes in each novel and examine their impact on the injustices they stand up against (Elish-Piper et al., 2014, p. 572).

The project required students to synthesize what they learned from exploring the concept of prejudice through a multimodal text set and to demonstrate their understandings by describing the ways characters in the two books addressed injustices.

Anchor Text

Text sets can be developed around an anchor text. In this case, text sets are created to build background knowledge, which is critical to understanding the anchor text. (An anchor text is similar to the *target text* or *complex text* described earlier.) For example, a high school English teacher in southeastern North Carolina selected the class novel *Suspect Red* (Elliott, 2017) as an anchor text. The theme of the study was the importance of students thinking for themselves. The historical fiction novel was set during the McCarthy era in the early 1950s, when a preponderance of accusations (some true, others false) about celebrities, government officials, and private citizens ran rampant. The parallels between the 1950s and today were quite stunning. Examples of stereotyping (i.e., profiling), not knowing who or what sources to believe (e.g., fake news), and attitudes toward minorities (including women) helped students better realize the importance of thinking for themselves.

Because students knew little about this era, the teacher provided informational, visual images (e.g., photographs that represented culture icons of the 1950s) to help build their knowledge of what it was like to live in the United States during that time. These images were a part of the text set. The images provoked not only much discussion but also enhanced student engagement. The students initially had no idea what or who some of the images represented, which raised many questions and predictions. They did on-the-spot online research to help them decipher the images. After a whole-class discussion of the images and the culture of the time, the teacher introduced the book and read the first two chapters aloud so students would be intrigued and want to continue reading.

Next, students read designated chapters of *Suspect Red* independently. After they read each portion of the text, engagements during class time included students' written aesthetic and efferent responses to the written and visual texts; students' queries about people, places, and events in the book; intertextual connections they made; and mini-inquiries on self-selected topics of interest. Sometimes students used their cell phones to answer their questions immediately. Other times, when more extensive research was needed, they used computers at school and at home to access information from Web-based resources. All of these experiences with texts helped students better understand the theme of the study.

When students finished reading the book, they participated in a Brown Bag Exam (Ousley, 2008), which is a nontraditional assessment. The purpose of this exam was to prompt students to continue to think more deeply and conceptually about the book. To prepare for the exam, the teacher and students brought in an object or image that was personally important to them, and that represented important themes or concepts related to the novel. Each artifact was placed in a small brown paper bag and distributed to students (making sure students did not receive the object they brought in themselves). Individually, students viewed their object and wrote about their first impressions, making initial (typically literal) connections between the book and the object. Individuals then proceeded to think about and record more abstract connections. Next, pairs of students shared their objects and connections with their partners; sharing connections provided students with different perspectives on each object. Then, to bring the students back to the text, individuals located quotes that supported the deep connections they made between the object and the book, followed by writing a culminating, synthesis statement that brought together students' thinking about the object and the connections they made with a text set's theme. A whole-class share followed. The Brown Bag Exam process encouraged students to discuss and think about the book long after the exam was completed. Thinking deeply as individuals and discussing multimodal texts with their peers furthered students' understanding of the book and the issues it addressed.

Effects of Text Sets

Incorporating a variety of texts also provides different contexts for reading instruction. In fact, teacher support as a means of helping students read difficult texts has been found to improve student comprehension (e.g., Cervetti et al., 2016), reading engagement, and conceptual learning (Guthrie et al., 1999). CORI's use of text sets (discussed earlier) was also found to be associated with increased motivation, engagement, and achievement (e.g., students' proficiency in reading to answer questions requiring conceptual integration of informational text content; Guthrie et. al., 2013, p. 10). In a study by Coombs and Bellingham (2015), students reported that text sets helped them better understand the novels they read. For example, one student reported that she was better able to empathize with the characters because the text set she read allowed her to better understand what it might be like to have a disability. Other students reported that text sets helped them better understand the parallels between their lives and the dystopian world of *The Giver* (Lowry, 1993). Text sets also supported students' writing. For example, some students reported that the different texts functioned as models for writing different genres. Still others reported that using text sets helped them better extract and synthesize evidence from multiple sources to support an argument.

Resources for Building and Teaching with Multimodal Text Sets

It is vitally important that the texts included in text sets are selected carefully so they support student engagement, development of background knowledge, and growth in strategic reading of print, nonprint, and multimodal material. Collecting resources can sometimes be challenging, so in this part of the chapter, I suggest resources for locating different types of texts. I begin with resources for books and move on to resources for multimodal texts.

Professional Organizations

Several professional organizations regularly publish recommendations of outstanding children's and young adult trade books, including picture books and novels. One of the first resources I consult when developing social studies-related text sets is the annual publication of an annotated bibliography for *Notable Social Studies Trade Books for Young People* (*www. socialstudies.org/publications/notables*). This publication is sponsored by the National Council of the Social Studies (NCSS) and the Children's Book Council. The books in this list focus primarily on human relations and diverse groups of people, and they address a broad range of cultural experiences in sensitive ways. Books that present a fresh perspective on traditional topics are also included.

The organization of the annotated bibliography is useful for identifying concepts related to the books. The list is arranged in categories, such as biography, contemporary concerns, environment/energy/ecology, folktales, history/life and culture in the Americas, reference, religion, social interactions/relationships, and world history and culture. Each annotation includes the bibliographic information, book summary, appropriate grade levels, book length, cost, ISBN number, and a note about front and back matter (e.g., Author's Note). In addition, each book is linked with thematic strands from the NCSS Curriculum Standards. These strands include culture; time, continuity, and change; people, places, and environments; individual development and identity; individuals, groups, and institutions; power, authority, and governance; production, distribution, and consumption; science, technology, and society; global connections; and civic ideals and practices.

The NCSS trade books list appears in the May/June issue of the journal *Social Education*. Although the current year's list is only available to members of the organization, lists from previous years are accessible to everyone (see *www.socialstudies.org/publications/notables*).

In addition to the NCSS, other professional organizations publish annual annotated lists of quality literature, which are available on the Internet. In Table 5.1, I provide a list of awards, their Web links, and what attributes the awards emphasize. All of these resources are especially useful for locating quality books to include in text sets.

Resources for Primary Sources and Multimodal Texts

Because text sets include not only books but also other kinds of texts, the following resources are useful for locating multimodal texts such as primary sources, film, and visuals.

The Library of Congress

The Library of Congress has collections of primary sources available online. For example, documents from the Veterans History Project include personal narratives, personal correspondence, diaries, and scrapbooks as well as visuals such as drawings and photographs. All of these primary sources are available on their website (*www.loc.gov/vets/about. html*). The purpose of this project is to collect, preserve, and make accessible personal accounts of U.S. veterans. Documents from veterans of World War I (1914) through the Iraq War (2011) are currently housed there. Resources are also available for teachers and students who wish to contribute to the project by interviewing veterans themselves. Such interviews can then be added to the database.

The National Archives

The National Archives website (*www.archives.gov*) includes a wealth of information, providing everyone with access to important government records. Information on their Home Page includes five major sections: Research Our Records, Veterans' Service Records, Educator Resources, Visit Us, and America's Founding Documents.

The Educator Resources component of the archives includes several sections. One is called DocsTeach (*www.docsteach.org*), which, as the name implies, provides access to a plethora of primary sources, such as letters, photographs, speeches, posters, maps, and videos, across different time periods in U.S. history, along with information about how to teach with these documents. Activities have been created to help students analyze and reflect on the documents and their significance. These documents are readily available for incorporation into a text set, and the activities provide ideas for teaching students to read print and nonprint documents. Also provided are online tools. Teachers can choose a particular primary source, then create learning engagements related to the concept being taught. Teachers and students can access the materials and instructions, as well as submit their work, through DocsTeach.

TABLE 5.1. List of Book Awards

Award	Years awarded	Website	Age/grade range	Description
Boston Globe–Horn Book Awards	1967–present	www.hbook.com/?page=boston-globe-horn-book-awards-landing-page	Grades PreK–12	Outstanding literature for children and young adults; awarded for nonfiction, fiction and poetry, and picture books
Carter G. Woodson Book Awards (American Library Association [ALA])	1974–present	www.socialstudies.org/awards/woodson	Grades K–12	Depicts ethnicity in the United States
Coretta Scott King Awards (ALA)	1970–present	www.ala.org/rt/emiert/cskbookawards	Grades PreK–12	Black experience, past, present, or future; awarded to African American authors and illustrators
Jane Addams Children's Book Award (Jane Addams Peace Association)	1993–present	www.janeaddamschildrens bookaward.org	Ages 5–14 years	Deepen young people's understanding of the world; engage children in thinking about peace, social justice, global community, and equity for all people
Notable Books for a Global Society (Children's Literature and Reading Special Interest Group)	2010–present	www.clrsig.org/notable-books-for-a-global-society-nbgs.html	Grades K–12	Enhance student understanding of people and cultures of the world

Award	Year	URL	Grades/Ages	Purpose
Orbis Pictus Award (National Council of Teachers of English [NCTE])	1990–present	*www2.ncte.org/awards/orbis-pictus-award-nonfiction-for-children*	Grades K–8	Excellence in nonfiction literature for children
Outstanding Science Trade Books (National Science Teachers Association [NSTA])	1996–present	*www.nsta.org/publications/ostb*	Grades K–12	Substantial, accurate, up-to-date science content
Pura Belpre Award (ALA)	1996–present	*www.ala.org/alsc/awardsgrants/bookmedia/belpremedal*	Up to age 15 years	Portray, affirm, and celebrate the Latino cultural experience; presented to Latino/a author and illustrator
Robert F. Sibert Informational Book Medal (ALA)	2001–present	*www.ala.org/alsc/awardsgrants/bookmedia/sibertmedal*	Ages birth–14 years	Most distinguished informational book published in the United States
Schneider Family Book Award (ALA)	2004–present	*www.ala.org/awardsgrants/schneider-family-book-award*	Ages birth–18 years	Honor an author or illustrator for a book that embodies an artistic expression of the disability experience
Best STEM Books (NSTA)	2017–present	*www.nsta.org/publications/stembooks*	Grades K–12	Substantial, accurate, up-to-date STEM content

Instruction regarding how primary sources should be read is crucially important if students are expected to analyze and use the information made available through the National Archives and other similar resources. In the Educator Resources file, there is a section called "Working with Primary Sources." On that page, information is provided about how to teach students to analyze different kinds of primary source documents. Links to worksheets with guiding questions are also provided for reading a wide range of sources such as photographs, written documents, objects or artifacts, maps, cartoons, videos, and sound recordings. These analysis guides provide support students need to read texts that differ from traditional print materials. One set of these guides is tailored especially for younger students, and the other set is more appropriate for older students (*www.archives.gov/education/lessons/worksheets*).

Reading Photographs

As noted earlier, the National Archives provides guidance on how to read photographs. Their recommendation is that students examine photographs by working through three steps: Observation, Inferences, and Questions. During the *Observation* step, students are directed to "study the photograph for 2 minutes to form an overall impression of the photograph," then zoom in to examine individual items in the photo. The next aspect of the Observation step is to divide the photograph into fourths and zoom in closer to study details in each quadrant of the photo. Then, using a three-column chart, students make a list of people in the photo, the activities in which they are engaged, and other objects that appear in the photo. Once students have examined a photograph for literal elements, they proceed to the second step, *Inference*. For this aspect of the analysis, students do much the same thing they do when making an inference with a print text. They look for clues about what events are occurring, the context of the photograph (by noticing people's clothing, vehicles, and other objects), and how people feel (by examining their facial expressions). Then students list three things they infer from the photo. The last step, is recording *Questions* they have about the photo. The Observations, Inferences, and Questions help students not only read the photograph but also view it from different perspectives and begin to wonder about it. See the photograph analysis worksheet in Figure 5.1 (available from the National Archives). All of these documents are in the public domain so they may be copied or modified for use in instruction.

Step 1. Observation

A. Study the photograph for 2 minutes. Form an overall impression of the photograph, then examine individual items. Next, divide the photo into quadrants and study each section to see what new details become visible.

B. Use the chart below to list people, objects, and activities in the photograph.

People	Objects	Activities

Step 2. Inference

Based on what you have observed above, list three things you might infer from this photograph.

Step 3. Questions

A. What questions does this photograph raise in your mind?

B. Where could you find answers to them?

FIGURE 5.1. Photo analysis worksheet. Created by Education Staff, National Archives and Records Administration, Washington, DC.

In keeping with the recommendations throughout this chapter that texts and concepts must be relevant to students, photographs can be culled from many different sources, including photographs students have taken, images from popular culture, or even the local or national news; the latter can be found easily using a basic image search on the Web. For example, students would undoubtedly be interested in viewing photographs (and videos) from the tragic shooting at the Marjory Stoneman Douglas High school in Parkland, Florida. Photographs can be analyzed not only to identify the literal and inferential aspects of the images but also to evaluate them from a critical (or skeptical) perspective. Questions such as the following help students better critique photographs. (1) Who took the photo and for what purpose? (2) Who benefits and who loses from the way the photograph is framed? (3) What story did the photographer want to tell? (4) What are the photographer's biases? (5) What influenced the composition of the photo? In other words, why were certain people, events, or objects featured and others cropped out? (6) From what vantage point was the photo taken? (7) What does this perspective reveal that another would not? (Leland et al., 2018).

Reading Moving Images

Students also need to be taught how to critically evaluate moving images such as video, film, documentaries, and public service announcements (Domke, Weippert, & Apol, 2018). Viewing moving images as texts is quite different from the passive viewing to which students are accustomed. The questions below provide guidance about what students should consider when evaluating moving images.

- "What does the title imply about the content of the film?"
- "When was the film made?"
- "Who made it? Who financed it, and what did they have to gain from it?"
- "What were the purposes of the film, and how are they implicitly or explicitly communicated?"
- "Identify the people, places, and activities in the film, and consider for what purposes particular people, places, and activities are included."
- "How do particular words in the narration influence the viewer to respond negatively or positively to the film?"

- "How was the music used? Consider the kind, volume, and purpose of music played in the background. Is there a lively cadence or an ominous tone? When does it change? How does the change affect the tone of the film at particular points? How is volume used and for what purposes?"
- "Whose viewpoint is the film made to support?"
- "What was life like in the United States (or another country) when the film was made?"
- "Whose voices are heard and whose voices are missing?"
- "Why do you think certain scenes are included and others neglected?"
- "About what aspects of the film are you skeptical?"

All these questions, and more, help viewers read more closely the complex text presented in a film (Domke et al., 2018). As I mentioned earlier, moving images from the past can be found in the National Archives and the Library of Congress. Moving images from the present may be found with a basic Internet search of "Videos." It is important to note that viewing a film in sections helps students better comprehend and analyze a film. Similarly, critically evaluating a moving image is vitally important and will undoubtedly require several re-viewings for different purposes.

Reading Political Cartoons

The political cartoon is another kind of multimodal source that tells much about the culture that existed when the cartoon was published. It is important that readers understand the context in which the cartoon appeared and in what resource it was published. Students can begin to analyze a cartoon in much the same way as they analyze a photograph, through examination of the visual elements of the cartoon and listing the people, objects, and activities that appear. This can be followed by an examination of the words in the captions, labels, or speech bubbles, and making a list of these words and where they appear in the cartoon. From here, students determine what words are the most important and how the typography may influence the power of the words. Next, students can examine the cartoon for any emotions that are portrayed. It is also useful to take note of any dates, numbers, and symbols that may appear in the cartoon, along with what they may represent. Students can then describe the action taking place, how the words help clarify the meaning of the symbols, and explain their understanding of the message of the cartoon. Finally, students should determine who (i.e., special interest groups) would agree or disagree with the cartoon's message, and discuss why students have drawn those conclusions. (See Figure 5.2 for details.)

Other Resources

It is important to mention that other resources available on the Internet also house materials that can be used for developing text sets. For example, the University of California Irvine History Project provides resources and a curriculum that teachers may find useful, particularly when teaching students to analyze primary source documents and other nonprint and multimodal resources. Although these analysis tools are somewhat similar to those of the National Archives, their four C's and six C's tools encourage students to consider information in the resources from a slightly different perspective. For example, the six C's of the primary source analysis worksheet uses six words, all of which begin with the letter C, to guide students' reading of primary sources. The six C's are Content (i.e., Describe the main idea in detail); Citation (Who created the source and when?); Context (What was going on in the world, region, or local community?); Connections (What do you already know about the resource?); Communication (Whose point of view is represented? Is the source reliable?); and Conclusions (How does this document help you better understand history?).[1]

The Stanford History Education Group (SHEG) also houses information and primary sources, along with resources to help teachers better instruct their students about ways to read like a historian (*https://sheg. stanford.edu/history-lessons*). These lessons focus on sourcing, contextualizing, corroborating, and close reading, skills that prove useful when students read and analyze both print and nonprint texts.[2]

In my own work designing text sets, I have found that once I identify the concept, subconcepts, and other related issues, a Google or Google image search and a YouTube video search almost always uncovers valuable

---

[1] This resource can be found at *https://doingsocialstudies.files.wordpress.com/2013/12/6cs_primary_source.pdf*.

[2] Videos of high school teachers teaching these skills are available at *www.teachingchannel. org/videos?q=reading+and+like+and+a+and+historian*.

Level 1	
Visuals	Words (not all cartoons include words)
1. List the objects or people you see in the cartoon.	1. Identify the cartoon caption and/or title. 2. Locate three words or phrases used by the cartoonist to identify objects or people within the cartoon. 3. Record any important dates or numbers that appear in the cartoon.

Level 2	
Visuals	Words
2. Which of the objects on your list are symbols? 3. What do you think each symbol means?	4. Which words or phrases in the cartoon appear to be the most significant? Why do you think so? 5. List adjectives that describe the emotions portrayed in the cartoon.

Level 3

A. Describe the action taking place in the cartoon.

B. Explain how the words in the cartoon clarify the symbols.

C. Explain the message of the cartoon.

D. What special interest groups would agree/disagree with the cartoon's message? Why?

FIGURE 5.2. Political cartoon analysis worksheet. Created by Education Staff, National Archives and Records Administration, Washington, DC.

primary sources and multimodal texts. After reviewing the materials' credibility (a crucial first step), I keep a record of those texts for possible use. As I mentioned earlier, searches such as these often result in many more texts than I would possibly use in a single text set. However, I suggest that you keep a list of these resources, so that students may use them for their self-initiated inquiry projects. In addition, you never know when those texts will come in handy for developing other text sets or teaching in other contexts.

Conclusion

To engage students in school, it is important to focus on concepts that are relevant and interesting to them. Furthermore, students must be taught how to read texts in a range of forms, that is, to "navigate, interpret, design and interrogate the written, visual and design elements of multimodal texts" (Serafini, 2012, p. 152). Developing text sets and teaching students how to negotiate multimodal text sets is one critical way to prepare young people to be responsible, reflective, and thinking citizens of the world.

● IMPLICATIONS FOR PROFESSIONAL LEARNING ●

- Providing students with opportunities to read, view, or listen to an unexpected nonprint or multimodal text (e.g., photograph, film clip, interview) at the beginning of an instructional unit can make a concept more relevant to students, thus, increasing their engagement and motivation to learn.
- Thoughtfully developed text sets that include print, nonprint, and multimodal texts provide students with a broader and deeper understanding of a concept. Equally important is teaching students how to construct meaning, critique, and synthesize information across multiple texts.
- When developing text sets, it is important to choose texts that reflect different perspectives and to teach students to weigh evidence, question whose voices are heard (and silenced), and to recognize authors' purposes for creating particular texts.

QUESTIONS FOR DISCUSSION

1. How might you take a topical unit and make the focus more comprehensive, so that the focus is on broad concepts rather than a specific topic?

2. Think about a novel or other text you are required to teach. What print, nonprint, and multimodal texts might you use to provide students with important foundational knowledge necessary for developing a broader and deeper understanding of the text?

3. Recognizing that real-world experiences, film, and cultural artifacts are powerful for generating student interest, what texts might you use to introduce a concept that is relevant to your students and engage them in further study of required curriculum?

4. How might you build student choice and collaboration into a text set that focuses on a particular concept?

REFERENCES

Adichie, C. N. (2009). Danger of a single story. Retrieved from *www.ted.com/talks/chimamanda_adichie_the_danger_of_a_single_story.*

Bersh, L. C. (2013). The curricular value of teaching about immigration through picture book thematic text sets. *The Social Studies, 104,* 47–56.

Boyd, F. B., & Ikpeze, C. H. (2007). Navigating a literacy landscape teaching conceptual understanding with multiple text types. *Journal of Literacy Research, 39*(2), 217–248.

Cappiello, M. A., & Dawes, E. T. (2013). *Teaching with text sets.* Huntington Beach, CA: Shell Education.

Cervetti, G. N., Wright, T. S., & Hwang, H. (2016). Conceptual coherence, comprehension, and vocabulary acquisition: A knowledge effect? *Reading and Writing, 29,* 761–779.

Coombs, D., & Bellingham, D. (2015). Using text sets to foster critical inquiry. *English Journal, 105*(2), 88–95.

Cooper, J., & Carlsmith, K. M. (2001). Cognitive dissonance. In N. J. Smelser & P. B. Baltes (Eds.), *International encyclopedia of the social and behavioral sciences* (pp. 2112–2114). Amsterdam, the Netherlands: Elsevier.

Crutcher, C. (1993). *Staying fat for Sarah Brynes.* New York: Greenwillow Books.

Domke, L. M., Weippert, T. L., & Apol, L. (2018). Beyond school breaks: Reinterpreting the uses of film in classrooms. *The Reading Teacher, 72*(1), 51–59.

Dunkerly-Bean, J., & Bean, T. W. (2015). Exploring human rights and cosmopolitan critical literacy with global young adult literature multimodal text sets. *New England Reading Association Journal, 50*(2), 1–7.

Elish-Piper, L., Wold, L. S., & Schwingendorf, K. (2014). Scaffolding high school students' reading of complex texts using linked text sets. *Journal of Adolescent and Adult Literacy, 57*(7), 565–574.

Elliott, L. M. (2017). *Suspect red.* New York: Disney-Hyperion.

Erikson, H. (2007). *Concept-based curriculum and instruction for the thinking classroom.* Thousand Oaks, CA: Corwin Press.

Erikson, H. L. (2008). *Stirring the head, heart, and soul: Redefining curriculum, instruction, and concept-based learning* (3rd ed.). Thousand Oaks, CA: Corwin Press.

Gelzheiser, L., Hallgren-Flynn, L., Connors, M., & Scanlon, D. (2014). Reading thematically related texts to develop knowledge and comprehension. *The Reading Teacher, 68*(1), 53–63.

Guthrie, J. T. (2013, April). *Fostering academic literacy engagement: Meeting CCSS expectations.* Presentation at a preconvention institute at the annual meeting of the International Reading Association, San Antonio, TX.

Guthrie, J. T., Anderson, E., Alao, S., & Rinehart, J. (1999). Influences of concept-oriented reading instruction on strategy use and conceptual learning from text. *Elementary School Journal, 99*(4), 343–366.

Guthrie, J. T., & Klauda, S. L. (2014). Effects of classroom practices on reading comprehension, engagement, and motivations of adolescents. *Reading Research Quarterly, 49*(4), 387–416.

Guthrie, J. T., Klauda, S. L., & Ho, A. N. (2013). Modeling the relationships among reading instruction, motivation, engagement, and achievement of adolescents. *Reading Research Quarterly, 48*(1), 9–26.

Guthrie, J. T., McRae, A., & Klauda, S. L. (2007). Contributions of concept-oriented reading instruction to knowledge about interventions for motivations in reading. *Educational Psychologist, 42*(4), 237–250.

Guthrie, J. T., Van Meter, P., McCann, A. D., Wigfield, A., Bennett, L., Poundstone, C. C., et al. (1996). Growth of literacy engagement: Changes in motivations and strategies during concept-oriented reading instruction. *Reading Research Quarterly, 31*, 306–322.

Hartman, D. K., & Hartman, J. A. (1993). Reading across texts: Expanding the role of the reader. *The Reading Teacher, 47*(3), 202–211.

Hoose, P. (2009). *Claudette Colvin: Twice toward justice.* New York: Farrar, Straus & Giroux.

Jang, B. G., Conradi, K., McKenna, M. C., & Jones, J. S. (2015). Motivation: Approaching an elusive concept through the factors that shape it. *The Reading Teacher, 69*(2), 239–247.

Kiefer, B. Z., & Tyson, C. A. (2014). *Charlotte Huck's children's literature: A brief guide* (2nd ed.). New York: McGraw-Hill.

Lanning, L. (2013). *Designing a concept-based curriculum for English language arts: Meeting the Common Core with intellectual integrity.* Thousand Oaks, CA: Corwin Press.

Lee, H. (1960). *To kill a mockingbird.* New York: HarperCollins.

Leland, C., Ociepka, A., Kuonen, K., & Bangert, S. (2018). Learning to talk back to texts. *Journal of Adolescent and Adult Literacy, 61*(6), 643–652.

Lewis, W., & Walpole, S. (2016). Designing your own text sets. *Literacy Today, 33*(4), 34–35.

Lowry, L. (1993). *The giver.* New York: Houghton Mifflin/Harcourt Books for Young Readers.

Lupo, S. M., McKenna, M. C., & Walpole, S. W. (2015, December). *Quad text sets: A formative approach to exploring how to scaffold adolescents in reading challenging texts.* Paper presented at the annual meeting of the Literacy Research Association, Carlsbad, CA.

Lupo, S. M., Strong, J. Z., Lewis, W., Walpole, S., & McKenna, M. C. (2017). Building background knowledge through reading: Rethinking text sets. *Journal of Adolescent and Adult Literacy, 61*(4), 433–444.

Ogle, D., & Correa-Kovtun, A. (2010). Supporting English-language learners and struggling readers in content literacy with the "Partner reading and content, too" routine. *The Reading Teacher, 63*(7), 532–542.

Ousley, D. (2008). Alternative assessment and the Brown Bag Exam: What does assessment have to do with lunch? *English Journal, 97*(6), 913–919.

Serafini, F. (2011). Expanding perspectives for comprehending visual images in multimodal texts. *Journal of Adolescent and Adult Literacy, 54*(5), 324–350.

Serafini, F. (2012). Expanding the four resources model: Reading visual and multimodal texts. *Pedagogies: An International Journal, 7*(2), 150–164.

Serafini, F., & Clausen, J. (2016). Typography as semiotic resource. *Journal of Visual Literacy, 31*(2), 1–16.

Short, K. G. (2018). What's trending in children's literature and why it matters. *Language Arts, 95*(5), 287–298.

Sipe, L. R. (1998). The construction of literary understanding by first and second graders in response to picture storybook read-alouds. *Reading Research Quarterly, 33*(4), 376–378.

Swafford, J., & McNulty, C. P. (2010). Experiencing history: Integrating cultural artifacts into a study of the Dust Bowl. *Social Studies Research and Practice, 8*, 55–67.

Swan, E. A. (2003). *Concept-oriented reading instruction: Engaging classroom, lifelong learners.* New York: Guilford Press.

t bro. (2010, November 25). *Jim Crow Laws 1930's Intro* [Video file]. Retrieved from *www.youtube.com/watch?v=_iflzgajomu*.

Tatum, A., Wold, L. S., & Elish-Piper, L. (2009). Adolescents and texts: Scaffolding the English canon with linked texts. *English Journal, 98*(6), 88–91.

Tracy, K. N., Menickelli, K., & Scales, R. (2017). Courageous voices: Using text sets to inspire change. *Journal of Adolescent and Adult Literacy, 60*(5), 527–536.

Tschida, C. M., Ryan, C. L., & Ticknor, A. S. (2014). Building on windows and mirrors: Encouraging the disruption of "single stories" through children's literature. *Journal of Children's Literature, 40*(1), 28–39.

Wineberg, S. (2016, Spring). Why historical thinking is not about history. Retrieved from *www.stanford.edu/search/?q=why+historical+thinking+is+not+about+history&search_type=web&submit=submit*.

Wright, T. S., & Gotwals, A. W. (2017). Supporting disciplinary talk from the start of school: Teaching students to think and talk like scientists. *The Reading Teacher, 71*(2), 189–197.

CHAPTER 6

Developing Conceptual Knowledge in the Content Areas

Overlooked Features of Texts That Influence Complexity

HEIDI ANNE E. MESMER

Within educational circles, when people use the term *conceptual knowledge*, they are referring to a rich network of relationships and interrelationships that inform broad understandings of the world (e.g., how raindrops form, how communities grow and flourish, how language works). In schools, students acquire conceptual knowledge through rich and varied processes, including discussion, experimentation, listening, writing, and reading. The building blocks of conceptual knowledge are words and their meanings, words that increasingly become connected and networked as understandings grow and develop over time.

Children's understanding of *water* and related terms provides an excellent example of the ways conceptual knowledge is built, networked, and extended. Very early in their schooling, children learn that water can take the form of a solid called *ice*, a liquid called *water*, or a gas called *vapor*. They learn what these words mean through experimentation, books, and illustrations. As they learn, they add labels for the various processes that describe how water transforms (i.e., *melt, condense, freeze, evaporate*). Then as they learn about weather, they extend and connect words such as *liquid, gas, freeze*, and *evaporate* to words such as *precipitate, snow, rain, cloud*, and *atmosphere*. Later they connect their knowledge of the forms of water to the ways that molecules act in solid, liquid, or gas forms. Thus, students are continually organizing and reorganizing words that they know into categories and groups to advance their conceptual knowledge. Printed texts play a crucial role in this development.

The purpose of this chapter is to examine how common approaches to estimating text complexity have overlooked features that make a text difficult. In this chapter, I tackle three features that have benefited from advances in both research and practice: (1) word familiarity or frequency and how it works differently in math, science/social science, and literary texts; (2) text cohesion; and (3) word concreteness.

Text Complexity: Some Background

The word *text* has become complicated by modern digital sensibilities and the unprecedented reconceptualization of literacy in the current era. When I write about *text,* I am speaking of an extended piece of writing, such as an article, a book, or a chapter. I mean a piece that comprises multiple sentences and paragraphs, often containing many parts, pages, or sections. Here, I am thinking mostly of printed pieces but, of course, increasingly, extended pieces are becoming digitally accessible as well, even in schools.

In 2012, my colleagues and I defined text complexity and provided a framework for thinking about it (Mesmer, Cunningham, & Hiebert, 2012). In our view, *text complexity* refers to the elements of text that can be counted, described, or captured (e.g., number of words, length of words, sentence length). *Text difficulty,* on the other hand, is an estimate of the challenge that a text poses to a particular reader. Text difficulty estimates, such as grades (e.g., 1.2, 1.3, 1.4), reflect how well a reader would comprehend the book with a certain collection of text features or text complexity. Some of the distinctions between text complexity and text difficulty are summarized in Table 6.1.

Text complexity contains three layers: words, syntax (sentences), and discourse. Complexity of words may be examined from the perspective of sound/spelling difficulty, meaning difficulty, length, familiarity, and many other elements. Often, tools used to estimate text difficulty collect the frequency of words to gauge how familiar they might be to a reader. The complexity of sentences, or syntax, might be thought of from the perspectives of sentence length, number of phrases or clauses, and/or the use of connectives and modifiers. Last, we argued that text complexity might also be described in terms of discourse layers. The discourse level of a text consists of units that cross sentence boundaries. So this would be paragraphs, chapters, or articles. In this chapter, the sections about familiarity and concreteness relate to the word layer, and the section about cohesion connects with the discourse layer.

TABLE 6.1. Distinctions between Text Complexity and Text Difficulty

Text complexity	Text difficulty
Based *only on the text*	Based on reader *performance* in a text
Analysis of words, syntax, or discourse	A label estimating how hard the text is (e.g., 2.4, 2.5, A, B, C, D; 450L, 460L)
Features of words, syntax, discourse Word familiarity, word length, age of acquisition Sentence length, number of clauses, number of phrases Genre, cohesion	The actual or predicted performance of multiple readers on a task based on that text or feature

How Does Text Enhance Conceptual Knowledge?

Although printed media are certainly not the only way to develop conceptual knowledge, it is difficult to imagine any discipline, be it science, math, history, or literature, that is not advanced by interactions with text. One of the specific contributions that text makes to conceptual knowledge is in the area of vocabulary development. This is because texts include words that people do not normally use orally or encounter in conversations with others. In fact, an often-cited analysis comparing the words in various language sources found that the words in "children's books" were less common, less frequent, or less familiar than the words used in the conversations of college-educated adults (Hayes & Ahrens, 1988). An updated comparison proves the same thing (Montag, Jones, & Smith, 2015); researchers have found that rich conversations that adults have with young children are fueled with the rich vocabulary of text rather than that of daily conversations. In other words, texts are building blocks of conceptual knowledge, and the words in the text are the fuel. Children need books to advance their vocabularies and conceptual understandings.

Text also enhances conceptual knowledge, but through syntax or sentences and how the ideas in sentences are connected to each other. Rich texts for children have complex sentences that require them to process and pay attention to multiple subjects, phrases, modifiers, or clauses. Authors create language that is interesting and complex, varied, and diverse. Readers must track ideas across sentences and retain important ideas throughout a passage.

The two text examples in Table 6.2 provide an excellent contrast between literary texts and those in content areas (i.e., science, social studies, and math). These examples convey how content-area texts differ from literary texts. Both of these texts are at the same approximate difficulty levels (670L). *Rotters!: Decomposition*, by John Townsend (2005), describes the decomposing process and includes words such as *microbes, bacteria,* and *microscope*. *Hedgie's Surprise,* a picture book by Jan Brett (2016), introduces the words *speckled, porridge, kettle, hayloft, piping,* and *goslings*. The sentences are lengthy, and they have phrases and clauses that add meaning.

In summary, text complexity and text difficulty are not the same thing. *Text complexity* is simply elements of the text, but *text difficulty* is a label that reflects a relationship between elements of the text and the reader's performance. Text difficulty tells us that a text with these kinds of words or sentences would likely be comprehensible to a student in the fourth month of second grade. Texts enhance conceptual knowledge, because they introduce words, syntactic patterns, and genres that students would not typically encounter in everyday speech. Although narrative and expository texts have different text features or text complexity, both advance knowledge, albeit in distinct ways.

TABLE 6.2. Contrasting a Content-Area Text (*Rotters!: Decomposition*) and a Literary Text (*Hedgie's Surprise*).

Rotters!: Decomposition	*Hedgie's Surprise*
All **microbes** are tiny, but **bacteria** are even smaller. They can only be seen under the **microscope**. A **microscope** is a machine that makes things look much bigger than they are.	Once there was a **speckled** hen who laid an egg every day, only to have it taken by a little Tomten every morning. It all started because the Tomten got tired of **porridge** for breakfast.
Bacteria are very tiny. They can feed on things that are too small for us to see. They can live on tiny drops of sweat or oil on your skin. They might find food in just a grain of dust. . . .	Each morning a rooster **crowed** as the sun came up. . . .
Microbes are everywhere. They float through the air. They live on plants. They live on animals. They live in your house. They even live on you. There are about 650,000 **bacteria** living on each square inch of your skin.	The Tomten climbed into the henhouse, took Henny's warm, smooth egg, and ran off to cook it in his little **kettle,** sprinkle it with salt, and gobble it down. Then he fell fast asleep in the **hayloft** until evening.
There are **billions** of **microbes** in the soil, too.	Henny didn't like Tomten taking her eggs, but she put up with it until one morning when she saw Goosey-Goosey sail forth, smiling and bowing with a stream of piping **goslings** following her.

Word Familiarity (Frequency) in Literary, Science/Social Science, and Math Texts

For decades, researchers have estimated the difficulty of a text, or its appropriateness for students at different grade levels, by thinking about the words and the sentences (Harrison, 1980; Klare & Buck, 1954; Mesmer, 2007). Although imperfect, analysis of both words and sentences does shed light on the conceptual difficulty of text. In order to decide whether a text is harder or easier, researchers have calculated the degree to which words in text are more or less familiar (Klare & Buck, 1954; Mesmer et al., 2012). Familiarity is typically measured by examining the frequency of words in a text. By *frequency*, I mean the number of times a word appears in written English (e.g., *the* = very frequent, *gall* = highly infrequent). Generally, but not always, rare or infrequent words are less familiar to the reader and therefore harder. For example, in *Hedgie's Surprise*, the words *porridge* and *goslings* are both infrequent and hard. In *Rotters!: Decomposition*, the words *microbes*, *bacteria*, and *microscope* are also infrequent and hard. However, the infrequent words in *Hedgie's Surprise* and *Rotters!: Decomposition* are hard in different ways. As I demonstrate in this section, all infrequent words are not the same (Graesser, McNamara, & Kulikowich, 2011; Mesmer, Hiebert, & Cunningham, 2019).

Science and Social Science Words

As demonstrated in the previous examples, the types of unfamiliar words that readers encounter in the texts of science and social science differ from those encountered in narrative fiction. There are four fundamental differences (see Table 6.3). First, the unfamiliar words in science and

TABLE 6.3. Contrasting Features of Narrative and Science/Social Studies Texts

Narrative fiction	Science and social studies text
Usually known conceptual category.	Often new schema or construct.
Concrete, easily represented nouns.	Heavily modified complex nouns.
New words rarely repeated.	Unfamiliar words are repeated frequently.
Ancillary to the primary concept.	Represent the target conceptual content.

social studies texts are more technical and complex. In *Rotters!: Decomposition*, the word *microbe* is conceptually more difficult to understand than, say, *kettle*. A *microbe* is a microscopic organism about which many young readers have no knowledge; they have not been exposed to the idea of microscopic organisms that cannot be seen with the eye. In comparison, the word *kettle*, while unknown, fits into a conceptual category with which a reader might be familiar—cookware. Thus, when reading infrequent words in a science or social science text, the reader has to build a new schema or construct, which is harder. The words of science also have multiple *morphemes*, or more meaningful word parts, and often word parts have Greek or Latin derivation, such as *micro*, *-ia*, and *-scope* (Fang, 2006).

Second, the unfamiliar, infrequent words in science and social studies also tend to be complex nouns. These nouns can often be more heavily modified. In addition, they often do not represent a person, animal, thing, or place. Instead, nouns can represent an entire process (Fang, 2006). For example, *evaporation* is the process of water being transformed from a liquid form to a vapor form. When a student reads the word *evaporation*, he or she cannot simply call up an item or color but must remember an entire process. When a verb, adjective, or adverb is converted into a noun, linguists call that *nominalization*, a text feature that makes the infrequent words of science and social science particularly challenging (Fang, 2006). For example, soil erosion is a modified nominalization of the word *erode*, which means to wash away slowly. In this example, a verb, *erode*, is turned into a noun meaning the process of *eroding*. In science or social science, one compact word can convey an entire multistep process (e.g., *meiosis*, *distillation*, *migration*).

The third feature that you may notice in the *Rotters!: Decomposition* science text can actually render text easier—repetition. Note that although *Rotters!: Decomposition* has a count of nine infrequent words, these nine actually comprise four words that are repeated (i.e., *microbe*, *microscope*, *bacteria*, and *billion*). In *Hedgie's Surprise*, on the other hand, there are six unique, unfamiliar words (i.e., none are repeated). The interesting thing about repetition, especially of more technical vocabulary, is that it helps students grasp the word and, in some respects, renders the texts easier. However, when formulas estimate difficulty, they do not take into account repetition. So each occurrence of the word *microbe*, for example, is treated as if it is an entirely new, unfamiliar word. This means that formulas may overestimate the difficulty of science and social science text.

Last, in science and social science texts, the unfamiliar words represent the target conceptual content. In narrative fiction, the unfamiliar words are usually more ancillary, adding a layer of meaning, or suggesting intensity or degree, or keeping the prose fresh and interesting. However, the unfamiliar words in science and social science texts are the very point. The words are the conceptual target and getting those words is critical to getting the main idea.

Math Words

Although we are increasingly seeing mathematics and literacy integrations, and even mathematics picture books, teachers and researchers rarely think about the words in books that focus on mathematics. What we found in an analysis of a historical dataset is that even when math texts had unfamiliar words, these words did not predict students' comprehension of the books (Mesmer et al., 2019). We wondered why. If a word is not familiar, shouldn't it be harder if it is in a math, science, or social studies book than in literature?

At first, we thought that perhaps mathematics texts simply did not have as many rare, infrequent words as, say, literature, science, and social science selections. But in actuality, when we tested this notion, mathematics texts and literary texts had the same levels of infrequent words, but science and social science texts had more infrequent words. Then we examined whether the frequency of words in math texts influenced comprehension and, to our surprise, we found that they did not. Infrequent words did influence comprehension of social science and science texts but not math texts. Below are two examples from grades 4–6 that illustrate what we uncovered about words in mathematics texts.

First, as I stated earlier, math texts *do* contain unfamiliar, infrequent words, but there are not as many as in science and social science texts. In the first example below (from Bormuth, 1969) are the words *billion*, *mathematician*, and *braces*.

> Think of the largest number you can. Regardless of what it is, you can always make it larger by adding the number one to it. Suppose your number is 1,000,000,000 (a **billion**); if you add 1 to it you get 1,000,000,001, which is larger than your largest number. That, by the way, is how **mathematicians** show that there is no such thing as the largest number in the world. For if anyone said that such-and-such a number is the largest, you could always add the number one to it and make it larger. Thus, there is no end to numbers; they keep on going forever.

What appears to be the case with at least some of these infrequent math words, is that although they are interesting, they are not integral to the main purpose or meaning of the passage. For example, knowing exactly how many 0's are in a *billion* is not exactly the point of the passage. That word, *billion,* is simply used to illustrate the point that a very big number can always be increased by adding one to it. The word *billion* is also duplicated with the number, which makes it more understandable. A student might comprehend the mathematical meaning of the word *billion* with the number but not know the word. The idea of the passage is that numbers are limitless. Similarly, the word *mathematicians* is also an infrequent word, but it is not essential to the meaning of passage. It appears that the ideas or concepts in mathematics texts are more complex than the actual words. In math, the collection of words is greater than the sum of its parts, a finding that leads to the next point.

The second example (from Bormuth, 1969) reflects a very common pattern in mathematics texts: familiar, frequent words taking on specific mathematical meanings.

> We think of a set as a collection of things. You can think of a set as a collection of people, of ideas, or of numbers; a collection of any things you can think of can be a set.
>
> The things that belong to a set are called the members of the set. You can name a set by using a capital letter. For example, a set whose members are letters might be named by writing Set L. Another way to name a set is to use **braces**. When you use **braces** to name a set, you must draw the braces and list every member of the set between the **braces**. (BL #821–829)

In this example, the word *set,* which is a frequent and familiar word, is the focus of the passage. In common measures of text difficulty, this word would not be flagged as a hard, infrequent word. However, *set,* in mathematical terms, is defined in very specific ways. Although the word *set* is not difficult, the specific, mathematical definition *is.* The other infrequent, familiar word in this passage, *braces,* is a British term for brackets {}. Although not understanding this term could lead to a misunderstanding about labeling a set, it would not impair a student's ability to understand the main idea of the passage: what a set is. It is very common in mathematical texts to use words that have multiple meanings or for a word that in other contexts is "easy" to be harder in a mathematical context (e.g., *balance, variable, line, plane*). In math, it is often the case that common, familiar terms take on specific mathematical meanings.

Narrative Fiction Words

What has been known for years is that literary genres often have fewer unfamiliar or infrequent words (Klare, 1984) compared to expository text. In an analysis of literary and expository texts, researchers found that expository texts comprise 29–34% unfamiliar words but language arts texts have 16–19% unfamiliar words (Lee, 2001). As I mentioned earlier, in an analysis that my colleagues and I conducted, we found that literature and math texts have more familiar words than social science and science texts (Mesmer et al., 2019). One of the reasons that narrative fiction possesses more familiar words is that there are high levels of dialogue that emulate the everyday language of speech. Narrative often stems from oral traditions that rely on oral language. In addition, the content of narrative fiction does not consist of technical explanations of the world.

Even when narrative fiction has unfamiliar words, the nature of these words can be quite different. For example, in *Hedgie's Surprise,* the words *speckled, kettle, porridge, hayloft, goslings,* and *piping* are quite different from the words in *Rotters!: Decomposition.* As I mentioned earlier, unfamiliar nouns, such as *porridge* and *hayloft,* are not conceptually complex. With these words, a simple synonym or brief definition could be used to convey the words' meanings: *porridge*—a type of hot breakfast cereal like oatmeal; *hayloft*—a place in a barn where hay is stored, usually in a second floor. Furthermore, the purpose of the text is not to convey the understanding of these words.

This trend with the nouns in narrative fiction is also mirrored with the adjectives, verbs, and adverbs. For example, in *Hedgie's Surprise,* the words *speckled, crowed,* and *piping* all have easy synonyms: *spotted, yelled,* and *chirping.* Note that the unfamiliar words in *Rotters!: Decomposition*—*microbes, bacteria, microscope, billions*—are all nouns. There are no adjectives, verbs, and adverbs, a trend that is very common in science and social science texts. The words in narrative fiction also tend to be what are called "Tier Two words" (Beck, McKeown, & Kucan, 2002, 2013). Tier One words, those that are known and used by students, do not need to be taught (e.g., *see, play, hug*). Tier Two words, such as *speckled, porridge,* and *crowed,* are unknown to students, but students usually possess a ready synonym. Tier Two words are not conceptually difficult (Beck et al., 2002, 2013). Furthermore, Tier Two words are not typically specific to a discipline and have broader applicability to a wide array of contexts. (*Speckled* need not apply only to the coloring of hens.) Tier Two words can be quickly taught by teachers and repeatedly used in future days and weeks. Tier Three words, such as those found in science texts, require the building of new schemas or concepts, and teaching them requires examples, descriptions, and illustrations. Tier Three words, such as *microbes* and *bacteria,* are words that are unknown and require substantive teaching, examples, and experiences to really be understood.

Because literary narratives have fewer unfamiliar or infrequent words, readability formulas often underestimate the difficulty of narrative texts as the Common Core writers remind us (National Governors Association, Council of Chief State School Officers, 2010). For example, the Lexile level of John Grisham's *The Firm* is about the same as that in *Rotters!: Decomposition* and *Hedgie's Surprise.* Clearly, these texts are not the same in terms of difficulty. Like math text, the whole is greater than the sum of its parts. The complexity of a narrative piece lies in the creative arrangement of words and phrases not in the complexity of individual words. Writers organize words figuratively. For example, they may use a metaphor by saying, "The columns were a row of dark soldiers, grimly guarding the memorial." In this example, the writer also personifies the columns by describing them as soldiers. Therefore, complex stories may be conveyed creatively using everyday language. Even a recent study of the latest readability formulas on the market found that most of the tools worked better for nonfiction, expository text than for narrative (Nelson, Perfetti, Liben, & Liben, 2012).

Text Cohesion

Until very recently, the approaches for quickly estimating the difficulty of a text, like Lexiles or other formulas, focused only on words and sentences. But new focus and energy has turned attention toward text cohesion, a discourse feature. Text cohesion can be thought of as the accumulated repetition of words within and across sentences (Givón, 1995; Grimes, 1975). Table 6.4 shows three examples of texts with low, medium, and high levels of cohesion.

Text cohesion, or the repetition of words and phrases, helps to create in a book, chapter, or article a balance between known and unknown information. Text cohesion creates a thread of meaning that winds through the passage and helps the reader to hang on to the important themes, concepts, and ideas. Notice that in the highly cohesive text, words such as *plant, seed,* and *grow* are repeated, as are *pistil, stamen,* and

TABLE 6.4. Examples of Texts with Low, Medium, and High Cohesion

Low cohesion: *Where Do Polar Bears Live?* (Thomson, 2011)	Medium cohesion: *Horses* (Simon, 2006)	High cohesion: *From Seed to Plant* (Gibbons & Mallon, 1991)
This island is covered with snow. No trees grow. Nothing has green leaves. The land is white as far as you can see. Then something small and round and black pokes up out of the snow. A black nose sniffs the air. Then a smooth white head appears. A mother polar bear heaves herself out of her den. A **cub** scrambles after her. When the **cub** was born 4 months ago, he was no bigger than a guinea pig. Blind and helpless, he snuggled in his mother's fur. He drank her milk and grew, safe from the long Arctic winter.	**Horses** move in four natural ways, called **gaits** or paces. They **walk, trot, canter,** and **gallop.** The **walk** is the slowest **gait** and the **gallop** is the fastest. When a **horse walks,** each hoof leaves the ground at a different time. It **moves** one **hind leg** first, and then the **front leg** on the same side; then the other **hind leg** and the other **front leg.** When a **horse walks,** its body swings gently with each stride. When a **horse trots,** its **legs** move in pairs, left **front leg** with right **hind leg,** and right front **leg** with left hind **leg.**	Most **plants** make **seeds.** A **seed** contains the beginning of a new **plant.** **Seeds** are different shapes, sizes, and colors. All **seeds** **grow** into the same kind of **plant** that made them. Many **plants grow flowers. Flowers** are where most **seeds** begin. A **flower** is made up of many **parts.** At the bottom of the **pistil** are tiny egg cells called ovules. In the center of the **flower** is the **pistil.** The sticky **part** at the top of the **pistil** is the **stigma.** The **parts** of the **flower** around the **pistil** are the **stamens. Stamens** make yellow powder called pollen.

stigma. These word repetitions help the reader infer the main idea of the passage. Notice that with the low cohesion text, the word *polar bear* only appears one time and, then, about halfway through the passage. The reader has to do some work to figure out the theme, concept, or ideas in the passage. Now, for some people, this makes a passage more interesting. Likely, for any adult reader, the low cohesion version is probably more interesting, but for children, the higher cohesion text is easier to follow and understand.

There are actually many different ways to capture or measure text cohesion (Graesser et al., 2011), all of which I do not discuss here. However, one indicator of text cohesion is *content word overlap*, which is the proportion of content words, such as *horse, gallop,* and *trot,* that repeat across adjacent sentences and within sentences in the passage. *Content words* are words that are related to the topic or story. Another indicator of text cohesion is *noun overlap*, which is the proportion of nouns that overlap. In the previous passages, words such as *stamen*, *pistil*, and *plant*, overlap, but additional nouns, such as *pond* or *log*, that are not directly connected to the topic might occur in the passage and would also be counted. In other words, unlike content word overlap, noun overlap might also include nouns that are not particular to the topic or theme of the passage. *Argument overlap* is the repetition of both nouns and pronouns between pairs of sentences (e.g., *it/it, plant/plants, stamen/stamen*).

A group of researchers has created a tool call Coh-Metrix that automatically analyzes the cohesion of a text (*http://cohmetrix.com*; Graesser et al., 2011). Figure 6.1 shows analyses of each of the earlier texts. (*Note.* For best results, Coh-Metrix requires passages of over 200 words.) The content word overlap, noun overlap, and argument overlap are all reflected in the bar called "referential cohesion." As you can see, the least cohesive text is *Where Do Polar Bears Live* (Thomson, 2011) and the most cohesive is *From Seed to Plant* (Gibbons & Mallon, 1991). These Coh-Metrix reports have many other components, such as word concreteness and narrativity, or the distinguishing factors between narrative and non-narrative terms. Word concreteness is an important text feature, one that wields a great deal of influence in elementary grades when learners are in the concrete operations stage (discussed further below).

You probably notice that these texts are all science informational texts. In a recent analysis of language arts, science, and social science texts in grades 2–11, researchers found that referential cohesion with the types of repetitions described here was highest in science texts (Graesser et al., 2011). This suggests that science text writers may control cohesion and repeat terms and words to make the texts more understandable to readers. Perhaps cohesion compensates for the difficult vocabulary and conceptual knowledge.

Now, if you are a teacher who works with young readers on a regular basis, you might be thinking, "OK, this cohesion stuff is interesting, but so what? What difference does it make?" What we know is that because more cohesive texts repeat words, noun phrases, and word roots across sentences, they help readers maintain a thread of understanding throughout their reading. It is as if cohesive passages remind the reader what the "big ideas" are, even if implicitly. In other words, the cohesive passage is saying to the reader, "This is about *plants* and *seeds*. Remember, we are talking about *plants* and *seeds* and *plant parts*." Generally, more cohesive passages are comprehended better (Graesser et al., 2011; Gernsbacher, Varner, & Faust, 1990). However, this pattern is influenced

Seed to Plant

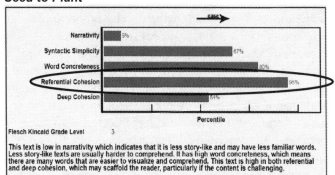

Horses

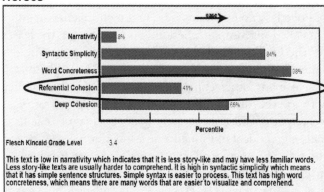

Where Polar Bears Live

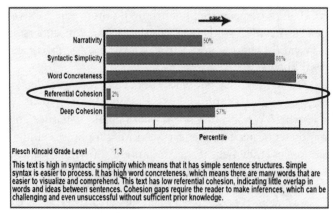

FIGURE 6.1. Coh-Metrix analyses for three texts.

by the readers' prior knowledge about a topic (McNamara, 2001). When readers have *less* background knowledge, their comprehension is better in *more cohesive texts*. However, when their background knowledge is higher, readers comprehend better in *less cohesive texts*. It is as if the lack of cohesion challenges them to stay engaged and make text-based inferences. For a reader who has done an animal study, the polar bears text would probably be intriguingly challenging and engaging. Conversely, a text such as *From Seed to Plant* would be boring for children studying plants. In fact, as an experienced educator, I actually found myself skimming this passage. As discussed in "Implications for Professional Learning," there are several strategies you can use to focus on cohesion.

Word Concreteness and Imageability

Another feature of words that influences the development of conceptual knowledge is word imageability, sometimes also called *concreteness*. *Imageabilty* is the degree to which a word evokes a mental image in the reader. Others have described it as the degree to which a word's meaning evokes "a semantic variable in that it refers to the extent to which a word's meaning incorporates sensorimotor properties" (Strain, Patterson, & Seidenberg, 1995, p. 1140). Words such as *blue*, *hop*, and *platypus*, if known to the reader, are imageable. Words such as *love*, *pride*, and *there* are not imageable. Often people use the word *concrete* in place of *imageable*, because the word *imageable* assumes that a word is known. If you don't know what a *platypus* is, for example, you cannot create an image of that word. The frequency or familiarity of a word and its concreteness actually interact, with the easiest words being frequent, highly concrete words and the hardest words being infrequent, not concrete words. Table 6.5 shows this relationship.

TABLE 6.5. Relationship between a Word's Frequency/Familiarity and Its Concreteness

Infrequent/unfamiliar		Frequent/familiar	
Not concrete	Highly concrete	Not concrete	Highly concrete
culture, gravity, revolution	precipitation, sedimentary rock, cerulean	love, the, to, like	cat, shoe, dog, red, jump

Word concreteness or imageability influences how easily people read words and remember the meanings of those words. Young readers learn more concrete words faster, especially if the words are also very frequent and regularly spelled (e.g., *cat* vs. *enough*) (Hargis & Gickling, 1978; Kolker & Terwilliger, 1981). More experienced readers tend to draw on the concreteness of a word as a compensatory strategy. When letters/sounds are more complex or the word is not frequent, the concreteness of a word tends to help readers remember the word (Raman & Baluch, 2001; Woollams, 2005).

In the previously mentioned analysis of language arts, science, and social science texts, researchers found that word concreteness is higher in science texts than in language arts and social science texts before grade 4 (Graesser et al., 2011). This is important to note, because it identifies yet another reason why science informational texts are well suited to young children. Whereas narrative fiction was previously assumed to be the easiest type of text for the early grades, we now know that this is not true. The work by Graesser and colleagues identifies one reason why this is the case: Science content in the early grades tends to be very concrete. In fact, the analyses of the early grades books *Where Do Polar Bears Live?*, *From Seed to Plant*, and *Horses* (Simon, 2006), all show this trend in concreteness. However, after grade 4, science texts decline in word concreteness, with words becoming less and less concrete as abstract concepts such as molecules, atoms, cellular processes, and physics begin to emerge.

Conclusion

Texts are a very important source for advancing conceptual knowledge. They have more rich language than speech and generally introduce students to an array of words that they would not encounter in conversations. Today's textbook market is replete with beautifully rendered texts for social studies and science, books that invite rich learning and growth. Thus, in the everyday rush of teaching, it is easy to dash into the book room, scan the shelves for books for the next social studies or science unit, find the right levels, and think the job done. What I'm saying in this chapter is that some very important elements of text are overlooked in those text levels.

I began the chapter by differentiating text complexity from text difficulty. Complexity is simply the features of the words, sentences, and discourse of the text, and text difficulty is the estimated challenge the text poses to a reader. Text difficulty labels, like levels, often do not address all the elements of texts that could possibly make a text challenging to a reader.

Specifically, I have addressed the ways in which word familiarity influences difficulty, how text cohesion comes into play, and how imageability or concreteness can make some texts easier. It is generally the case that more familiar words are the easiest to read and understand, and that content-area texts have fewer of these words. Often science and social studies texts have unfamiliar, dense nouns that are complex. However, this basic pattern is actually disrupted a bit. For example, even though science texts may have unfamiliar words, those words, unlike the hard words in narrative fiction, are often repeated. On the other hand, in math texts, very familiar words such as *set, point, line,* or *variable* take on specific meanings that make these words harder. Another feature that makes text complex is *cohesion,* or the degree to which words, phrases, or clauses are repeated, overlapping in sentences throughout a paragraph. Generally, less experienced readers find texts written with a high degree of cohesion easier to read. A final text complexity facet I have addressed in this chapter is word concreteness or imageability. As it turns out, when words are more concrete, they are easier for the younger reader. Of course, we all know that selecting materials to advance conceptual knowledge in the content areas is never a matter of "grab and go"; this chapter pinpoints some specific and overlooked features of text that are worth considering in the assessment of text difficulty.

● IMPLICATIONS FOR PROFESSIONAL LEARNING ●

- If you are a teacher, you might find all of this information interesting. But you might be asking yourself, "What do I do with this? How will it help me teach kids?" In the following list, I extend the ideas in the chapter to instructional decision making.

Don't Depend on Levels and Formulas Alone

- Labels are *estimates.* Use them as "a place to start."
- Leveling systems have a standard error of measure. The "true" level of a book can be *as much as* one whole to one half-year above or below the label.

- Labels can *underestimate* difficulty in narrative fiction and *over-estimate* difficulty in informational/expository texts (due to word repetition).

Be on the Lookout for Uncommon Uses of Common Words

- Mathematics have "easy" words used differently or outside of their common vernacular uses (*balance, line, angle,* and *variable*). Look for common words that are conceptually complex from a math standpoint.

- Science also can use common words that have specific science meanings (e.g., *fault, stable, react*).

- In narratives, authors will take common words and use them figuratively comparing unlike things. For example, in *Hedgie's Surprise* the author writes about Goosey-Goosey *sailing* forth, with a *stream* of goslings.

- Narratives also use allegory, metaphor, personification, simile, and hyperbole to convey levels of meaning with simple, commonplace words.

Science and Social Studies Unfamiliar Words Need More Time

- In science and social science, unfamiliar words *are often the entire point* of the reading.

- Students have to *build* new cognitive categories for the new words they learn in science and social studies. They do not have a ready synonym.

- Words in the science or social studies text take more time to learn and teach.

- Unfamiliar words tend to be more conceptually dense, with nominalizations that represent complex processes in one word.

Look for Cohesion, Especially in Science and Social Science Texts

- Text cohesion, or the repetition of content within and across sentences, makes texts easier for readers with less background knowledge or skill.

- Check to see whether these repeated words in science or social studies can help the students extract a main idea from the text.

- Students with minimal background usually benefit from more cohesive texts.

- Toward the end of a unit or study, when students have more background on a topic, they may enjoy the challenge of a text with less cohesion.

QUESTIONS FOR DISCUSSION

1. The chapter describes some differences in how complexity at the word, sentence, and discourse levels play out differently in math, literacy, science, and social science texts. What have been your observations about the difficulty of words, syntax, and discourse in different content areas? Do your observations reflect those in the chapter?

2. This chapter identifies three text features—word familiarity, text cohesion, and word concreteness—that tend to be overlooked in estimating text difficulty. Which of these do you see most often ignored in texts that you use to teach? Why do you think that feature is ignored?

3. This chapter makes the point repeatedly that formulas can both underestimate and overestimate text difficulty depending on content. What have been your observations about the ways that systems under- or overestimate difficulty?

REFERENCES

Beck, I. L., McKeown, M. G., & Kucan, L. (2002). *Bringing words to life: Robust vocabulary instruction: Solving problems in the teaching of literacy.* New York: Guilford Press.

Beck, I. L., McKeown, M. G., & Kucan, L. (2013). *Bringing words to life: Robust vocabulary instruction.* New York: Guilford Press.

Bormuth, J. R. (1969). *Development of readability analyses* (U.S. Office of Education Final Report, Project No. 70052, Contract No. OEC-3-7-070052-0326). Chicago: University of Chicago.

Brett, J. (2016). *Hedgie's surprise.* New York: Putnam.

Fang, Z. (2006). The language demands of science reading in middle school. *International Journal of Science Education, 28*(5), 491–520.

Gernsbacher, M. A., Varner, K. R., & Faust, M. E. (1990). Investigating differences in general comprehension skill. *Journal of Experimental Psychology: Learning, Memory, and Cognition, 16*(3), 430.

Gibbons, G., & Mallon, E. (1991). *From seed to plant.* New York: Holiday House.

Givón, T. (1995). *Functionalism and grammar.* Philadelphia: Benjamins.

Graesser, A. C., McNamara, D. S., & Kulikowich, J. M. (2011). Coh-Metrix providing multilevel analyses of text characteristics. *Educational Researcher, 40*(5), 223–234.

Grimes, J. E. (1975). *The thread of discourse.* The Hague, the Netherlands: Mouton.

Grisham, J. (1991). *The firm*. New York: Doubleday.

Hargis, C. H., & Gickling, E. E. (1978). The function of imagery in word recognition development. *The Reading Teacher, 31*(8), 870–874.

Harrison, C. (1980). *Readability in the classroom*. Cambridge, UK: Cambridge University Press.

Hayes, D., & Ahrens, M. (1988). Vocabulary simplification for children: A special case of "motherese"? *Journal of Child Language, 15,* 395–410.

Klare, G. R. (1984). Readability. In P. D. Pearson, R. Barr, M. Kamil, & P. Mosenthal (Eds.), *Handbook of reading research* (Vol. 1, pp. 681–744). New York: Longman.

Klare, G. R., & Buck, B. (1954). *Know your reader: The scientific approach to readability*. Oxford, UK: Hermitage House.

Kolker, B., & Terwilliger, P. N. (1981). Sight vocabulary learning of first and second graders. *Reading World, 20*(4), 251–258.

Lee, D. Y. W. (2001). Genres, registers, text types, domains and styles: Clarifying the concepts and navigating a path through the BNC jungle. *Language Learning and Technology, 5*(3), 37–72.

Mesmer, H. A. E. (2007). *Tools for matching readers to texts: Research-based practices*. New York: Guilford Press.

Mesmer, H. A., Cunningham, J. W., & Hiebert, E. H. (2012). Toward a theoretical model of text complexity for the early grades: Learning from the past, anticipating the future. *Reading Research Quarterly, 47*(3), 235–258.

Mesmer, H. A., Hiebert, E. H., & Cunningham, J. W. (2019). *Does one size fit all?: Examining text complexity and text difficulty across grade and content*. Manuscript under review.

Montag, J. L., Jones, M. N., & Smith, L. B. (2015). The words children hear: Picture books and the statistics for language learning. *Psychological Science, 26*(9), 1489–1496.

National Governors Association Center for Best Practices, Council of Chief State School Officers. (2010). *Common Core State Standards for English language arts and literacy in history/social studies, science, and technical subjects*. Washington, DC: Authors. Retrieved from *www.corestandards.org/assets/ccssi_ela%20standards.pdf*.

Nelson, J., Perfetti, C., Liben, D., & Liben, M. (2012). *Measures of text difficulty: Testing their predictive value for grade levels and student performance*. Washington, DC: Council of Chief State School Officers.

Piaget, J. (1936). *Origins of intelligence in the child*. London: Routledge & Kegan Paul.

Raman, I., & Baluch, B. (2001). Semantic effects as a function of reading skill in word naming of a transparent orthography. *Reading and Writing, 14*(7/8), 599–614.

Simon, S. (2006). *Horses*. New York: HarperCollins.

Strain, E., Patterson, K., & Seidenberg, M. S. (1995). Semantic effects in single-word naming. *Journal of Experimental Psychology: Learning, Memory, and Cognition, 21*(5), 1140–1154.

Thomson, S. L. (2011). *Where do polar bears live?* New York: New York: HarperCollins.

Townsend, J. (2005). *Rotters!: Decomposition*. New York: Raintree Fusion: Life Science.

Woollams, A. M. (2005). Imageability and ambiguity effects in speeded naming: Convergence and divergence. *Journal of Experimental Psychology: Learning, Memory, and Cognition, 31*(5), 878–890.

CHAPTER 7

Teaching and Learning in a Digital World

Digital Literacies for Disciplinary Learning

JILL CASTEK
MICHAEL MANDERINO

In this chapter, we approach digital and disciplinary literacies as inextricably linked concepts that, when coupled together, offer powerful opportunities to harness the learning potential of the Internet to engage learners across disciplines (Goss, Castek, & Manderino, 2016; Manderino & Castek, 2016; Castek & Manderino, 2017). We are both teachers and researchers, each with a strong commitment to improving instructional practice, teacher development, digital inclusion, and student engagement. Jill researches online reading, digital literacies and inquiry, and the use of digital texts and tools to support learning in science, technology, engineering, and mathematics (STEM). Michael studies disciplinary literacies in digital contexts in history and English language arts and examines the use of multimodal texts for disciplinary learning. This chapter unites our complementary perspectives across disciplinary fields as well as across K–12 and adult education in formal and informal settings.

Over the course of a 2-year period, we have been discussing digital and disciplinary learning with our colleagues in schools and universities. These discussions revealed three important potentials for linking disciplinary and digital literacies. These three potentials recognize that teaching and learning with digital technologies require us to think differently about classroom organization. They also introduce synergistic practices centered around teaching literacies in ways that cut across disciplinary boundaries. The three potentials we discuss in this chapter are (1) bidirectional expertise, (2) democratizing knowledge production, and

(3) expanded inquiry approaches that include both problem posing and problem solving.

Additionally, we describe a framework of organizing principles that dovetails with these potentials. The framework addresses three organizing principles for planning classroom instruction: (1) accessing and evaluating information, (2) using and representing information, and (3) producing and exchanging information. The chapter focuses on the potential for transforming instruction when digital and disciplinary learning are tied together.

Learning in a Digital World

Digital texts and tools have proliferated into every facet of our lives in the past few decades. Digital devices and networks have affected the ways we share ideas and communicate. In a recent survey, 95% of teens reported possessing a smartphone, with 45% reporting they are online constantly and another 44% reporting being online several times per day (Anderson & Jiang, 2018). Unfettered access to online resources and collaborative platforms creates opportunities to use and produce a vast range of materials that can be shared, revised, and remixed. These digital potentials allow us to connect with individuals and groups both locally and globally, and to contribute to an ever-expanding base of knowledge.

The Internet, online information, and networked communication tools mediate the ways we learn, especially in the disciplines, but the tools to develop knowledge have traditionally been implemented offline and face-to-face. However, the availability of digital texts and tools widens and amplifies opportunities to develop conceptual knowledge in the disciplines. In today's world, digital devices are increasingly used for accessing and sharing information, creating representations of conceptual thinking, and encouraging dialogic interchanges. Internet use and global networking that address these purposes unleash vast potential and a multitude of real-world contexts in which learners may engage as critical and agentive citizens.

Digital literacies are multifaceted and multidimensional. They are needed to use digital tools to both consume and produce knowledge. Learners who are digitally literate need to develop flexible mindsets and competencies to make choices, interact, and engage in an open, networked society (Lankshear & Knobel, 2006; Phillips & Manderino, 2015). In addition, digital literacies represent the multitude of ways people collaborate, create, and communicate using digital texts and tools. Furthermore, they are critical to fully accessing disciplinary learning whether a learner is an expert or novice. As such, the role of disciplinary practices as situated in classrooms has been theorized and researched in terms of habits of practice (Wickens, Manderino, Parker, & Jung, 2015). This research considers the situated nature of learning within a disciplinary community and how participation in such a community impacts an individual's knowledge construction. Habits of practice also recognize the wider range of disciplinary practices, including the distinct habits of thinking within a discipline that are needed to develop deep disciplinary knowledge and understanding.

Classroom and youth practices have driven the need for comprehensive policies regarding literacy and technology in education. School adoption of 1:1 computing has accelerated access to new technologies, but has not necessarily created equity in terms of use, instruction, or assessment. As educators, we can no longer sideline the learning of these essential literacies; doing so leaves digital literacies instruction to chance. Under-resourced communities and students who find themselves on the wrong side of the digital divide may not have regular access to tools, devices, nor have opportunities for contextual practice in using them to advance their learning (Leu, Forzani, & Kennedy, 2015; Leu, Forzani, Rhoads, et al., 2015). For many learners, school is the best place to learn digital literacies in a formal way. However, many schools have not provided such instruction. All students need opportunities and instruction to learn the full range of digital literacies in the disciplines and across the curriculum in order to be fully literate in a digital age.

The Growing Importance of Disciplinary Literacies

Recent scholarship on literacy has focused specifically on how the disciplines (e.g., history, literature, science) shape individuals' ways of knowing, and how those ways of knowing impact an individual's construction of meaning when interacting with domain-specific texts or in domain-specific contexts. For example, the way that an expert reads a science text differs from that of a nonexpert. In other words, readers who are steeped in a discipline such as science possess habits of thinking that support the comprehension of the text. A scientist may approach a text skeptically because she knows that an individual scientific text must be congruent with scientific evidence. The scientist may also adjust her reading to account for the integrated nature of graphics and text to identify a claim made within the text. Finally, a scientist may use a particular text to inform her construction of a model or to generate a hypothesis for an experiment. Discipline-specific teaching helps learners understand the ways in which disciplinary texts are constructed and encourages them to employ particular practices when learning from such texts.

A historian, on the other hand, likely approaches a text differently. She may look specifically for divergent perspectives and seek to disrupt a particular narrative based on the historical evidence provided. A historian may also consider who wrote the text and the context in which it was written to ascertain the veracity of the account as a credible perspective. Finally, a historian may use a set of resources to construct a written argument about the role of a particular event in history.

The purpose of these two examples—one in science and the other in history—is to show that the goals of the reader and the context/domain in which they are constructed impact how an individual makes meaning from a text. No matter the discipline, however, the development of conceptual knowledge is vital to its disciplinary practice.

Today's classrooms hold the potential to become engaged learning environments in which students are immersed in authentic disciplinary practices. In such an environment, students regularly engage in analysis, think for themselves about the information they collect, and share ideas from different perspectives to make sense of the content they find both online and face-to-face. Disciplinary instruction involves asking questions, constructing meaning from data, generating creative solutions, and reflecting on how to improve these solutions for different contexts; this occurs through inquiries into solving real-world problems that impact learners and their understanding of the world.

Changes to education contexts call for shifting mindsets and embracing literacies as multiple, situated, and social (Gee, 2000; Street, 2003). Designing instruction within a frame of multiple, situated, and social literacies opens up space to address social and textual practices that are central to digital and disciplinary learning. Paying attention to sociocultural aspects of learning (e.g., dialogue and collaboration) in addition to cognitive components (e.g., strategies and processes) opens new possibilities for innovative digital and disciplinary instructional design. As Shanahan, Silvestri, and McVee (2018) suggested, it is critical for students to participate in learning contexts that are reimagined to provide three types of opportunities: (1) they should allow for language-in-use as students work through problem solving with hands-on, minds-on involvement; (2) they should enable the solving of student-identified problems;

and (3) they should incorporate digital documentation as a mediational tool. These practices, when applied in instructional contexts, facilitate students' development of insider discourse, agency, and identity.

Disciplinary literacies that rely solely on print resources are no longer sufficient to fully convey complex and multilayered meanings given that learning in the digital age traverses digital/print, in- and out-of-school, face-to-face, and virtual communication. Full participation in the disciplines cannot be possible without a commitment to understanding digital literacies and their associated practices, and digital literacies are critical to fully accessing the literacies required for disciplinary learning.

Digital Literacies for Disciplinary Learning

Digital literacies are shaped by disciplinary learning. For example, scientific inquiry often includes the construction and testing of a representational model that is driven by scientific principles and concepts (NGSS Lead States, 2013). Examples of scientific models may include representations of the water cycle, cell division, or particle acceleration. Digital tools help learners visualize what they cannot readily see and provide the means to explore these models in a fully immersive way. Virtual reality applications and headsets allow learners to examine digital models from all angles, up close and in the round, as if the object were held in their hands. The construction of three-dimensional (3-D) models of cell division, for example, and the use of interactive digital features within these models, may be more effective at communicating dynamic processes than traditional two-dimensional figures. Moreover, the higher-order thinking processes used to interpret the 3-D models can be more generative and applicable to visualizing related concepts.

Digital literacies also shape the ways that individuals construct and communicate disciplinary knowledge. For example, if a learning goal is to communicate an analysis of a historical event, consideration of the medium is important. One task learners may be assigned is to write a critical interpretation for the teacher. However, digital contexts allow individuals to communicate with a wider audience that includes the public. Digital literacies, and the selection of a particular digital tool or medium, shape the possibilities for that knowledge construction and communication. Decisions to blog or create a digital artifact, and decisions about where to share the representation (e.g., on Twitter or on one's Web page), all impact the audience that the creator intends to engage. No matter how the information is shared, the digital and disciplinary literacies used to create it are interdependent and central to the learning experience.

Since print resources no longer sufficiently convey the complex and multilayered requirements of disciplinary literacies, it is important to use the wide range of communication tools available in the digital age. For example, disciplinary and digital literacies are necessary to disentangle and critically evaluate online texts, because authorship, credibility, and accuracy can be veiled on the open Web. Similarly, digital literacies are critical to fully accessing the literacies required for disciplinary learning. As a result, we argue that digital and disciplinary literacies should be thought of as inextricably linked rather than as separate areas of focus.

Most disciplinary practices in fields such as science, journalism, engineering, and other careers include digital resources as part of their inquiry. These inquiry processes include gathering information, visualizing data, generating visual representations, and communicating. These practices require both digital and disciplinary literacies to read, write, and express ideas in multiple forms. Linking digital and disciplinary learning uses the Internet's networking and knowledge-building resources toward this end. Likewise, using digital media can help shape learners' understanding of the social and intellectual practices of the discipline.

As the pace of digital innovation accelerates, educators at all levels must make space for instructional practices that build on the synergies between digital and disciplinary learning. To achieve this aim, educators must break through those typically predefined spaces bounded by school and help learners find ways to deepen their involvement with online resources, learning materials, and networks. Some schools and communities have jointly made strides in helping students gain access to the Internet both in and out of school by issuing one laptop, Chromebook, or tablet to each student through 1:1 computing. These programs open new avenues for learners, encouraging them to inquire, connect, and create, by providing everyone, both students and teachers, access to the digital tools for deeper learning within and across disciplines.

Three Potentials Addressed by Interweaving Digital Literacies for Disciplinary Learning

The power of digital texts and tools is clear; however, we argue that this power lies in the form of three potentials for deep learning: bidirectional expertise, democratizing knowledge production, and inquiry approaches that include both problem posing and problem solving.

First, given youth affinity for, and experience with, digital environments, we propose that knowledge production become more bidirectional *between* teacher and student, rather than *from* teacher to student. Second, the purposeful interweaving of digital literacies for disciplinary learning can democratize knowledge production within the disciplines and open new opportunities for inquiry within and across disciplines. Finally, digital literacies for disciplinary learning create opportunities for inquiry that extend beyond traditionally prescribed classroom-controlled inquiry and into inquiry processes that focus on both problem posing and problem solving. These inquiry processes transcend both the physical space of the classroom and the temporal confines of the traditional school day and calendar.

However, simply providing access to digital texts and tools alone does not create opportunities to build political or social consciousness, increase civic engagement, or generate solutions to problems facing communities and the world at large. Developing this kind of consciousness involves instruction around both problem posing and problem solving, and also requires disciplinary understanding—the sort of disciplinary practice that requires educators to think in flexible ways about designing instruction. These three specific potentials can be used to facilitate deep learning and wide knowledge construction. In the sections that follow, we describe and explain these three potentials. The discussion of these three potentials is intended to prompt consideration of shifts in teaching and learning paradigms, and to offer new ways of thinking about engaged learning and instructional approaches for classrooms.

Potential 1: Bidirectional Expertise

The digital world is constantly changing, but a persistent trend is that the digital world is a collaborative world. Learning in the 21st century is marked by greater access to texts in multiple formats, multiple forms of representation, multiple means of knowledge construction, and varied communication vehicles to organize, collaborate, and disseminate knowledge. These realities necessitate new ways of organizing teaching and learning. One promising approach is apprenticeship. This approach emphasizes the role of the teacher in providing demonstrations, engaging students, monitoring their understanding, providing timely support, and ultimately withdrawing that support as students gain independence. However, when applied to disciplinary learning, this model regards the teacher as expert and the student as novice. Studies of digital practice often show youth as digitally proficient (e.g., Barron, Gomez, Martin, &

Pinkard, 2014), suggesting that expert/novice labels only serve to reify, or solidify, learning as didactic. Reimagining apprenticeship models when digital literacies are leveraged for disciplinary learning suggests reinventing collaborative relationships (Greenleaf, Schoenbach, Cziko, & Mueller, 2001) to achieve the goals of both teachers and learners. Learners bring their extensive experiences using digital technologies with them to the classroom, and these experiences, when shared, can be transformative. Distributing knowledge and expertise widely across the learning landscape is beneficial for the whole community, and even more so when it emanates from students' expertise. Benefits include increased relevance, buy-in, and student empowerment. Shifting traditional notions of expert–novice relationships to more bidirectional knowledge exchanges between adults and youth can potentially encourage more collaborative forms of inquiry.

Creating opportunities for youth to demonstrate ways they access, make sense of, and dialogue about online resources repositions students from passive learners into active participants and decision makers about their own learning experiences and outcomes. With this greater agency, however, students need guidance in their evaluation of media sources (Wineburg & McGrew, 2017).

In a media-saturated environment, the need for critical evaluation of sources is just as important as the ability to access sources. Traditionally, teachers are the arbiters of what texts are consumed; therefore, the texts are assumed to be credible. By making use of bidirectional expertise, teachers can also help students develop agency in text selection; teachers and students can co-construct the processes for critically evaluating sources of all kinds.

There are two areas that can become powerful levers for digital literacies engagement in the disciplines: (1) having youth select texts and (2) co-constructing inquiry. First, data from a recent survey of 1,200 English language arts teachers show that in comparison to teachers' responses in a 2013 survey, more teachers are selecting texts based on reading level rather than grade level (Griffith, with Duffett, 2018). This approach is problematic not only in terms of using authentic texts for disciplinary inquiry, but it also reinforces a lack of agency for adolescents in terms of their own selection of texts within their disciplinary inquiry.

Rather than singularly focusing on texts that are perceived to be readable, we argue that the focus should instead be on disciplinary inquiry that is supported by digital texts and tools. It is also the case that when students are active participants in the inquiry, the level of complexity in texts with which they engage accelerates. As such, when students participate in this process by accessing and evaluating the sources that drive their inquiry themselves, they become a part of disciplinary production.

An example of this type of approach was advanced within a high school English class in which students brought in media texts to analyze with their classmates in a practice called #litanalysis4life (Rainey & Storm, 2017). In this instructional practice, young people bring their unique ways to use and represent information in digital spaces. Images, graphics interchange formats (GIFs), and videos dominate the media landscape. As this researcher–teacher collaboration seeks to apprentice students in disciplinary approaches to inquiry, the students actively engage in the medium that allows them to best share their knowledge construction. In this particular example, the texts that students brought into the classroom were analyzed through multiple interpretive lenses, such as a historical lens, a race lens, and a socioeconomic lens (Rainey & Storm, 2017). The disciplinary practices that are highly valued within the literary community are then brought to bear on the types of texts that are highly valued by students. As evidenced in this example, while there are norms for disciplinary communication, new forms of media are embraced as vehicles for sharing disciplinary knowledge.

In disciplines beyond English language arts, students' experiences with podcasts or video creation can be ideal for creating a medium that allows for broadly sharing disciplinary knowledge construction. The norms and practices of the disciplines can be brought to bear in not only the analysis of student-selected texts but also the production of new texts by students. Such texts allow students to represent and communicate disciplinary knowledge to others in ways that mirror the exchange of ideas in the digital world beyond school. Furthermore, by enabling students to make broad use of social media to connect ideas in networks that are familiar to them (e.g., Twitter, Facebook, Instagram) (Anderson & Jiang, 2018), teachers are able to scaffold students as they decide how best, and where, to share that knowledge with others online.

Potential 2: Democratizing Knowledge Production

Many scholars have argued that digital interactions offer students opportunities to discover multiple ways of knowing the world—including how to participate within and across academic discourse communities—and that providing these spaces is a matter of social justice (Lee & Spratley, 2010; Moje, 2007). All students deserve access to rich, intellectual conversations, information, and digital literacies instruction that prepare them for college and careers. Such activities are key components of participation in a digital information age, leading to participatory citizenship and personal fulfillment. Moreover, disciplinary communities are enriched through the participation of linguistically and culturally diverse voices.

Multiple text types, various modes of meaning making (New London Group, 1996), and online and offline cognitive practices are all situated in disciplinary contexts. Digital texts and tools used for disciplinary learning should be grounded in social participation that is mediated by both the discipline *and* the learning environment. In other words, digital texts, digital tools, and the disciplinary specific ways to use them in many different learning contexts (e.g., classrooms, outdoors, in fieldwork, and in the community) should all be taken into consideration.

In the broadest sense, the Internet is a participatory culture (Jenkins, 2006), one that is marked by low barriers to entry, in which all members' contributions are valued. In fact, in the digital age, barriers to texts, audiences, production tools, and disciplinary experts are greatly reduced. Theories of multiliteracies, new literacies, and participatory cultures can converge in this setting to offer dynamic potentials for disciplinary learning. However, this potential has gone largely untapped.

The digital world—including social networking spaces and digital texts and tools—can be used to open up spaces for students to participate in discovery that is even more authentic and empowered than ever before, regardless of the discipline. Unfortunately, approaches to disciplinary content in many classrooms fall short of these aims. As the democratization of the Internet opens access to historical and scientific documents for individuals to read and make sense of, learners require a second layer of disciplinary thinking that accounts for a source's digital presence. As educators, we must teach our students to ask questions, such as who wrote this material, for what purpose, what implicit biases are attached to it, whether and to what extent the information is shaped by commercial interests, and whether and to what extent it may be trustworthy, along with other means of interrogating the text.

On the other hand, rich examples of this type of democratization, such as *makerspaces* (collaborative work spaces for making, learning, exploring, and sharing ideas) have occurred inside and outside of school and in afterschool settings, libraries, or other public and private facilities (Phillips, Woodard, & Killian-Lund, 2016; Tucker-Raymond, Gravel, Wagh, & Wilson, 2016). In makerspaces, learners of all ages act as mentors when working with and alongside more and less experienced peers.

Through this process of knowledge sharing, skilled makers apprentice those more novice as part of their projects.

Tucker-Raymond et al. (2016) provided an example of Nakim, a young mentor, who was working on a woodcut design for a book jacket as part of a community makerspace focused on the arts. He had access to expert woodcutters, both in person and through his extended maker online community. As he designed his own woodcut book jacket, he also shared making tips for other learners on his blog. What is unique about this example, as well as this learning space, is that the learners drove the task and products. In the process of engaged learning, learners exchange the tips and lessons learned from mentors with other peers and learners. This circular flow of ideas, practices, and information through digital and nondigital means results in new products and approaches to learning-through-making.

Despite recognized potentials such as those in the previous example (Tucker-Raymond et al., 2016), disciplinary educators have given too little attention to the democratizing potential of digital literacies and have not fully embraced synergies between digital and disciplinary learning. Disciplinary insiders have served as gatekeepers regarding what information is made accessible. In contrast, the Internet makes access to knowledge and the ability to communicate and critique that knowledge within a worldwide forum largely open and free. To capitalize on the open and free Internet, and to problem-solve and communicate solutions, we advocate that such democratizing platforms be used more widely to provide greater access to, and participation in, the disciplines.

Potential 3: Expanded Inquiry Approaches That Link Problem Posing and Problem Solving

Inquiry learning is an engaging way to design instruction, one that links problem posing with problem solving. By foregrounding these constructs in instruction, disciplinary and digital literacies are not simply learning tasks to be mastered, but rather tools that help individuals' attempts to solve intellectual and real-world problems. The confluence of digital and disciplinary literacies for these purposes expands opportunities for learning beyond the walls of secondary schools, postsecondary institutions, and formalized learning spaces.

Inquiry as a stance for learning has long been espoused (e.g., Dewey, 1938). As astrophysicist Neil DeGrasse Tyson (2015) remarked in one of his speeches, people are perpetually engaged in science and are constantly questioning the world around them. However, school structures have tended to stifle this sort of natural inquiry. While many school tasks focus on teacher-initiated questions (Cazden & Beck, 2003; Wells, 1993), even inquiry-labeled activities are typically designed with prescribed answers in mind. If digital literacies for disciplinary learning are used to leverage bidirectional expertise and capitalize on the democratization of knowledge consumption and production discussed earlier, then inquiry must also be student driven and allow for nonlinear processes to pose and solve social and intellectual problems.

Shanahan et al. (2018) captured the potential of inquiry by using engineering journals in an afterschool club. In this club, students shared their design decisions through multimedia texts in their engineering journals. The journals made use of content-rich vocabulary and provided students with opportunities to represent their inquiry through multimodal artifacts, allowing English language learners to engage in rich disciplinary practices while developing their language skills. Just as with the example on democratizing knowledge production (Potential 2), we see examples of inquiry, design, and apprenticeship in spaces outside the confines of the classroom in this sequence of events.

One key to incorporating digital tools in disciplinary learning is to match disciplinary inquiry goals with a range of digital tools that support those goals. Students then have voice, choice, and agency in their learning. If we aim to invite inquiry learning across disciplines in ways that will benefit those learners who are often the most marginalized in academic contexts, then we must create opportunities for these types of inquiry practices in classrooms. In the next section, we describe a planning framework that can guide teachers who are working to create spaces for teaching digital literacies within disciplinary learning.

Addressing the Three Potentials:
An Instructional Framework

We previously introduced three potentials that address instructional practices to link digital literacies and disciplinary learning. The benefits of the three principles can be maximized for designing classroom instruction when they are examined alongside a planning framework. The planning framework we have designed (Castek & Manderino, 2017) suggests ways to organize and embed digital literacies for disciplinary learning into classroom instruction that can make the most of the synergies that exist between these areas. The framework is not meant to suggest hierarchical steps or linearity. Instead, it introduces multiple points of entry for flexible instructional planning and execution, offering three areas that should be thought about and addressed across extended instructional sequences. Planning instruction in this way provides the means to teach students a range of digital and disciplinary practices, such as how to critically evaluate disciplinary information, ways to examine multiple perspectives using different disciplinary lenses, and suggestions for expressing their interpretation of disciplinary concepts. As shown in Figure 7.1, the three areas of the framework include (1) accessing and evaluating online information, (2) using and representing online information, and (3) producing and exchanging online information.

Accessing and Evaluating Online Information

In today's information-rich digital spaces, it is critically important to determine which resources offer the most knowledgeable perspectives and come from the most reliable sources. Disciplinary learning relies on compiling discipline-specific information that comes from many sources, both online and offline. However, it is not always clear where information or even data found online originates. It is essential that we teach students

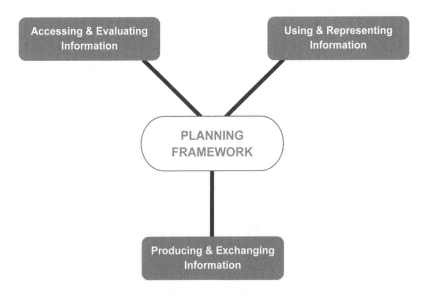

FIGURE 7.1. Planning framework.

a critical, evaluative stance when it comes to considering sources and source material found online. An essential aspect of developing such a stance lies in providing students with disciplinary expertise, so they can evaluate and interpret what they are gathering, using the same specific considerations that an expert within that discipline might use.

Teaching critical evaluation as both a discipline-specific and digital practice will not only help students better understand the disciplinary content they encounter but also aid them in becoming critical consumers of all content they find online. Students' ability to evaluate online information is strengthened when they are presented with the criteria used in a discipline and are encouraged to use these criteria (Duncan, Tate, & Chinn, 2014; Schwarz & White, 2005). The evaluation of online information must converge with digital practices for accessing quality content. Leveraging both areas in an integrated way invites learners to become informed, yet critical, consumers of disciplinary knowledge—an indispensable and fundamental condition for participation in an information-rich digital world.

Using and Representing Online Information

Today's classrooms require learners to be adept and flexible when in working across different modalities and between online and offline learning spaces, all the while synthesizing and making sense of information that comes from a wide variety of sources and perspectives. Experts within different disciplines explore topics in depth, using a range of resources. These experts collect data, debate ideas, and explore multiple perspectives. The information sources they use include digital simulations, animated 3-D models, or embedded images, audio, and video segments that are linked within and between different texts. These resources are generally read in a less linear manner than text-only information and require instructional scaffolding and extended practice if students are to engage in quality synthesis.

Gathering ideas from the multiple types of representations identified earlier involves layers of interpretation. In a digital world, meaning making is also a collaborative, networked activity that involves many individuals with different kinds of expertise. Discussion is often part of this process and includes both face-to-face and virtual discussion, the latter often being mediated through a shared, networked collaborative space such as Hypothes.is (*https://web.hypothes.is*). This space provides an online forum to hold discussions, read socially, organize a collection of reading materials and research archives, and take personal notes. Hypothes.is and other similar digital tools provide a collaborative context for synthesizing ideas drawn from multiple resources and offers a means for discussing them with other learners. Such digital activities mirror the forums disciplinary experts use to exchange ideas, track the evolution of their thinking, and post ideas for critique and discussion with other disciplinarians. Incorporating this type of flexible digital form into classroom instruction invites multiple perspectives and encourages the examination of ideas from different points of view. These practices are commonplace in the disciplines and can readily be included as part of disciplinary learning in classrooms.

Producing and Exchanging Online Information

When individuals engage digitally and collaborate dynamically, multiple opportunities exist to create and build knowledge. In the discipline of science, drawing conclusions that come from first- and secondhand investigations is a critical component of the inquiry process. These conclusions can then be discussed, debated, and circulated within the disciplinary community. However, disciplinary learning should also lead to knowledge production and critique of the models and representations generated. Students need to possess both digital and disciplinary literacies to produce such representations of their own learning. The digital tools that they employ, the representations that they create, and the media that they use to communicate their ideas offer valuable practice in constructing knowledge.

Disciplinary learning requires discussion, data gathering, synthesis, argumentation, and data interpretation. Digital networks can support these processes in authentic and meaningful ways. For example, digital tools afford opportunities for students to engage in both synchronous, or concurrent, and asynchronous discussions that promote idea sharing and authentic argumentation. Additionally, digital networking can be used to connect learners with disciplinary experts via tools such as Zoom, Skype, Google Hangouts, and Twitter. Finally, digital tools afford opportunities for students to construct knowledge using multiple modes, such as video, audio, image, text, and combinations thereof. Digital and disciplinary literacies are not simply additive, they are generative, providing possibilities for creating, comprehending, communicating, and critiquing knowledge.

Implementing Digital Literacies for Disciplinary Learning

In this section, we introduce important implications for turning the three potentials discussed in this chapter into pedagogical realities across in- and out-of-school learning environments. The implications are aimed to spark changes in practice and possibilities for future research.

Implication 1: Contextualize Digital Literacies within and across Meaningful Learning: Make Connections across Content and Grade Levels

Teaching digital literacies for disciplinary learning requires a commitment to coherent and sustained instructional design and practice. As a result, the use of digital texts and tools needs to be orchestrated in ways that build both new strategies and new content knowledge. However, limited integration or one-off uses of digital texts and tools will not lead to the types of disciplinary knowledge building and sharing that is needed to solve the intellectual and social problems of the 21st century. Rather, instructional design and formative assessments of students' disciplinary learning should progress across grade levels and deepen over time. Only then can fluid, flexible use of digital literacies be applied independently in the context of the disciplines. Ideally, integrated digital and disciplinary approaches to learning would be introduced and continue across instructional sequences that extend across disciplines, so that they become tools for deepening disciplinary inquiry.

Implication 2: Overcome Limited Instructional Time: Increase Interdisciplinary Instruction, Materials, and Lesson Sharing

Given the limited instructional time most teachers face, they understand the tension between depth and breadth of instruction. However, we argue that instruction should be driven by learning outcomes rather than discrete digital or disciplinary activities; nor should the use of a particular digital tool to represent knowledge serve as the driver of the learning task (International Literacy Association, 2018). Rather, intentionally designed and sequenced learning outcomes, grounded in disciplinary content and practices, should be used to create spaces to develop digital literacies for disciplinary learning. Planning strategically for interdisciplinary instruction and implementing collaborative curation of learning materials can provide these open spaces for learning.

The first tension that exists in classrooms is the finite amount of time available to move through the curriculum. We advocate for the design of learning environments that capitalize on 24/7 access of digital texts and tools that can extend access beyond the traditional hours of the school day. Additionally, interdisciplinary approaches to learning offer opportunities to deepen skills across disciplines, and can be used to develop disciplinary lenses toward problem solving. These lenses can be used to build connections between the disciplines with the end goal of solving intellectual and social problems using the most innovative instructional approaches and cutting-edge tools.

The second tension that exists centers around time pressures—the finite amount of time teachers have to keep pace with the seemingly infinite possibilities of digital literacies for disciplinary learning. We advocate for collaborative curation of digital resources that converge with disciplinary practices. Twitter chats, Google docs and sites, and TES Teach with Blendspace (*www.tes.com/lessons*) are great places for teachers to connect, curate, and share resources for digital literacies for disciplinary learning. The next level for this type of sharing in schools involves building professional learning communities and providing professional learning that extends capacity through an iterative design process aimed at testing and retesting teaching innovations (see Hobbs & Coiro, 2016, 2018).

Implication 3: Build a Community Aimed at Testing Out Teaching Innovations: Collaborative Professional Learning

Research on professional learning demonstrates that sustained and collaborative learning communities make a difference in student learning (Desimone, 2009; Yoon, Duncan, Lee, Scarloss, & Shapley, 2007). We advocate for professional learning that makes space for teachers, along with their colleagues, to design, iterate, and test learning tasks within and across disciplines. If teachers are to build students' disciplinary knowledge, then they themselves must develop their own means of digital and disciplinary engagement. Teachers rarely get opportunities to build, tinker, and create their own disciplinary inquiry. Making time for such activities supports their development, instructional planning, and implementation as they guide their students through similar processes.

As we discussed in the section on bidirectional expertise, we support collaborative professional learning, because it creates spaces for teachers to engage in their own learning while sharing the texts and tools used by students, and to develop digital and disciplinary skills and knowledge while being apprenticed by, and along with, their students.

Conclusion

Digital and disciplinary literacies are inextricably linked concepts that when coupled together, offer powerful opportunities to harness the learning potential of the Internet. This chapter argues that educators at all levels must make space for instructional practices that build on the synergies between digital and disciplinary learning. We describe synergistic practices centered around (1) bidirectional expertise, (2) democratizing knowledge production, and (3) expanded inquiry approaches, and suggest ways to use our planning framework (Castek & Manderino, 2017) to organize and embed digital literacies for disciplinary learning into classroom instruction. Taken together, the three synergies and framework of organizing principles provide guidance for teachers who seek to transform instruction and create powerful learning.

● IMPLICATIONS FOR PROFESSIONAL LEARNING ●

- Digital literacies feed students' motivation by tapping into their interest in accessing and sharing digital texts and tools widely. This engagement can be used to deepen and broaden disciplinary inquiry.
- The fluid nature of online and offline practices can be considered in the creation of an environment for students to engage in authentic disciplinary practices.
- The sharing of student work digitally, so that peers and teachers benefit, can serve to empower students.
- The power of digital texts and tools should be harnessed to make disciplinary knowledge and practice accessible to all learners.

QUESTIONS FOR DISCUSSION

1. How are digital literacies and disciplinary literacies connected and mutually interdependent?

2. What types of learning potentials exist when digital literacies for disciplinary learning become intentionally interwoven?

3. How do the elements in the planning framework work together to facilitate instruction around teaching digital literacies for disciplinary learning?

4. What lessons and learning principles can be drawn from research around in- and out-of-school contexts and after school learning environments?

5. What types of disciplinary practices can be taught through digital literacies?

REFERENCES

Anderson, M., & Jiang, J. (2018). Teens, social media and technology 2018. Retrieved from *www.pewinternet.org/2018/05/31/teens-social-media-technology-2018*.

Barron, B., Gomez, K., Martin, C. K., & Pinkard, N. (2014). *The digital youth network: Cultivating digital media citizenship in urban communities*. Cambridge, MA: MIT Press.

Castek, J., & Manderino, M. (2017). A planning framework for integrating digital literacies for disciplinary learning. *Journal of Adolescent and Adult Literacy, 60*(6), 697–700.

Cazden, C. B., & Beck, S. W. (2003). Classroom discourse. In A. C. Graesser, M. A. Gernsbacher, & S. R. Goldman (Eds.), *Handbook of discourse processes* (pp. 165–197). Mahwah, NJ: Erlbaum.

DeGrasse Tyson, N. (2015, December 16). *It's OK not to know*. Commencement address. University of Massachusetts, Amherst, Amherst, MA.

Desimone, L. M. (2009). Improving impact studies of teachers' professional development: Toward better conceptualizations and measures. *Educational Researcher, 38*(3), 181–199.

Dewey, J. (1938). *Experience and education: The Kappa Delta Phi lecture series*. New York: Kappa Delta Phi.

Duncan, R. G., Tate, C., & Chinn, C. A. (2014). *Students' use of evidence and epistemic criteria in model generation and model evaluation*. Boulder, CO: International Society of the Learning Sciences.

Gee, J. P. (2000). Teenagers in new times: A new literacy studies perspective. *Journal of Adolescent and Adult Literacy, 43*(5), 412–420.

Goss, M., Castek, J., & Manderino, M. (2016). Disciplinary and digital literacies: Three synergies. *Journal of Adolescent and Adult Literacy, 60*(3), 335–340.

Greenleaf, C., Schoenbach, R., Cziko, C., & Mueller, F. (2001). Apprenticing adolescent readers to academic literacy. *Harvard Educational Review, 71*(1), 79–130.

Griffith, D., with Duffett, A. M. (2018). Reading and writing instruction in America's schools. Retrieved from *https://edex.s3-us-west-2.amazonaws.com/publication/pdfs/%2807.19%29%20reading%20and%20writing%20instruction%20in%20america%27s%20schools.pdf.*

Heller, R., & Greenleaf, C. L. (2007). Literacy instruction in the content areas: Getting to the core of middle and high school improvement. Retrieved from *https://all4ed.org/reports-factsheets/literacy-instruction-in-the-content-areas-getting-to-the-core-of-middle-and-high-school-improvement.*

Hobbs, R., & Coiro, J. (2016). Everyone learns from everyone. *Journal of Adolescent and Adult Literacy, 59*(6), 623–629.

Hobbs, R., & Coiro, J. (2018). Design features of a professional development program in digital literacy. *Journal of Adolescent and Adult Literacy, 62*(4), 401–409.

International Literacy Association. (2018). Improving digital practices for literacy, learning, and justice: More than just tools (Literacy leadership brief). Retrieved from *www.literacyworldwide.org/docs/default-source/where-we-stand/ila-improving-digital-practices-literacy-learning-justice.pdf.*

Jenkins, H. (2006). *Convergence culture: Where old and new media collide.* New York: New York University Press.

Lankshear, C., & Knobel, M. (2006). *New literacies: Everyday practices and classroom learning.* London: Open University Press.

Lee, C. D., & Spratley, A. (2010). *Reading in the disciplines: The challenges of adolescent literacy.* New York: Carnegie Corporation of New York.

Leu, D. J., Forzani, E., & Kennedy, C. (2015). Income inequality and the online reading achievement gap: Teaching our way to success with online research and comprehension. *The Reading Teacher, 68*, 422–427.

Leu, D. J., Forzani, E., Rhoads, C., Maykel, C., Kennedy, C., & Timbrell, N. (2015). The new literacies of online research and comprehension: Rethinking the reading achievement gap. *Reading Research Quarterly, 50*(1), 37–59.

Manderino, M., & Castek, J. (2016). Digital literacies for disciplinary learning: A call to action. *Journal of Adolescent and Adult Literacy, 60*(1), 79–81.

Moje, E. B. (2007). Chapter 1. Developing socially just subject-matter instruction: A review of the literature on disciplinary literacy teaching. *Review of Research in Education, 31*(1), 1–44.

New London Group. (1996). A pedagogy of multiliteracies: Designing social futures. *Harvard Educational Review, 66*(1), 60–92.

NGSS Lead States. (2013). *Next Generation Science Standards: For states, by states.* Washington, DC: National Academies Press.

Phillips, N. C., & Manderino, M. (2015). *Access, equity, and empowerment: Supporting digital literacies for all learners* (Policy brief). Chicago: Center for Literacy, University of Illinois at Chicago.

Phillips, N., Woodard, R., & Killian-Lund, V. (2016). Cultivating disciplinary futures in a school-based Digital Atelier. *Journal of Adolescent and Adult Literacy, 60*(4), 461–465.

Rainey, E. C., & Storm, S. (2017). Teaching digital literacies in secondary English Language Arts. *Journal of Adolescent and Adult Literacy, 61*(2), 203–207.

Schwarz, C. V., & White, B. Y. (2005). Metamodeling knowledge: Developing students' understanding of scientific modeling. *Cognition and Instruction, 23*(2), 165–205.

Shanahan, L. E., Silvestri, K. N., & McVee, M. B. (2018). Digital engineering design team journals: Providing multimodal opportunities for English learners to explain design choices. *Journal of Adolescent and Adult Literacy, 61*(4), 445–451.

Street, B. (2003). What's "new" in New Literacy Studies?: Critical approaches to literacy in theory and practice. *Current Issues in Comparative Education, 5*(2), 77–91.

Tucker-Raymond, E., Gravel, B. E., Wagh, A., & Wilson, N. (2016). Making it social: Considering the purpose of literacy to support participation in making and engineering. *Journal of Adolescent and Adult Literacy, 60*(2), 207–211.

Wells, G. (1993). Reevaluating the IRF sequence: A proposal for the articulation of theories of activity and discourse for the analysis of teaching and learning in the classroom. *Linguistics and Education, 5*(1), 1–37.

Wickens, C. M., Manderino, M., Parker, J., & Jung, J. (2015). Habits of practice. *Journal of Adolescent and Adult Literacy, 59*, 75–82.

Wineburg, S. S. (1991). Historical problem solving: A study of the cognitive processes used in the evaluation of documentary and pictorial evidence. *Journal of Educational Psychology, 83*(1), 73–87.

Wineburg, S., & McGrew, S. (2017, October 6). Lateral reading: Reading less and learning more when evaluating digital information (Stanford History Education Group Working Paper No. 2017-A1). Retrieved from *https://ssrn.com/abstract=3048994*.

Yoon, K. S., Duncan, T., Lee, S. W. Y., Scarloss, B., & Shapley, K. L. (2007). Reviewing the evidence on how teacher professional development affects student achievement (Issues and Answers REL 2007-No. 033). Retrieved from *http://ies.ed.gov/ncee/edlabs*.

CHAPTER 8

Teaching to Write and Writing to Learn

Conceptual Development
through Discipline-Specific Writing

ESTANISLADO S. BARRERA IV
KIM SKINNER

The recent demands from the Common Core State Standards (National Governors Association Center for Best Practices, Council of Chief State School Officers [NGA & CCSSO], 2010) and Next Generation Science Standards (NGSS Lead States, 2013) have caused a substantial shift in not only what is being taught but also how we teach. This new model, in which the focus is college and career readiness for all, increasingly influences teaching and learning in PreK–12 classrooms. With these multidisciplinary shifts in content, disciplinary literacy has moved to the fore. In fact, according to the "What's Hot in Literacy 2017 Report" (International Literacy Association, 2017), disciplinary literacy is the fifth hottest topic at both national and community levels.

However, despite the much-deserved attention, current instructional practices are not fostering the necessary skills required to navigate the reading and writing of complex text types specific to the disciplines of literature, science, social studies, and mathematics (Perle, Grigg, & Donahue, 2005; Perle & Moran, 2005; T. Shanahan & Shanahan, 2008). Through these specialized texts, ideas are communicated that are both discipline-specific and essential for participation in society. Thus, the role of content-area teachers extends beyond teaching students to read and write texts as a means of acquiring content knowledge; instead, content-area teachers need to support students in reading and writing about the range of texts used to negotiate, express, create, and understand disciplinary content (Draper, Broomhead, Jensen, & Siebert, 2010).

Since students usually do not know how to read and write the specialized texts found in each discipline, content-area teachers are left with the task of providing students with this instruction. However, approaching disciplinary literacy through the teaching of various discrete skills allows for only surface-level learning. In this chapter, we provide guidance for content-area teachers to address the reciprocal nature of disciplinary reading and writing, and provide some pedagogical recommendations that demonstrate how writing can facilitate learning and comprehension within the disciplines. First, we discuss the importance of teaching the reading and writing relative to specialized texts unique to each discipline. Then, we describe the nature of writing instruction, specifically as related to the understanding and creation of nonfiction texts. Finally, we discuss the particular discipline-specific literacy needs of learners in mathematics, science, and social studies classrooms.

Teaching Discipline-Specific Literacy

Numerous researchers have addressed the complexities of literacy in the content areas. Referring to the current interest in content-area literacy, Phillips and Wong (2010) argued that "as the Common Core of Standards make clear, literacy skills cross subject-area boundaries . . . all core content teachers have a responsibility to teach literacy" (p. 40). Much attention now swirls around *disciplinary literacy* as a conceptual framework for addressing literacy demands in the content areas. As defined by T. Shanahan and Shanahan (2008), *disciplinary literacy* includes "the specialized skills and codes that someone must master to be able to read and write in the various disciplines (science, math, literature, history) and technical fields" (p. 49).

While still valuing content literacy strategies, these scholars argued that literacy within the disciplines involves attention to specialized language skills and cognitive processes. Moje (2008) further described disciplinary literacy as an investigation of what words, symbols, and phrases mean in a particular discipline. She argued that students need practice in reading, writing, thinking, and talking in ways valued within each particular discipline, as there are key differences among the disciplines (Moje, 2007).

Literacy Skills Do Not Just Evolve

In the field of literacy, there has been an understanding that students typically learn to read from kindergarten through second grade; then, from third grade on, the focus shifts to reading to learn. This concept is important, because "strong early reading skills do not automatically develop into more complex skills" (T. Shanahan & Shanahan, 2008, p. 43). Efforts put forth by teachers have often focused on developing basic and intermediate literacy ability. When one thinks of reading instruction, the basics of decoding and mastery of sight words immediately comes to mind. Then, to continue the development, strategies are introduced that facilitate vocabulary acquisition and comprehension. The skills taught in this manner may be applicable for engaging with fictional texts and most common everyday tasks, but they are not enough to access and participate actively in disciplines such as science, math, and history.

These basic and intermediate skills need to be developed further to meet the demands for disciplinary literacy. This process of literacy development is a continuum that must be supported throughout each of the grade levels and the content areas relative to the grades (see Figure 8.1).

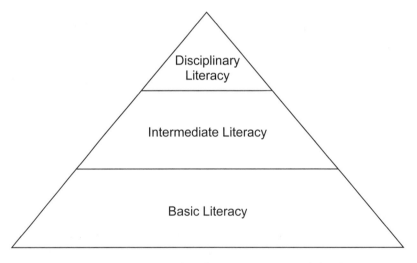

Basic Literacy: Literacy skills such as decoding and knowledge of high-frequency words that underlie virtually all reading tasks.

Intermediate Literacy: Literacy skills common to many tasks, including generic comprehension strategies, common word meanings, and basic fluency.

Disciplinary Literacy: Literacy skills specialized to history, science, mathematics, literature, or other subject matter.

FIGURE 8.1. The increasing specialization of literacy development.

Often, we see what C. Shanahan, Shanahan, and Misischia (2011) have referred to as "literacy avoidance" (p. 395). Content-area teachers, unsure of how to support their students with respect to developing specific literacy skills, convert discipline-specific texts into presentations or lectures and remove the opportunity to engage with an authentic text-type representative of the discipline.

Teachers who are instructors of the disciplines must find ways to engage students with the practices, materials, equipment, and texts that are specific to their content areas and to the vocations and professions of their fields. Without these authentic interactions, students will not be able to develop the specific literacy practices associated with the demands of these fields. For example, a teacher in the discipline of science should be providing students with opportunities to draw information from multiple sources, write laboratory reports, and create informational pieces based on science experiments. Practitioners in mathematics education realize the production and consumption of written texts in mathematics involves competence in the unique and specific language of mathematics, such as the comprehension and construction of word problems, so that learners can recognize the ways in which mathematical understanding can be applied.

Disciplinary Questions and Problems

Students engaged in disciplinary learning need a central and authentic question or problem to investigate; they need a reason to read and write in a particular way (Moje, 2015). Engaging in the work of a mathematician, a historian, a literary critic, or a scientist requires investigating a genuine problem with a real-world purpose; it is the same with students. For example, without a guiding question or problem, the learners are unlikely to be engaged, and the practices will likely be meaningless as a result. Moje (2015, p. 262) identified six shared practices that constitute a cycle of inquiry (see Figure 8.2) across any disciplinary community:

1. Problem framing
2. Working with data
3. Using varied media to consult and produce multiple texts
4. Analyzing, summarizing, and synthesizing findings
5. Examining and evaluating claims
6. Communicating claims

By implementing these practices, writing instruction can begin to intersect with discipline-specific authentic purposes. These recommended practices also allow teachers to gradually develop writing skills and differentiate their instruction.

Multiple Data and Multiple Texts

Members of all disciplinary communities work with some form of data, though what counts as data often varies considerably across disciplines

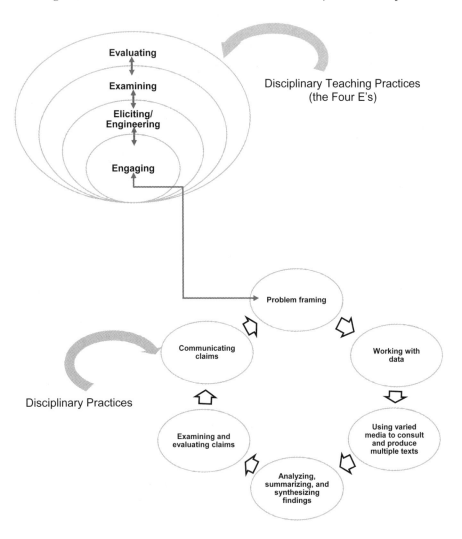

FIGURE 8.2. The four E's heuristic with disciplinary practices. From Moje (2015, p. 262). Copyright © Harvard Education Publishing Group.

(Nokes, 2013; Rainey, Maher, Coupland, Franchi, & Moje, 2017; Spires, Kerkhoff, & Graham, 2016). What is important, however, is that learners find ways to interact with data in meaningful ways, for example, as a literary critic finding evidence within a text or a scientist combining substances to produce a new substance (Moje, 2015). Moje argued that besides opportunities to work with the materials, tools, and texts for collecting data, learners need to read and produce multimodal forms of texts, "using social media, email, charts, maps, photographs, video recordings, presentations, logs and journals, and traditional publications" (p. 264). When students understand and produce multimodal texts in each subject area, they make visible what counts as authentic disciplinary literacy practices in content learning.

Disciplinary Cycle

Drawing from her experience as a practitioner and researcher, Moje (2015) created a heuristic that frames the crucial pedagogical practices for disciplinary literacy instruction. The heuristic consists of four E's: *engage, elicit/engineer, examine,* and *evaluate.* The first E—*engage*—reminds teachers "to ask how much daily classroom practices are like those of the disciplines." The second E—*elicit/engineer*—"helps the teacher remember that adolescents are not experts and that their engagement in literacy practices needs to be engineered" (p. 260). Moje explained that the third E—*examining*—prompts students to pay close attention to words and words-in-use, while the fourth E—*evaluating*—asks students to determine when, why, and in what ways disciplinary language is–is not useful.

Typically, the teaching of writing and the act of writing are separated from the content areas, resulting in a dissected and lock-step approach governed by formulas, rules, and conventions (Barrera, 2017). Current approaches to writing instruction often lack authentic purpose and are void of specific literacy practices relevant to domains found in the real world. For writing to be truly discipline-specific, it must be nested within a discipline, so that its intention is "making associations across knowledge bases and application to novel situations" (Frey, Fisher, & Hattie, 2016, p. 570). Students cannot evolve in disciplinary literacy practices on their own; they need support as they develop through the literacy progression (T. Shanahan & Shanahan, 2008), and they must develop an understanding and recognition of the disciplines and their specific cultures (Moje, 2015; O'Brien, Stewart, & Moje, 1995).

How We Can Learn by Writing

Research on writing instruction indicates that teachers need to provide time, opportunities, and guidance (Barrera, 2017; Cruz, 2008; Horowitz & Samuels, 1987; National Writing Project, 2007) to students, though studies also indicate teachers rarely provide either writing instruction or opportunities to write during class (Graham & Perin, 2007; Hillocks, 2008; Murphy & Yancey, 2008). The act of writing for different audiences and purposes is complex, and research advocates the use of modeling and multiple exposures to a wide range of writing forms (Graham & Perin, 2007; T. Shanahan & Shanahan, 2008).

With the recent demands and widespread adoption of the Common Core State Standards across the United States, writing instruction is now commonly addressed in curriculum development across the content areas. The Standards include the following guidelines for writing:

> For students, writing is a key means of asserting and defending claims, showing what they know about a subject, and conveying what they have experienced, imagined, thought, and felt. To be college- and career ready writers, students must take task, purpose, and audience into careful consideration, choosing words, information, structures, and formats deliberately. They need to know how to combine elements of different kinds of writing—for example, to use narrative strategies within argument and explanation within narrative—to produce complex and nuanced writing. They need to be able to use technology strategically when creating, refining, and collaborating on writing. They have to become adept at gathering information, evaluating sources, and citing material accurately, reporting findings from their research and analysis of sources in a clear and cogent manner. They must have the flexibility, concentration, and fluency to produce high-quality first draft text under a tight deadline as well as the capacity to revisit and make improvements to a piece of writing over multiple drafts when circumstances encourage or require it. (NGA & CCSSO, 2010, p. 41)

As most states are now implementing these, or similar state standards, in their public schools, the demand for teaching and learning about writing across content classrooms is likely to continue to increase (Graham & Perin, 2007; McCarthey, 2008).

In addition to increased writing instructional time and opportunities for students, teachers must understand how to teach the numerous and unique genres of writing relative to the disciplines they are teaching (Draper & Siebert, 2010). This means that an elementary teacher with a self-contained classroom is responsible for instructing his or her students about written texts across a number of disciplines, such as mathematics, history, and science. And those teachers who are departmentalized in elementary schools or teach a specific content area at the secondary level are responsible for teaching the text types or genres of their respective disciplines.

Addressing the particular challenges of nonfiction writing construction, Dorfman and Cappelli (2009) argued, "It makes sense if we want our students to write good nonfiction, we need to immerse them in the work of good nonfiction authors" (p. 3). "Teachers of young writers have clamored for research-based strategies for teaching the numerous subgenres of nonfiction writing, as well as ways to motivate and engage students throughout the writing process" (Skinner, Barrera, Brauchle, & Valadez, 2012, p. 12). Explicit instruction on the unique structures and features of nonfiction is important to the construction of nonfiction texts. Also important is the use of mentor texts as models of the author's craft—models that illuminate the reading–writing connection. Instructional strategies designed to increase motivation empower students to develop agency and independence.

The Uniqueness of Nonfiction Reading and Writing

For some time now, Stead (2002) has challenged the overemphasis on narrative writing found in many primary grade classrooms and has instead recommended that both teachers and students experience the many different writing genres to understand their purposes and the ways they work. This is significant because, as Dreher and Kletzien (2015) pointed out, as adults, we primarily read and write informational texts. Therefore, the genres of nonfiction reading and writing must be taught with authentic purpose given their broad encompassing natures. Young learners need to have access to informational texts and opportunities to experience them beginning in preschool (Purcell-Gates, Duke, & Martineau, 2007). Only recently in our primary schools are we seeing an intentional instructional shift from fiction reading and writing to nonfiction reading and writing. However, it requires more than just exposing our students to nonfiction texts and nonfiction writing prompts. This is particularly significant because Casbergue and Plauché (2003) found that "when children read and write expository texts without the knowledge they need, their reading comprehension and writing development is hampered" (p. 286). The time to move from exposure to nonfiction reading and writing in the classroom toward opportunities for the application of nonfiction reading comprehension through nonfiction writing has never been more crucial and necessary (Skinner et al., 2012).

So, how do we impart the knowledge to which Casbergue and Plauché referred? According to Stead and Hoyt (2011), we need to begin by teaching our students "to gain control over the unique structures, language, and visual features that comprise the heart of nonfiction texts" (p. 2). Turning our attention to the "uniqueness" of these text types fosters the understanding of what it means to be an author of nonfiction texts.

Nonfiction Text Types

According to the Common Core State Standards (NGA & CCSSO, 2010), "students must read widely and deeply from among a broad range of high-quality, increasingly challenging literary and informational texts" (p. 10). It is also important that students be taught how to transfer the knowledge they have gained and produce writing that demonstrates understanding, synthesis, application, and evaluation. One way to accomplish this is by teaching students that each piece of nonfiction writing has a purpose and was written with a specific intent. Stead and Hoyt (2011) categorized the primary purposes of nonfiction writing as the following: to inform, to instruct, to narrate, to persuade, and to respond. Being able to determine the purpose then allows the writer to identify an appropriate genre and use the specific characteristics and features associated with the text type.

Features of Nonfiction Texts

In addition to teaching purpose and text types, the features specific to a particular text must also be taught. Duke, Caughlan, Juzwik, and Martin (2011) argued that "teaching genre features explicitly can help develop students' ability to think about texts as text—what some call *authors' craft* or *metatextuality*" (p. 17, emphasis in original). They further posited that "writing strategies are often taught as though they apply equally to all texts or all strategies work equally well for most texts, but this is not the case" (p. 18). According to these researchers, it is crucial that the teaching of procedural texts needs to be distinct from teaching how to write a personal narrative. In fact, Duke et al. (2011) emphasized that it is no longer just about teaching "composition"; what is important is the composition "*of what for what*" (p. 6, emphasis in original).

To attend to the "of what for what," the author must consider the purpose, type of text, and the nature of the information in order to determine the organizational structure for a text. Once students have determined the purpose of their writing, they then must decide how to organize their writing. For students to make that determination, they should consider the type of information they are using for their text, how the information might be chunked or divided up, and what kind of organization would be best for the readers of their writing. This can be accomplished by teaching about the common organizational structures of nonfiction: enumerative, chronological, sequential, compare–contrast, question–answer, cause–effect, and narrative (Kristo & Bamford, 2004).

Mentor Texts

Current research on writing instruction recommends that teachers gain an understanding of how to teach the specific genres of writing. Students can become accomplished content-area writers through both consistent and explicit instruction and by having teachers who "marinate" them in the various types and constructions of nonfiction texts (Kristo & Bamford, 2004, p. 266). One way to accomplish this is by providing exemplars of the various writing genres with mentor texts. In fact, Stead and Hoyt (2011) recommend that preparing students to navigate and create nonfiction texts with confidence and intent will make them more successful readers and writers.

When it comes to the teaching of writing, many teachers become anxious; they begin to question themselves, the process, and even the abilities of their students. In fact, previous research by Skinner et al. (2012) raised some very important questions related to writing:

1. How can teachers model the key components of writing instruction through mini-lessons, in light of the expectations for nonfiction writing for students at each grade level?
2. How do the authors of nonfiction texts begin writing about a topic?
3. How do authors decide what to write about and how to organize their writing? (p. 13)

To address these anxieties, Dorfman and Cappelli (2009) posited that the first step for any nonfiction writer is to form an essential question. Finding texts that model this first step helps young writers grasp how writing topics are chosen. Dorfman and Cappelli provide examples of mentor texts in which the title reveals the origin of the ideas for each book: Kaner's (1999) *Animal Defenses: How Animals Protect Themselves* and Gehman's (2007) *Hummingbirds: Tiny but Mighty.*

In addition to serving as exemplars of specific nonfiction writing genres, mentor texts also serve to expose students and readers to the numerous text features associated with and utilized by nonfiction. According to Stead and Hoyt (2011), text features have two specific purposes when used to write nonfiction text—to visually communicate information and to draw attention to important concepts and ideas. Visual communication of information is accomplished through photographs, diagrams, illustrations, graphs, charts, tables, storyboards, flowcharts, and arrows. The other purpose of nonfiction text features, to draw attention to important concepts and ideas, is accomplished through titles, bold words, headings, subheadings, tables of contents, captions, indexes, and glossaries.

The best way to introduce young writers to these text features is by explicitly teaching about them using exemplars, such as mentor texts. As you go through a text, draw your students' attention to specific text features, discuss the author's choice to include it, and evaluate whether it achieves its purpose. You can also use text features to demonstrate how to navigate effectively through a text to find a particular chapter, section, or even information more efficiently. Then, as they construct their own nonfiction texts, students learn to consider which visual features they could add to increase their readers' understanding of their own works.

With respect to mentor texts, it is important to point out that these can also be teacher-created. Portalupi and Fletcher (2001) stated that teacher modeling and creation of nonfiction writing can help students "uncover the experiential knowledge they already possess" (p. 9). Following Stead and Hoyt's (2011) suggestion, teachers can create a mentor text on the spot while conducting a focused mini-lesson using particular forms of nonfiction writing. The mini-lesson should incorporate a think-aloud, and the teacher should facilitate the writing of the text. This provides the opportunity for students to both see and hear the writing process. By experiencing the creation of the on-the-spot mentor text the students take ownership of the writing process. The mentor text also "becomes a part of the fabric of the classroom, allowing reflection and revisiting by the teacher and students alike" (Skinner et al., 2012, p. 14). Additionally, teachers can create models of visual texts (e.g., maps, illustrations, and diagrams) for students during their mini-lessons, once again accompanying the writing by thinking aloud about both the construction of and purpose for the visual text.

Allowing students to get to know authors is another way to mentor burgeoning authors. Sharing the personal lives and experiences of authors who have struggled with their own writing helps students to understand that writing is challenging. For example, well-known authors such as Jon Scieszka confess that writing is hard work—a task he compares to "ditch-digging"—allows students to feel that they are not alone in experiencing the struggle of getting words on paper (Scieszka, Smith, & Leach, 2001, p. 37). Another way to encourage young authors who may feel overwhelmed is by putting up inspirational quotes and words of perseverance on a classroom bulletin board.

Motivation

When asked how they motivate students to write, Fletcher and Portalupi (2001) responded, "There's no magic answer, and it's a fact that certain kids will stubbornly resist the invitation to write. But it starts by giving them regular time, real choice, and your genuine interest in what they put down on paper" (p. 24). In her book for teachers, *A Quick Guide to Reaching Struggling Writers*, Cruz (2008, p. xii) explored strategies teachers can use to address the causes behind the six most common statements made by students who lack motivation to write. Her strategies for addressing motivation issues with young writers are categorized according to these frequently recurring statements:

> "I'm not a good writer."
> "My hand hurts."
> "I don't know how to spell."
> "I don't have anything to write about."
> "I never get to write anything I want to write."
> "I'm done."

Of particular relevance to the writing of nonfiction are issues related to generating ideas and choice. As all teachers of writers know, many students find generating and developing a topic to write about very challenging. To have students believe they truly have something to write about, teachers need to teach numerous strategies for originating topics and ideas (Cruz, 2008). One strategy for generating writing topics is to have students develop personal lists of things with which they are familiar, such as places, people, and objects, to give them a starting point for writing that draws on their own experiences. Another strategy ties back to the previous section on mentor texts: Students can identify ideas for their own writing by reading the writing of others. What is important is that students gain independence by knowing ways they can get "unstuck" when writing.

Classrooms that support quality nonfiction writing instruction give students ample opportunity to "bring their passion, knowledge, quirky humor, and authentic voice to this kind of writing" (Portalupi & Fletcher, 2001, p. 2). Many writers struggle because they feel they are not given choice or allowed a voice when they write. Hill and Ekey (2010) stated, "Our decisions about *what* to teach will be based on our curriculum and standards, the focus for our unit of study, and what we know about each individual writer" (p. 12, emphasis in original). While knowledge of the different forms of writing is essential, so is student agency. Decisions concerning what to write and what form that writing will take should not always rest solely with the teacher.

Supporting Discipline-Specific Writing

Supporting discipline-specific writing must occur within and across grade levels and content areas. As students matriculate through their learning careers, both the complexity and the types of texts increase. This upturn in sophistication in reading is expected to be reflected in the written pieces produced by the students, which is best accomplished by continuous literacy development and an understanding of disciplines as cultures with specific disciplinary knowledge. Harris, Graham, Mason, and Friedlander (2008, p. ix) argued, "There are many reasons why students have problems with writing. One of the most obvious is simply that they've never been taught how to write." Research conducted on teacher perceptions about ability and preparedness to teach writing (Coker & Lewis, 2008; Kiuhara, Graham & Hawken, 2009) revealed that many teachers have low perceptions of themselves as writing instructors.

Though often assumed to be the literacy experts on elementary and secondary campuses, English language arts (ELA) teachers have their own particular disciplinary demands. ELA teachers are first and foremost content teachers. In a study of secondary content teachers' knowledge of learners' literacy needs, Meyer (2013) indicated that the focus in ELA teachers' classrooms is on literacy skills related to English as a discipline. Furthermore, many of the literacy skills needed by students today (e.g., visual literacy, digital literacy, media literacy) are outside the realm of an ELA classroom. In fact, ELA teachers' knowledge of students' literacy needs is similar to that of secondary science and social studies teachers (Meyer, 2013). Ultimately, subject-area teachers are responsible for integrating literacy instruction into content-area instruction. Draper and Siebert (2010) explained:

> Content-area teachers are knowledgeable about the texts and literacies central to the discipline. Indeed, we could not expect language arts teachers to understand the differences between how to frame and support historical and scientific arguments, much less how to write a mathematical proof or critique of a painting. Rather, content-area teachers must support the development of the discipline-specific literacies of the adolescents in their classrooms. (p. 35)

Disciplinary teachers are experts on the content knowledge and demands particular to their field. What counts as the literacy practices for a disciplinary community are the "shared language and symbolic tools that members of academic disciplines (e.g., biology, philosophy, musical theater, architecture and design, psychology) use to construct knowledge alongside others" (Rainey et al., 2017, p. 371). Production of knowledge within any discipline requires the disciplinarian to engage in a cycle of inquiry, which includes "articulating questions or problems for pursuit, investigating those questions using discipline-specific methods, communicating results of investigations to specific audiences, and evaluating one's own claims and those of others" (Moje, 2015, p. 254).

Writing and Conceptual Knowledge in Social Studies

What counts as writing like a historian? What counts as history literacy teaching?

Research conducted on disciplinary literacy teaching by Rainey and colleagues (2017) used the previously discussed four E's heuristic created by Moje (2015) to represent four overlapping categories of instructional practice. This heuristic is helpful for delineating what disciplinary literacy teaching must include, and why. In addition to illustrating Moje's heuristic, Rainey et al. (2017) provided the following specific definitions of the four E categories:

1. *Engaging* students in work that aligns with the problem- and text-based work of disciplinarians.
2. *Eliciting and engineering* students' learning opportunities, so that they are able to successfully accomplish classroom tasks and learn disciplinary practice from them.
3. *Examining* words, language, and representations.
4. *Evaluating* words and ways with words within and across domains. (p. 372)

In their study, Rainey et al. (2017) analyzed a history literacy lesson taught by a veteran teacher. This teacher was considered an "expert educator" largely due to his commitment to inquiry-based teaching, his use of multiple forms of text, his leadership at his school, and the consistent success of his students on measures of academic achievement.

Data indicated that by using the four E's as a framework for analysis, the expert educator of history made use of a guiding question, primary source documents, analysis of reading, creation of a written text to represent one's viewpoint (a graphic organizer followed by a text-based claim), and student debate to represent contrasting points of view. His students created texts that made visible the way he used "writing to learn" and "writing to demonstrate knowledge" as tools for increasing conceptual knowledge in history. In the report "Writing across the Curriculum: Social Studies" (n.d.), writing to learn activities are described in the following way:

- Writing-to-Learn activities encourage the kind of reflection on learning that improves students' metacognitive skills. The key to effectively using writing activities in every subject lies in matching the right activity to the learning situation. As you select writing strategies, ask yourself, "How well suited is this task for the objective the students are learning?" "Does this strategy fit my students' abilities and needs?" "Will this strategy complement the way my students will be assessed on the content later?"
- Writing-to-Learn fosters critical thinking. It is writing that uses impromptu, short/informal writing tasks designed by the teacher and included throughout the lesson to help students think through key concepts. Attention is focused on ideas rather than correctness of style, grammar or spelling. This approach frequently uses

journals, logs, micro themes, responses to written or oral questions, summaries, free writing, and notes, that align to learning ideas and concepts. (pp. 3–4)

While impromptu writing tasks foster critical thinking, students can use writing in content-area classrooms to demonstrate knowledge in numerous ways. In "Writing Across the Curriculum: Social Studies" (n.d.), writing to demonstrate knowledge is described as

- Writing in which students show what they have learned by synthesizing information and explaining their understanding of concepts. Students write for an audience with a specific purpose.
- Examples include essays that deal with specific questions, letters, projects, and formal papers prepared over weeks. Students adhere to format guidelines when writing reports, article reviews, and research papers. These should be checked before being submitted by the student for correctness of spelling, grammar, and transition word usage. (p. 4)

Furthermore, examples of forms of writing in social studies include essay writing, persuasive civic writing, report writing, research reports, and narrative writing to demonstrate knowledge.

Writing and Conceptual Knowledge in Mathematics

In "Writing across the Curriculum: Mathematics" (n.d.), some of the following strategies are provided to increase students' conceptual knowledge of mathematics:

- In order for writing in mathematics to impact student learning, it must be more than just copying the notes given in class. Information must be personalized. Students must be expected to include reflections and questions when they write. By making these personal connections, students begin to develop a conceptual understanding of the mathematics they are exploring in their studies.
- Many mathematics educators feel that students should already know how to write effectively when they come to their classrooms. Students have learned to write from their English language arts teachers, but they usually do not know how to apply these skills to mathematics. Mathematics teachers will find that they have to explicitly teach and provide scaffolding for each strategy before

their students will be able to implement writing in mathematics.
(p. 4)

Why write as part of mathematics instruction? Children's writing gives us glimpses of their thinking. For example, reviewing their writing of procedures for carrying out an operation allows us to analyze their thoughts to see how fully they comprehend what has been taught; if a student only partially understands the material, then analyzing the writing can help to determine where the misconception(s) exist or whether they are part of the learning process. Writing demands that you find out what you know and don't know. According to the National Council of Teachers of Mathematics (NCTM) Standards (2000), "Opportunities to explain, conjecture, and defend one's ideas orally and in writing stimulates deeper understandings of concepts and principles" (p. 78).

One prewriting strategy is to have the students discuss their thinking in small groups before they write. This gives them a chance to verbalize their ideas and prepares them for putting their ideas down on paper. Furthermore, hearing other students' points of view can provide options that individuals might not have thought of independently. For example, writing topics for math class include the following: How do my math experiences mirror the experiences of others? What have I learned about math in class? How did I solve that problem?

Additionally, students can write to introduce a process or concept (e.g., fractions, decimals, multiplication, division, problem solving, prime/composite numbers). Concepts, processes, and vocabulary can be developed by having the students initially write what they know, then add on as their knowledge increases. Another strategy involves keeping math journals, not just for notes or solving problems, but for reflecting on learning; these might include responding to prompts such as the following: Write about what you did. Write about what you learned. Write about what you're not sure of or what you are wondering about. What is multiplication? What is division? Write all you know about angles.

When children attempt to read and create written solutions to mathematical word problems, they need opportunities to not only present their answers but also explain their reasoning. Students need to write in ways that may not only convince the reader that their solutions are correct but also reveal how they arrived at their solutions. As such, it is important to remind students to include as much detail as possible. Finally, writing can be utilized in math teaching and learning to assess understanding; for example, you can use it to determine the following:

What have your students learned? Was their reasoning adequate? Are students using the mathematics presented during class lessons? Are there noticeable gaps in understanding? Thus, writing can be used for many pedagogical purposes in the mathematics classroom.

Writing and Conceptual Knowledge in Science

The "Writing across the Curriculum: Science" (n.d.) report suggests that learning science is complex, involving much more than the memorization of sets of facts and examples. While writing instruction and practice are crucial components for teaching and learning in all disciplines, they are particularly critical for producing innovative scientists. This report suggests:

> Increasing student science literacy means that explanations harbored prior to instruction must be explored and often challenged. In order to develop new or improved conceptual frameworks, students must be given the opportunity to process their ideas—before, during and after new learning takes place. Scientists need to be able to write clearly and effectively. Not only do they have to keep clean and complete records of their ideas and work, but they also have to communicate their findings to world-wide audiences. Teaching students to write well must also be a part of any comprehensive science program. Strategies that require students to demonstrate their knowledge of science also provide opportunities to practice writing for authentic audiences.
>
> In order for writing in science to impact student learning, it must be more than just recording notes or data collected. Students must be expected to include reflections, questions, predictions, claims linked to evidence and conclusions when they write. By making these personal connections, students begin to challenge prior misconceptions they may still harbor and start to develop a conceptual understanding of the scientific phenomena they are exploring in their studies. (p. 5)

Examples of science writing that develop content knowledge in students include journals, logs, summaries, notes, essays, letters, projects, reports, article reviews, and research papers.

Why write as part of science instruction? "Scientists assume that not all arguments or claims will be equally valid" (Rainey et al., 2017, p. 377) and therefore must be able to critique, discuss, and disseminate their understandings to others within their discourse community and beyond.

As is the case in the other disciplines, writing serves very specific purposes in science and requires knowledge of specific text types.

Informally, writing can be used in science to assess students' schemas with respect to concepts and issues. This can be accomplished by having the students engage in quick-writes or daily entries in a journal. Analysis of students' written responses can assist with determining prior knowledge, misconceptions, range of discipline-specific vocabulary, lesson plan design, and flexible grouping for instruction. Informal writing activities can also serve to assess students' understanding of assigned readings or as a method for evaluating how much content was understood at the end of a lesson or part of a lesson (e.g., exit ticket). Another prevalent method of writing in science is using interactive notebooks for the purpose of taking notes about the content and also recording observations and data.

Formally, writing as part of science instruction is very natural, as it serves many crucial purposes—capturing observations through note taking; documenting experimental procedures; recording and analyzing data and reporting findings; and adding to the field of knowledge through dissemination. Capturing information from an observation, for example, is a written practice that is specific to the discipline of science and can require specific components such as the documenting of start, elapsed, and end times. Illustrating layouts, positions, perspectives, and mapping the environment is also something very relevant to observing. This written practice may also include using special codes or abbreviations similar to shorthand.

Documenting the process of conducting an experiment is a crucial written practice in the field of science and is a text type that deserves much attention, because it requires knowledge of the procedural or "how-to" genre. This particular written assignment lends itself well to modeling writing or engaging in shared writing. Writing procedures for how an experiment was conducted is also a perfect activity for coauthoring—in pairs or as a small group.

Another written practice associated with science is that of recording and analyzing data and reporting the findings. The act of recording data provides opportunities for students to engage in specific writing tasks that can involve unique forms, templates, and/or formats. Among examples of recording data that include opportunities to experience logging measurements in different formats are using a 24-hour clock (e.g., 13:05 instead of 1:05 P.M.) and codes, abbreviations, or symbols (e.g., placing a "~" before a number to indicate approximately). Similar to documenting the procedures for an experiment, the process of analysis must also be explained and requires concise writing that conveys logical thinking. Composing the findings is another written practice in science that places specific demands on students due to the use of data tables and figures such as bar and line graphs. Students must not only know how to use these text features, they must also know how to skillfully navigate the reader's attention to these more visual elements.

Most importantly, both teaching of writing and developing the skill of writing in the discipline of science allow for the dissemination of new knowledge to the field. Teaching students how to write arguments and claims not only allows them to become members of an important discourse community, but it also prepares them to be critical consumers of the scientific arguments and claims they encounter. Expecting students to share their scientific work gives rise to developing awareness of an audience, because scientific information is reported to different consumers for different purposes and in varying formats.

Conclusion

Content-area teachers have expertise in disciplinary discourses, texts, and instruction (Gee, 1996). They are familiar with the demands of the specialized texts of their discipline and the ways these texts should be read and written. However, content teachers need continued knowledge and support to teach reading and writing in their discipline if their students are to master the literacy demands of the 21st century. Research on content-area teachers' resistance to literacy integration indicates that a fundamental reason for this resistance includes their feelings of inadequacy as literacy instructors (Draper, 2008; T. Shanahan & Shanahan, 2008). Similarly, elementary teachers are now expected to provide effective, albeit fundamental, writing instruction across content areas. This is not an easy task.

Simply put, no one should be blamed for the growing pains. This shift in disciplinary literacy is new; therefore, teachers need time to learn and develop their understanding of writing. In fact, most teachers are actually doing discipline-specific writing. They are just not aware they are doing it, or they are not intentionally teaching about those specific written practices and why they are important. Luckily, the easiest way to resolve this situation is to allow students to actually exist within each discipline—allow them to exist as historians, mathematicians, and scientists—as part of their disciplinary learning.

• IMPLICATIONS FOR PROFESSIONAL LEARNING •

- Content-area teachers need to develop the discipline-specific literacy practices relevant to the particular professions and discourse communities.

- Literacy skills do not evolve. Instead, they must be supported in distinct ways and developed over time based on discipline-specific practices and levels of rigor.

- Students need opportunities to engage with authentic discipline-specific text types and genres in order to develop the ability to navigate content and produce new texts that demonstrate knowledge and understanding of key concepts.

- Engagement in disciplinary learning must use real-world issues or authentic questions and go through the six practices associated with the cycle of inquiry.

- Students need mentor texts that can be used as a reference for learning about and producing discipline-specific texts and text features.

QUESTIONS FOR DISCUSSION

1. With significant attention now being given to disciplinary literacy, what are the successes and challenges being encountered in your classroom, department, or professional learning community? What specifically allowed for the successes you experienced? What supports, resources, or solutions are needed to address the challenges you identified?

2. Moje (2015) suggests that students need a central and authentic question or problem to investigate in order to become engaged in disciplinary learning. How does this approach to instruction allow for opportunities to have students write during each of the six practices associated with the cycle of inquiry?

3. Mentor texts play a significant role in developing students' ability to not only navigate texts as a reader, but also to create or write texts as a writer. What specific text types or genres are relevant to your particular discipline? Identify exemplars for each relevant text type or genre and determine the specific text features that need to be taught.

REFERENCES

Barrera, E. S., IV. (2017). Developing fluency in writing: How features of speech can support acts of writing. *Writing and Pedagogy, 9*(1), 103–143.

Casbergue, R. M., & Plauché, M. B. (2003). Immersing children in nonfiction: Fostering emergent research and writing. In D. Barone & L. M. Marrow (Eds.), *Literacy and young children: Research-based practices* (pp. 243–288). New York: Guilford Press.

Coker, D., & Lewis, W. E. (2008). Beyond writing next: A discussion of writing research and instructional uncertainty. *Harvard Educational Review, 78,* 231–251.

Cruz, M. C. (2008). *A quick guide to reaching struggling writers K–5.* Portsmouth, NH: Heinemann.

Dorfman, L. R., & Cappelli, R. (2009). *Nonfiction mentor texts: Teaching informational writing through children's literature, K–8.* Portland, ME: Stenhouse.

Draper, R. J. (2008). Redefining content-area literacy teacher education: Finding my voice through collaboration. *Harvard Educational Review, 78,* 60–83.

Draper, R. J., Broomhead, P., Jensen, A. P., & Siebert, D. (2010). Aims and criteria for collaboration in content-area classrooms. In R. J. Draper, P. Broomhead, A. P. Jensen, J. D. Nokes, & D. Siebert (Eds.), *(Re)Imagining content-area literacy instruction* (pp. 1–19). New York: Teachers College Press.

Draper, R. J., & Siebert, D. (2010). Rethinking texts, literacies, and literacy across the curriculum. In R. J. Draper, P. Broomhead, A. P. Jensen, J. D. Nokes, & D. Siebert (Eds.), *(Re)Imagining content-area literacy instruction* (pp. 20–39). New York: Teachers College Press.

Dreher, M. J., & Kletzien, S. B. (2015). *Teaching informational text in K–3 classrooms: Best practices to help children read, write, and learn from nonfiction.* New York: Guilford Press.

Duke, N. K., Caughlan, S., Juzwik, M., & Martin, N. (2011). *Reading and writing genre with purpose in K–8 classrooms.* Portsmouth, NH: Heinemann.

Fletcher, R., & Portalupi, J. (2001). *Writing workshop: The essential guide.* Portland, ME: Stenhouse.

Frey, N., Fisher, D., & Hattie, J. (2016). *Visible literacy for learning, grades K–12: Implementing the practices that work best to accelerate student learning.* Thousand Oaks, CA: Corwin.

Gee, J. P. (1996). *Social linguistics and literacies: Ideology in discourses* (2nd ed.). London: RoutledgeFalmer.

Gehman, J. (2007). *Hummingbirds: Tiny but mighty.* Eaglewood, CO: Reading Matters.

Graham, S., & Perin, D. (2007). *Writing next: Effective strategies to improve writing of adolescents in middle and high schools—A report to Carnegie Corporation of New York.* Washington, DC: Alliance for Excellent Education.

Harris, K. R., Graham, S., Mason, L. H., & Friedlander, B. (2008). *Powerful reading strategies for all students.* Baltimore: Brookes.

Hill, B. C., & Ekey, C. (2010). *The next-step guide to enhancing writing instruction.* Portsmouth, NH: Heinemann.

Hillocks, G., Jr. (2008). Writing in secondary schools. In C. Bazerman (Ed.), *Handbook of research on writing: History, society, school, individual, text* (pp. 311–330). Mahwah, NJ: Erlbaum.

Hillocks, G., Jr. (2010). Teaching argument for critical thinking and writing: An introduction. *The English Teacher, 99*(6), 24–32.

Horowitz, R., & Samuels, S. J. (Eds.). (1987). *Comprehending oral and written language.* San Diego, CA: Academic Press.

International Literacy Association. (2017). What's hot in literacy 2017 report. Retrieved from *www.literacyworldwide.org/docs/default-source/resource-documents/whats-hot-2017-report.pdf.*

Kaner, E. (1999). *Animal defenses: How animals protect themselves.* Tonawanda, NY: Kids Can Press.

Kiuhara, S. A., Graham, S., & Hawken, L. S. (2009). Teaching writing to high school students: A national survey. *Journal of Educational Psychology, 101,* 136–160.

Kristo, J. V., & Bamford, R. A. (2004). *Nonfiction in focus.* New York: Scholastic.

Langer, J. A., & Applebee, A. N. (2007). *How writing shapes thinking: A study of teaching and learning.* Fort Collins, CO: WAC Clearinghouse.

McCarthey, S. J. (2008). The impact of No Child Left Behind on teachers' writing instruction. *Written Communication, 25,* 462–505.

Meyer, C. K. (2013). The literacy needs of adolescents: What do content-area teachers know? *Action in Teacher Education, 35,* 56–71.

Moje, E. B. (2007). Developing socially just subject-matter instruction: A review of the literature on disciplinary literacy. In L. Parker (Ed.), *Review of research in education* (Vol. 31, pp. 1–44). Washington, DC: American Educational Research Association.

Moje, E. B. (2008). Foregrounding the disciplines in secondary literacy teaching and learning: A call for change. *Journal of Adolescent and Adult Literacy, 52*(2), 96–107.

Moje, E. B. (2015). Doing and teaching disciplinary literacy with adolescent learners. *Harvard Educational Review, 85*(2), 254–278.

Murphy, S., & Yancey, B. (2008). Construct and consequence: Validity in writing assessment. In C. Bazerman (Ed.), *Handbook of research on writing: History, society, school, individual, text* (pp. 365–385). New York: Routledge.

National Council of Teachers of Mathematics. (2000). *Principles and standards for school mathematics.* Reston, VA: Author.

National Governors Association Center for Best Practices, Council of Chief State School Officers. (2010). *Common Core State Standards for English language arts and literacy in history/social studies, science, and technical subjects.* Washington, DC: Authors.

National Writing Project. (2007). The 2007 survey on teaching writing: American public opinion on the importance of writing in the schools. Retrieved from *www.nwp. org/cs/public/print/resource/2389.*

NGSS Lead States. (2013). *Next generation science standards: For states, by states.* Washington, DC: National Academic Press.

Nokes, J. D. (2010). (Re)imagining literacies for history classrooms. In R. J. Draper, P. Broomhead, A. P. Jensen, J. D. Nokes, & D. Siebert (Eds.), *(Re)imagining content-area literacy instruction* (pp. 54–68). New York: Teachers College Press.

Nokes, J. (2013). *Building students' historical literacies: Learning to read and reason with historical texts and evidence.* New York: Routledge.

O'Brien, D. G., Stewart, R. A., & Moje, E. B. (1995). Why content literacy is difficult to infuse into the secondary school: Complexities of curriculum, pedagogy, and school culture. *Reading Research Quarterly, 30,* 442–463.

Pearson, P. D., Moje, E., & Greenleaf, C. (2010). Literacy and science: Each in the service of the other. *Science, 328*(5977), 459–463.

Perle, M., Grigg, W., & Donahue, P. (2005). *The nation's report card: Reading 2005.* Washington, DC: U.S. Department of Education, National Center for Education Statistics.

Perle, M., & Moran, R. (2005). *NAEP 2004 trends in academic progress: Three decades of student performances.* Washington, DC: U.S. Department of Education, National Center for Education Statistics.

Phillips, V., & Wong, C. (2010). Tying together the Common Core of Standards, instruction, and assessments. *Phi Beta Kappan, 91*(5), 37–42.

Portalupi, J., & Fletcher, R. (2001). *Nonfiction craft lessons: Teaching information writing K–8.* Portland, ME: Stenhouse.

Purcell-Gates, V., Duke, N. K., & Martineau, J. A. (2007). Learning to read and write genre-specific text: Roles of authentic experience and explicit teaching. *Reading Research Quarterly, 42,* 8–45.

Rainey, E. C., Maher, B. L., Coupland, D., Franchi, R., & Moje, E. B. (2018). But what does it look like?: Illustrations of disciplinary literacy teaching in two content areas. *Journal of Adult and Adolescent Literacy, 61*(4), 371–379.

Scieszka, J., Smith, L., & Leach, M. (2001). The stinky cheese man and other fairly stupid tales. In L. S. Marcus (Ed.), *Side by side: Five favorite picture-book teams go to work* (pp. 28–37). New York: Walker.

Shanahan, C., Shanahan, T., & Misischia, C. (2011). Analysis of expert readers in three disciplines: History, mathematics, and chemistry. *Journal of Literacy Research, 43*(4), 393–429.

Shanahan, T., & Shanahan, C. (2008). Teaching disciplinary literacy to adolescents. *Harvard Educational Review, 78*(1), 40–59.

Skinner, K., Barrera, E. S., IV, Brauchle, J. P., & Valadez, C. (2012). Motivating and engaging K–5 writers: Teaching the construction of nonfiction texts. In J. Cassidy, S. Grote-Garcia, E. Martinez, & R. Garcia (Eds.), *What's hot in literacy 2012 yearbook* (pp. 8–14). San Antonio: Specialized Literacy Professionals and Texas Association for Literacy Education.

Spires, H. A., Kerkhoff, S. N., & Graham, A. C. K. (2016). Disciplinary literacy and inquiry: Teaching for deeper content learning. *Journal of Adolescent and Adult Literacy, 60*(2), 151–161.

Stead, T. (2002). *Is that a fact?: Teaching nonfiction writing K–3.* Portland, ME: Stenhouse.

Stead, T., & Hoyt, L. (2011). *A guide to teaching nonfiction writing.* Portsmouth, NH: Heinemann.

Writing across the curriculum: Mathematics. (n.d.). Retrieved from *www.michigan.gov/documents/mde/writing_to_learn_mathematics_306722_7.pdf.*

Writing across the curriculum: Science. (n.d.). Retrieved from *www.michigan.gov/documents/mde/science_wac_2_3_264454_7.pdf.*

Writing across the curriculum: Social Studies. (n.d.). Retrieved from *www.michigan.gov/documents/mde/sswac_225020_7.pdf.*

CHAPTER 9

Addressing Complexities of Science Texts to Facilitate English Language Learners' Conceptual Development

MARCO A. BRAVO
SAÚL I. MALDONADO
JORGE L. SOLÍS

English language learners (ELLs) are the fastest growing sector of the school-age population (McFarland et al., 2017), making up nearly 10% of the kindergarten through 12th-grade student population. They represent twice the growth rate of the overall student enrollment rate (4.9%) in the past decade. This demographic change in the student population has recently seen significant growth in particular states. Wyoming, for example, experienced an increase of 48.1% in the ELL population between school year 2009–2010 and 2014–2015. During the same time period, Louisiana experienced an increase of over 40% in the ELL population (42.7%), and West Virginia's ELL population grew 83.5%. Addressing the needs of ELLs is a national concern.

In addition to being the fastest growing student population, ELLs do not perform as well as their non-ELL counterparts in reading measures (August & Shanahan, 2006). On the 2015 National Assessment of Educational Progress (NAEP) reading assessment, the average reading scale score for fourth-grade ELLs was 37 points lower than that of their non-ELL counterparts (National Center for Education Statistics, 2015). The difference between ELLs and non-ELLs becomes more pronounced as ELLs reach middle and high school; 2015 NAEP data show that the reading gap between these two groups was 45 points in eighth grade and 49 points by 12th grade.

These reading achievement disparities can be partially attributed to differences in opportunities to build conceptual knowledge from texts through oral and written language. And due to their emerging proficiency with the English language, ELLs' written and oral language development may be compromised and, subsequently, their building of new understandings from texts may be inhibited. One key finding from the synthesis of research concerning the literacy development of second-language learners (e.g., August & Shanahan, 2006) is that a strong relationship exists between English oral proficiency and reading comprehension for this population. The more developed the oral proficiency of ELLs, the stronger the outcomes on reading comprehension measures.

New instructional models designed to amplify ELLs' experiences with texts have shown promise in terms of supporting reading comprehension. For example, science texts require particular instructional attention to their text structure (Cervetti, Barber, Dorph, Pearson, & Goldschmidt, 2012); language use, such as figurative language (Bravo, 2016); and nature of vocabulary (Lee, 2017). Reading comprehension is critical for acquiring conceptual knowledge for all students, but especially for ELLs interacting with science texts. Scaffolds are needed for ELLs, so that they may gain access to the rich conceptual development possible from both oral conversations and writing about science texts.

In this chapter, we present an analysis of the Common Core State Standards and Next Generation Science Standards to illustrate potential opportunities for integrating science and literacy instruction. We also review some of the pertinent literature that suggests specific approaches for developing conceptual knowledge through oral language with science texts. Finally, we present three instructional approaches that have the potential to facilitate ELLs' conceptual development in science and English language acquisition simultaneously.

English Language Arts and Science Standards

The Common Core State Standards for English Language Arts (CCSS-ELA; National Governors Association Center for Best Practices, Council of Chief State School Offices, 2010), the English Language Proficiency Standards (ELPS; 2014), and the Next Generation Science Standards (NGSS; NGSS Lead States, 2013) provide some distinct challenges and learning possibilities for ELLs. The challenges include particular literacy difficulties in the integration of language and content (Bunch, Kibler, &

Pimentel, 2012; Hakuta, Santos, & Fang, 2013). The language-intensive elements in the NGSS, such as science concepts and the language/ discourse of science, add an additional cognitive load for ELLs (Lee, Quinn, & Valdés, 2013). The CCSS-ELA, the ELPS and the NGSS promote a view of language in which "[it] is both the path to content and part of the content itself" (Hakuta et al., 2013, p. 454). Language arts and science standards further advance literacy-rich learning opportunities that are inseparable from content learning. Figure 9.1 illustrates this pedagogical shift. At the same time, disciplinary boundaries are being blurred, and ELLs are in a position to benefit from integrated instruction, allowing them to sharpen their English language skills as they learn a content area such as science.

CCSS-ELA

In the CCSS-ELA, students are asked to engage with complex texts like those found in the science discipline (Bunch et al., 2012). All students experience text complexity challenges, including the nature of the vocabulary in the text, the complexity of sentences, and the complexity of the ideas represented in the text. ELLs face additional challenges when engaging with complex informational texts, as they may be less

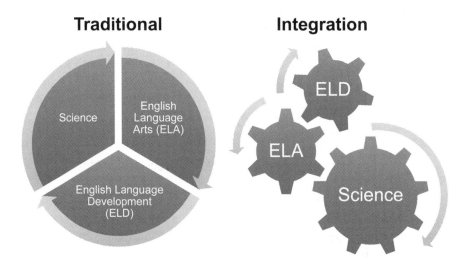

FIGURE 9.1. Pedagogical shifts in standards.

familiar with the language features that are used, the cultural knowledge needed to understand the meanings in the texts, and the text structures of disciplinary texts such as science texts. Engaging with complex texts in a second language is cognitively taxing (Bunch, Walqui, & Pearson, 2014). However, several instructional practices can help ELLs have more success with complex texts: These include contextualizing topics with ELLs background knowledge; preteaching critical vocabulary; giving students opportunities to discuss texts; and providing explicit support with the specialized features of disciplinary texts, such as reviewing figurative language and the text structure. Examples of how this can be done are explained in a later section of this chapter.

NGSS

Implications of the NGSS for ELLs are visible in the science framework in which language plays a central role in making sense of science concepts and practices:

1. *Science and Engineering Practices* (e.g., constructing arguments and designing solutions).
2. *Disciplinary Core Ideas* (e.g., Earth's systems, communicating with peers about proposed design solutions).
3. *Crosscutting Concepts* (e.g., cause and effect, structure and functions).

Language becomes central to understanding and accessing key science practices and concepts. For example, it is not enough to identify a design solution, as called for under the Disciplinary Core Ideas; these solutions must also be communicated to peers. Such communication requires student understanding of the form and function of science language (Lee et al., 2013). For example, teachers need to ensure that students' science explanations respond to a question with a claim and provide evidence to support the claim. Science explanations follow a genre of writing used by scientists, just as novelists follow certain literary conventions (e.g., including plot, resolution, beginning, middle, and end).

Similarly, constructing scientific argumentation is a goal of the Science and Engineering Practices framework. Argumentation in science endorses or challenges a claim by leveraging evidence, with the goal of promoting new scientific understandings (Norris, Philips, &

Osborne, 2007). A claim in scientific argumentation, as explained in the NGSS, is not simply an opinion, but a conjecture or conclusion that is supported by evidence, such as data resulting from an investigation or an experiment. Scientific arguments have a particular organizational structure and require certain grammatical constructions, such as conditionals (*if* this evidence, *then* this claim), declaratives (Pluto should not be classified as a planet.), and researchable questions (Does a chemical reaction happen when you mix salt and water?). Whether in written or oral form, scientific explanations and argumentation conform to the discourse of science, and it is this type of language that has been elusive for ELLs.

ELPS

ELPS levels are categorized according to language type (receptive or productive) and are further defined by what ELLs at various proficiency levels can perform. These standards provide a guide as to the type of language that is to be acquired by ELLs. This is evident in Table 9.1.

These standards also intersect with the ELA-CCSS and the NGSS. Ten ELPS represent the language proficiency that ELLs must have to access the disciplinary content and language practices in science, math, and English language arts. The greatest overlap between ELA practices, Science practices, and ELP standards occurs with respect to ELPS 4 and 6 (Council of Chief State School Officers, 2014, p. 34). These two ELPS draw attention to the importance of scaffolding ELLs' oral and written language construction of evidence-based reasoning and for engaging in argumentation. For example, second-grade teachers engaging in content-specific practices can address how ELLs analyze and critique the arguments of others orally and in writing (ELPS 6) by providing different kinds of prompting and support for ELLs (Level 1–Level 5).

Integration

Both the CCSS-ELA and the NGSS focus on building conceptual knowledge through language. This is evident in Table 9.2, in which key CCSS-ELA and ELPS practices and disciplinary core ideas within the CCSS-ELA are presented. These six CCSS-ELA practices represent core and overlapping disciplinary practices, driving the need to support receptive (oral, written) and productive (oral, written) literacy functions and tasks in science.

TABLE 9.1. Written Language Functions for K–3 Associated with Engaging in Argument from Evidence[a]

ELL Level 2	ELL Level 3
Receptive language	
Can identify arguments and evidence given in a text if provided with support and examples.	Can comprehend arguments and identify evidence in age-appropriate written texts on topics covered in class.
Can sort statements into for and against positions.	Can comprehend and relate written arguments to one another, with support of background knowledge or accompanying illustrations.
Can ask clarification questions or respond to text in ways that demonstrate some comprehension of the written argument.	Can elicit clarification or respond to text in ways that indicate comprehension.
Productive language	
Can produce a written argument and provide supporting evidence by closely imitating a sample text. Will draw on segments of others' speech in the classroom as well as memorized chunks and expressions.	Can write the arguments he or she can produce orally and provide supporting evidence using illustrations, drawings, and other devices that communicate meaning. Will draw substantially from written examples provided as well as from language of teacher and peers.

[a]Informed by ELPS (Council of Chief State School Officers, 2014).

Furthermore, these CCSS-ELA practices require additional instructional attention to support the varied English language proficiency (ELP) levels of ELLs. ELLs at beginning ELP levels require more intense and different scaffolding (e.g., leveraging ELLs' native language; more time to complete tasks) than ELLs at advanced ELP levels (e.g., graphic organizers, posing higher-order questions). The guidelines offered by the Council of Chief State School Officers (2012) suggest that state ELPS can be used to map these overlapping literacy practices across CCSS-ELA standards. For example, with respect to the NGSS Practice 7 (engaging in argument from evidence; National Research Council, 2012), the degree of instructional support for ELLs can vary while attending to disciplinary receptive and productive language functions.

TABLE 9.2. Key Practices and Disciplinary Core Ideas of the CCSS-ELA Related to Reading and Writing

Key CCSS-ELA practices	Disciplinary core ideas from the CCSS
1. Support analyses of a range of grade-level complex texts with evidence. 2. Produce clear and coherent writing in which the development, organization, and style are appropriate to task, purpose, and audience. 3. Construct valid arguments from evidence, and critique the reasoning of others. 4. Build and present knowledge through research by integrating, comparing, and synthesizing ideas from texts. 5. Build on the ideas of others and articulate one's own when working collaboratively. 6. Use English structures to communicate context-specific messages.	Reading • Read complex literature closely and support analyses with evidence. • Read complex informational texts closely and support analyses with evidence. • Use context to determine the meaning of words and phrases. • Engage in the comparison and synthesis of ideas within and/or across texts. Writing • Write analytically (e.g., write to inform/explain and to make an argument) in response to sources. • Write narratives to develop the craft of writing. • Develop and strengthen writing through revision and editing. • Gather, synthesize, and report on research. • Write routinely over various time frames.

Note. Adapted from Council of Chief State School Officers (2012). Copyright © 2012.

Oral Language and Conceptual Development

Improving students' achievement on reading assessments requires developing both fluency in language conventions and literacy in domain knowledge (Hirsch, 2003). Additionally, reading assessments may evaluate decoding and fluency mechanics, as well as meaning-making and conceptual measures (Chall, 1996). Yet Lee and Spratley (2010) describe reading to learn as *disciplinary literacy*, a sophisticated mode of reasoning that requires particular types of reading knowledge and skills. Heller and Greenleaf (2007) defined *sophisticated literacy* skills as "the capacity to draw inferences from academic texts, synthesize information from various sources, and follow complicated directions" (p. 5) and characterize the unique literacy practices of domains such as science. ELLs reading science texts are required to develop decoding and fluency skills in English and simultaneously develop disciplinary literacy in science

(Cervetti, Bravo, Duong, Hernandez, & Tilson, 2008; Thier & Daviss, 2002).

The development of ELLs' disciplinary literacy requires synergistic instruction across all domains of language: reading, writing, listening, and speaking. August and Shanahan (2006) concluded that developing ELLs' reading comprehension and writing proficiency requires extensive instructional support of oral English language development, specifically in terms of metalinguistic awareness, syntactic skills, and listening comprehension. ELLs' conceptual development in science further requires an oral language context that promotes disciplinary literacy (Bravo, 2016), and culturally and linguistically responsive pedagogical approaches for ELLs learning science (Solís, 2017). This can be seen in an examination of classroom listening and speaking activities of ELLs, in which Bunch (2014) found productive forms of students' engagement in academic language use when considering students' varied language resources (language of ideas and the language of display) in connection to academic language tasks involving a range of language registers.

Teaching ELLs through listening and speaking opportunities in the classroom is aligned with the instructional conversations standard for effective pedagogy and learning recommended by research literature for students across all cultural and linguistic groups in the United States (Tharp & Dalton, 2007). Bravo, Mosqueda, Solís, and Stoddart (2014, p. 606) defined *instructional conversations in the context of science* as "using the language of science in ways of talking and representing the natural world through discourse, interaction, and collaboration." Pedagogical features of instructional conversations are listening and speaking interactions that include (1) clear conversational goals, (2) more student–student talk than teacher talk, and (3) monitoring and assessing student talk to scaffold science instruction in ways that integrate the learning of both concepts and processes (National Research Council, 1996). Clear purposes for discussion and structured guides for scaffolding instruction are pedagogical practices aligned with Michaels and O'Connor's (2012) productive talk framework, in which conversations are "focused, coherent, rigorous, and lead to deep conceptual understanding" (p. 1).

In one of the most recognized models for ELL instruction—*Sheltered Instruction Observation Protocol*—Short, Fidelman, and Louguit (2012) noted that opportunities for students to talk and learn about language and content from each other are pivotal in supporting ELLs' academic language development alongside their conceptual development. As students develop their knowledge of scientific ideas through generalizations of facts and experiences, teachers of ELLs need to consider differentiated participation structures (whole-group, small-group, partners) as a means of developing ELLs' argumentative thinking through both listening and speaking domains. Structured opportunities to discuss what is read, as recommended by this model, are an instructional practice that concurrently develops ELLs' oral language competence in English and conceptual knowledge in science.

Scaffolding Oral Language with Science Texts

To optimize ELLs' conceptual development from text-based science discussion requires understanding both the complexities learners bring to the literacy task and the texts with which they interact during instruction. English learner variables include the English proficiency of the learner, the degree of prior knowledge of the content under study, and familiarity of the discussion format being used. One additional learner variable to consider is how the ELL handles anxiety in the target language, as participating in discussion can be a risky business for ELLs (Yan & Horwitz, 2008). Text considerations include the many linguistic blind spots that ELLs encounter, including the use of metaphors, similes, and presence of dual-meaning words. In addition, the type and quantity of text features (diagrams, captions, tables) inform how much support ELLs will require to utilize available information to build understandings about the text and meaningfully participate in discussions.

Individual ELL Differences

English Proficiency Level

ELLs are not a homogenous group. ELLs have different levels of English proficiency that often mediate how involved they are during instruction. Krashen and Terrell (1983) suggested there are at least five stages of second-language acquisition (preproduction, early production, speech emergence, intermediate fluency, advanced fluency). ELLs at each stage are able to perform certain linguistic tasks, such as extracting key information from texts that they read, or that are read to them, with varying success. An ELL at beginning stages of English language development may be at the silent period of second-language acquisition (preproduction), a stage defined by receptively taking in and understanding language but not producing language as a learner. ELLs at this stage spend much of their time listening and responding nonverbally (shaking their heads, raising a hand). Learners have been documented to remain in this stage for up to 6 months. In comparison, an ELL at an intermediate fluency stage of English is producing written and oral language but will have gaps in understanding academic terms and less familiar expressions.

The type of scaffold needed by ELLs at these two distinct stages of second-language acquisition, when asked to discuss a text they have read, would require careful consideration of their English proficiency level. A teacher's directions for a student at the beginning stage would require an emphasis on listening comprehension and opportunities for student participation with nonverbal responses (e.g., thumbs up/down; confirm by nodding). An ELL at an intermediate fluency level would require instructional attention to the academic vocabulary in the text, as well as any special format that is used as part of the oral responses by students. For example, if students are to respond with evidence from the text, a sentence stem that has specific components is required: "I think that _____ because _____. This information I found on page _____ of the book."

Degree of Prior Knowledge

Cummins (1981) distinguished between social and academic language in his framework that unpacks elements of Basic Interpersonal Communicative Skills (BICS) and Cognitive Academic Language Proficiency (CALP). The amount of prior knowledge an ELL has about the subject under study is one of the defining features of a task's cognitive demand (or lack of demand). The less one knows, for example, about the phases of the moon, the more cognitive energy is pulled to understand what causes the phases of the moon; this means that less cognitive energy is available to devote to responding to teacher questions or class discussions about the topic. What students know, and whether they bring to bear the right prior knowledge, also mitigates how ELLs participate and learn from instruction that involves discussion about texts, especially science texts. Moreover, prior knowledge can refer to students' home language. The shifting use of more than one language for ELLs, when possible, is a potential learning resource for both language and content development; that is, *translanguaging*, or the strategic shift between one and another language in conversation, can be a productive form of student sense making to promote greater awareness of science-related home and community experiences (García & Wei, 2014).

The implementation of *anticipation guides* has been found to be one successful strategy for activating and building the appropriate prior knowledge with students (Duffelmeyer, 1994). This before-reading strategy has students listen to several statements about key concepts in the book they will read. Subsequently, students agree or disagree with the statements, and a short discussion ensues as to why they agree or disagree. The teacher then tells students to listen for information in the book about whether the statements are true or false. This strategy sets the purpose for reading and piques the curiosity of students. Science texts often have many key concepts. Using anticipation guides helps ELLs cull through multiple concepts in science texts and identify those that are critical.

Personality Traits

ELLs also vary by personality traits that influence how they handle interaction with others (Kębłowska, 2012; Lightbown & Spada, 2013). Kębłowska (2012) suggested that motivation, anxiety, and risk taking, among other individual factors, mediate how learning and language acquisition unfold through and in a second language. ELLs who are risk takers are more likely to try out their English-speaking skills than are ELLs who are introverted, shy, and hence more likely to get access to English input and feedback on their English-speaking skills. Moreover, ELLs may exhibit stronger elements of some of these traits (e.g., risk taking, anxiety) at earlier stages of second-language acquisition. Part of the reason anxiety is heightened for ELLs during whole-class discussions is their fear that classmates will judge their English pronunciation abilities.

Knowing ELL's personality traits can assist teachers in molding appropriate scaffolds for their students' discussions of science texts, allowing ELLs to participate more freely in these discussions. Some potential modifications to the text discussion can include turning the student contribution segment into a game-type activity. One such game is a Discussion Mixer, in which the teacher tells students that they will play a game in which they walk around the classroom, mixing and talking with various classmates. Students are informed that they are to walk around the room, and when the teacher signals with a hand clap or by ringing a bell, students stop and discuss a question posed by the teacher, based on the text they are reading. After a few rounds of the Discussion Mixer, the teacher can ask ELLs who have a higher threshold for anxiety to share their responses. This type of discussion format reduces the high-stakes nature of discussions and allows ELLs to lower their affective filter (Krashen & Terrell, 1983) by focusing on communicative success rather than on form.

Text Factors

Figurative Language

Figurative language is part and parcel of science texts and scientific discourse, and is an important part of the language of scientists. It is critical not only for the construction of more comprehensible examples but also for engaging and creating new scientific models (Darian, 2000; Duit, 1991; Lancor, 2014b; Solís, 2017). While often thought to be written free of figurative language, science texts written for children and youth actually use various forms of these devices; these are an authentic aspect of the language used by a range of scientific communities (e.g., physicists, chemists, biologists). Analogies, hypotheticals, personification, similes, and metaphors are literary devices used to define "our everyday realities," to influence our thinking, and to concretize scientific concepts that are sometimes abstract or difficult to grasp (Lancor, 2014a; p. 1247). For example, during one observation we conducted in San Francisco of a third-grade science lesson, the teacher used hypothetical constructions to create an imaginary scenario; students were asked to consider the local weather patterns by imagining "you're a giant walking across the Golden Gate Bridge" as the teacher sketched the Northern California landscape on the chalkboard (Solís, Kattan, & Baquedano-López, 2009). Several of the cognitive benefits related to the use of figurative language are relevant to scientific sense making, including (1) providing visualizations of the abstract, (2) leveraging students' prior knowledge on a familiar subject, and (3) supporting students' understanding of abstract ideas by connecting similar examples in the real world (Duit, 1991).

Dual-Meaning Words

One aspect of vocabulary learning from science texts involves understanding authors' intended meaning when they use terms that have dual meanings (e.g., cell, current). Cloud, Genesee, and Hamayan (2009) suggest that this can cause comprehension difficulties for ELLs and requires direct and explicit instruction to draw their awareness to the polysemous nature of science vocabulary. Almost three-fourths (70%) of the words identified as critical science vocabulary for students in the elementary grades have multiple meanings (Johnson, Moe, & Baumann, 1983). This creates a special challenge for ELLs, who often come to the science text with an everyday meaning for particular words, even when the author intends a more academic meaning. Consider the term *test* in the science text that states, "He decided to test these ingredients." ELLs are likely to relate to the meaning with which they are familiar (an exam) even though they may know that the meaning does not quite fit the context (i.e., a trial to see whether a relationship exists; Laufer, 1997).

To problematize the issue a bit further, we note that many academic words have different meanings across content areas. In social studies, the term *property* often refers to land that is owned by an individual or entity, whereas in science, the term often means something you can see, smell, or feel in relation to an ingredient. In mathematics, the intended meaning for *property* is often the rule for solving a problem (e.g., associative property, distributive property). Other terms that have unique meanings across content areas include *solution, matter,* and *product.* ELLs need to learn to use their knowledge of these terms flexibly as they receive instruction across content areas. Additionally, teachers need to provide some instructional time familiarizing students with these terms before the science texts are read to or by the ELLs, particularly when the students are at the beginning and early intermediate stages of English language proficiency.

Science Text Features

Science texts have unique features that are not found in narrative texts (Cervetti & Barber, 2008). Science texts can contain an index, headings, a table of contents, bulleted list, diagrams, realistic illustrations, data in a table format, and unique text structures to convey information. An additional feature of science texts is that they serve the purpose of communicating information about the natural world (Duke, 2014). When ELLs interact with science texts, they have to contend with language and content learning goals simultaneously. Understanding the features of informational texts, like science texts, and how they are utilized to convey information, is a scaffold that can support the content learning goals of ELLs, consequently lessening the cognitive burden that they have to bear (Lesaux, 2006).

In Figure 9.2, the text feature diagram illustrates the information processing that students have to perform in order to comprehend how gas chromatography separates molecules by size (Curley & Chase, 2008) and shows how students need to understand the various elements associated with the diagram, including the captions and directionality (illustrated by arrows), as well as the size and color of molecules, which collectively detail the process of molecular separation. These nuanced pieces of information require explicit instructional attention to help students fully comprehend the text and participate actively in discussions about the text with others.

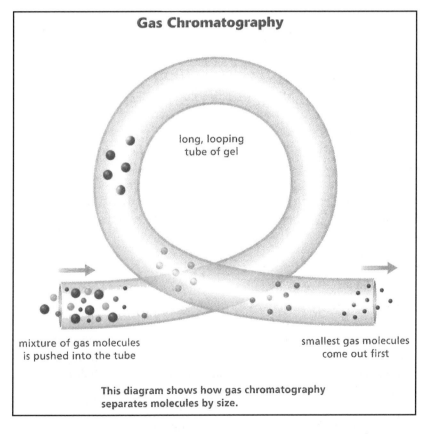

FIGURE 9.2. Text feature diagram for gas chromatography. From Curley and Chase (2008). Copyright © The Regents of the University of California.

Instructional Models

ELL pedagogy calls for direct and explicit instruction of learning goals, along with opportunities for ELLs to practice these goals through interaction with others (Echevarria, Short, & Powers, 2006). In the following examples, we provide three instructional models for teaching figurative language, dual-meaning vocabulary, and text features that are found in science texts. If this type of instruction takes place prior to conceptual discussions, it can deepen ELLs' understandings of the concepts presented in the science text and better prepare students to actively participate in discussions.

Figurative Language

Different types of figurative language (analogy, simile, personification, reification, metaphor, and hypotheticals) may be found in science texts, depending on the material's grade level and scientific field (Darian, 2000). However, the meanings and significance that these constructions bring to bear on scientific sense making differs, depending both on their use in instruction and how students connect to these constructions. Science teachers are usually aware of figurative language in texts and in everyday speech, but this awareness is not usually included in their instruction. Conversely, ELLs are rarely familiar with science-related metaphors, analogies, and similes. Therefore, teachers can approach the appearance of figurative language as an opportunity for amplifying disciplinary content comprehension and language development. Below are some instructional examples that can help students grapple with figurative language in science.

• Make a point of including and discussing metaphors that appear in science texts. Students can discuss how these constructions highlight or obscure characteristics attached to a scientific concept. For example, the idea that "energy is like money" suggests that energy is a substance that can be accounted for in some form, highlighting the idea of conservation, while obscuring its transformational qualities (Lacor, 2014b).

• Students can learn to identify how figurative language is expressed by looking for features such as quotation marks, italics, and prototypical lexical markers (i.e., *like, as, just as, imagine, in the same way,* X *can be likened to*; Darian, 2000). These literary features are resources for understanding and using scientific discourse patterns.

- Students can create their own figurative language examples as way to construct an argument or demonstrate their comprehension of big ideas.

Dual-Meaning Vocabulary

Explicit instruction designed to determine the author's intended meaning of dual-meaning words can increase ELLs' awareness of these terms, while giving them a strategy to use when they confront these words in text on their own. Parent (2012) suggests that ELLs develop a stronger grip on understanding multiple meanings when they see the multiple definitions and try to select the meaning that best fits the author's use of the term. Here, we provide an example for teaching dual-meaning science vocabulary.

- Locate a few science words that have multiple meanings from the science text that students will read or that you will read to them. Try to select words with which students may be familiar. For example, students may know the everyday meaning of *marine* (a type of military person) but not the scientific meaning that refers to something found in the ocean.

- Create a class chart with three columns labeled Science Vocabulary, Everyday Meaning, Science Meaning. Label the chart "Multiple Meanings Chart." Write the science vocabulary you selected from the science book and add the dual meanings of the word. You may also want to have student copies of the chart for students to fill in as you complete the chart on the board.

- Before students read, or you read the text to students, explain that science books have vocabulary that has multiple meanings. Explain that many of these vocabulary words have an everyday meaning and a very specialized meaning in science. Provide the example of *marine*. Ask students to select which meaning they think would be intended by the author of a science text.

- Work with students to complete the chart for the multiple meanings using the vocabulary words you selected. Depending on your ELLs'

English proficiency levels, complete the science meaning and have students think of the everyday meaning as an additional scaffold.

- Elicit sentences with the science words that make use of the everyday meaning and others that use the science meaning.

Teachers can expand on this level of direct instruction by having ELLs illustrate the everyday and science meaning or use a dictionary to support their definitions (as appropriate). Teachers can also have ELLs go on a hunt in the text to find other words that have multiple meanings.

Textual Features and Structures

In addition to figurative language and dual-meaning vocabulary, teachers can explicitly address features and structures in science texts to foster learning conditions that facilitate ELLs' conceptual development. In the process of acquiring English, ELLs require instruction regarding how textual features in science materials communicate important information; these include text features in both the printed text and the illustrations. For example, teachers can explicitly review indices, illustrations, and headings to show how science materials organize ideas. Additionally, teachers developing ELLs' conceptual understanding in science may review the following textual features: diagrams, tables and tables of contents, glossaries, captions, and notation markers (lists); and italicized, bolded, and underlined words and phrases. ELLs may also benefit from explicit instruction about the ways science texts are organized into recognizable structures, such as description, cause–effect, problem–solution, compare–contrast, time–order, and question–answer. Similar to genres in the English language arts, familiarity with textual structures in science materials serves ELLs as a framework for conceptual development.

To develop ELLs' conceptual knowledge and skills in science, teachers may consider selecting introductory activities from among the following:

1. *Prereading.* Have students complete a graphic organizer that records examples, page numbers, and observations of the textual features.
2. *Prereading.* Have students create and participate in a gallery walk of structures that occur in science texts.
3. *During reading.* Have students co-create a word wall of signal

words and phrases that are associated with specific textual structures.

4. *During reading.* Have students participate in structured student–student conversations about the ways that textual features and structures communicate the importance of information.

5. *Postreading.* Have students communicate their understanding of science processes and knowledge by using multiple textual structures.

6. *Postreading.* Have students develop a glossary of text feature distinctions between their first and second languages (L1 and L2).

Teachers who address textual features and structures in their science instruction provide ELLs with an opportunity to better comprehend science texts and, subsequently, to actively participate in discussions of these texts. Such opportunities to build content knowledge and sharpen literacy skills are critical for the academic success of ELLs. ELLs are working against the clock as they attempt to keep up with native English speakers in their development of content and simultaneously develop English proficiency in time to graduate from high school and be prepared for college or careers.

Conclusion

In this chapter, we have offered some instructional models for supporting ELLs' access to rich science texts through discussion and attention to linguistic blind spots that can impede both their comprehension and their subsequent contribution to class discussions. Through the contextualized and authentic use of literacy in science, students can develop and practice complex language forms and gain conceptual knowledge about the natural world. This approach to teaching science, along with English language and literacy, to ELLs is consistent with the NGSS, ELPS, and the ELA-CCSS. Yet conceptual development from rich science texts through discussions necessitates that we give some considerations to the challenges these texts and discussion formats present to ELLs. Figurative language, dual-meaning words, and text features and structures are a few of the elements of science texts that require instructional attention. Similarly, student variables, such as their prior knowledge of the subject, their personality characteristics, and their ELP, also require consideration. Last, familiarity with the discussion format utilized after reading can also act as an obstacle for ELLs. However, with some adaptations to their instruction, this population can develop rich conceptual knowledge through discussions about the science texts they read.

● IMPLICATIONS FOR PROFESSIONAL LEARNING ●

- Making instructional adaptations that include discussing certain linguistic features of science texts (e.g., presence of dual-meaning words, idiomatic expressions) is critical for ELLs to fully participate in and take advantage of discussions of science texts.
- Consideration of ELLs' English proficiency, prior knowledge, and personality traits is necessary when crafting instruction that involves discussions of science texts.
- Explicitly teaching the format that will be utilized to discuss texts ensures that ELLs have equal access to the learning opportunities as their native English-speaking peers.

QUESTIONS FOR DISCUSSION

1. What are the challenges that informational texts (e.g., science) present to ELLs?

2. How can teachers prepare ELLs to have productive discussions about the science texts they read?

3. How can teachers take advantage of the presence of language in and across new standards to support their ELLs' language and content learning?

REFERENCES

August, D., & Shanahan, T. (2006). *Developing literacy in second-language learners: Report of the National Literacy Panel on Language Minority Children and Youth.* Mahwah, NJ: Erlbaum.

Bravo, M. (2016). Situating the English Language Arts Common Core Standards in science: Enhancing access to language for emergent bilingual students. In C. P. Proctor, A. Boardman, & E. H. Hiebert (Eds.), *Teaching emergent students: Flexible approaches in an era of new standards* (pp. 179–194). New York: Guilford Press.

Bravo, M. A., Mosqueda, E., Solís, J. L., & Stoddart, T. (2014). Possibilities and limits of integrating science and diversity education in preservice elementary teacher preparation. *Journal of Science Teacher Education 43*, 601–619.

Bunch, G. C. (2014). The language of ideas and the language of display: Reconceptualizing "academic language" in linguistically diverse classrooms. *International Multilingual Research Journal, 8*, 70–86.

Bunch, G. C., Kibler, A., & Pimentel, S. (2012). Realizing opportunities for English learners in the Common Core English Language Arts and Disciplinary Literacy Standards. Retrieved March 25, 2013, from *https://ell.stanford.edu/sites/default/files/events/bunch-kibler-pimentel_aera_2013-04-08.pdf*.

Bunch, G. C., Walqui, A., & Pearson, P. D. (2014). Complex text and new common standards in the United States: Pedagogical implications for English learners. *TESOL Quarterly, 48*(3), 533–559.

Cervetti, G. N., & Barber, J. (2008). Text in hands-on science. In E. H. Hiebert & M. Sailors (Eds.), *Finding the right texts: What works for beginning and struggling readers* (pp. 89–108). New York: Guilford Press.

Cervetti, G. N., Barber, J., Dorph, R., Pearson, P. D., & Goldschmidt, P. G. (2012). The impact of an integrated approach to science and literacy in elementary school classrooms. *Journal of Research in Science Teaching, 49*(5), 631–658.

Cervetti, G. N., Bravo, M. A., Duong, T., Hernandez, S., & Tilson, J. (2008). A research-based approach to instruction for English Language Learners in science (Report prepared for the Noyce Foundation). Retrieved March 6, 2018, from *www.science-andliteracy.org/research/english_language_learners*.

Chall, J. S. (1996). *Stages of reading development*. Fort Worth, TX: Harcourt Brace.

Cloud, N., Genesee, F., & Hamayan, E. (2009). *Literacy instruction for English language learners: A teacher's guide to research-based strategies*. Portsmouth, NH: Heinemann.

Council of Chief State School Officers. (2012). *Framework for English language proficiency development standards corresponding to the Common Core State Standards and the Next Generation Science Standards*. Washington, DC: Author.

Council of Chief State School Officers. (2014). *English language proficiency standards with correspondences to the K–12 Practices and Common Core State Standards*. Washington, DC: Author.

Cummins, J. (1981). Age on arrival and immigrant second language learning in Canada: A reassessment. *Applied Linguistics, 2*(2), 132–149.

Curley, J., & Chase, A. (2008). *Break it down: How scientists separate mixtures*. Nashua, NH: Delta Education.

Darian, S. (2000). The role of figurative language in introductory science texts. *International Journal of Applied Linguistics, 10*(2), 163–186.

Duffelmeyer, F. (1994). Effective anticipation guide statements for learning from expository prose. *Journal of Reading, 37*, 452–455.

Duit, R. (1991). On the role of analogies and metaphors in learning science. *Science Education, 75*(6), 649–672.

Duke, N. K. (2014). *Inside information: Developing powerful readers and writers of informational text through project-based instruction, K–5*. Newark, DE: International Literacy Association.

Echevarria, J., Short, D., & Powers, K. (2006). School reform and standards-based education: A model for English-language learners. *Journal of Educational Research, 99*(4), 195–211.

García, O., & Wei, L. (2014). *Translanguaging and education*. London: Palgrave Macmillan.

Hakuta, K., Santos, M., & Fang, Z. (2013). Challenges and opportunities for language learning in the context of the CCSS and the NGSS. *Journal of Adolescent and Adult Literacy, 56*(6), 451–454.

Heller, R., & Greenleaf, C. (2007). *Literacy instruction in the content areas: Getting to the core of middle and high school improvement*. Washington, DC: Alliance for Excellent Education.

Hirsch, E. D. (2003). Reading comprehension requires knowledge of words and the world: Scientific insights into the fourth-grade slump and the nation's stagnant comprehension scores. *American Educator, 27*, 10–13, 16–22, 28–29, 48.

Johnson, D., & Moe, A., & Bauman, J. (1983). *The Ginn word book for teachers: A basic lexicon*. Lexington, MA: Ginn & Co.

Kębłowska, M. (2012). The place of affect in second language acquisition. In M. Pawlak (Ed.), *New perspectives on individual differences in language learning and teaching* (pp. 157–167). Berlin: Springer.

Krashen, S. D., & Terrell, T. D. (1983). *The natural approach: Language acquisition in the classroom*. New York: Pergamon Press.

Lancor, R. (2014a). Using metaphor theory to examine conceptions of energy in biology, chemistry, and physics. *Science and Education, 23*(6), 1245–1267.

Lancor, R. A. (2014b). Using student-generated analogies to investigate conceptions of energy: A multidisciplinary study. *International Journal of Science Education, 36*(1), 1–23.

Laufer, B. (1997). The lexical plight in second language reading: Words you don't know, words you think you know and words you can't guess. In J. Coady & T. Huckin (Eds.), *Second language vocabulary acquisition* (pp. 2–34). New York: Cambridge University Press.

Lee, C. D., & Spratley, A. (2010). *Reading in the disciplines: The challenges of adolescent literacy*. New York: Carnegie Corporation of New York.

Lee, O. (2017). Common Core State Standards for ELA/literacy and Next Generation Science Standards: Convergences and discrepancies using argument as an example. *Educational Researcher, 46*(2), 90–102.

Lee, O., Quinn, H., & Valdés, G. (2013). Science and language for English language learners in relation to Next Generation Science Standards and with implications for Common Core State Standards for English language arts and mathematics. *Educational Researcher, 42*(4), 223–233.

Lesaux, N. K. (2006). Building consensus: Future directions for research on English language learners at risk for learning difficulties. *Teachers College Record, 108*(11), 2406–2434.

Lightbown, P., & Spada, N. (2013). *How languages are learned* (3rd ed.). London: Oxford University Press.

McFarland, J., Hussar, B., de Brey, C., Snyder, T., Wang, X., Wilkinson-Flicker, S., et al. (2017). *The condition of education 2017* (NCES 2017-144). Washington, DC: U.S. Department of Education, National Center for Education Statistics. Available at *https://nces.ed.gov/pubsearch/pubsinfo.asp?pubid=2017144*.

Michaels, S., & O'Connor, C. (2012). *Talk science primer*. Cambridge, MA: TERC.

National Center for Education Statistics. (2015). *The nation's report card: Reading. 2015.* Washington, DC: Institute of Education Sciences, U.S. Department of Education.

National Governors Association Center for Best Practices, Council of Chief State School Officers. (2010). *Common Core State Standards for English language arts and literacy in history/social studies, science, and technical subjects.* Washington, DC: Authors.

National Research Council. (1996). *National science education standards.* Washington, DC: National Academies Press.

National Research Council. (2012). *A framework for K–12 science education: Practices, crosscutting concepts, and core ideas.* Washington, DC: National Academies Press.

NGSS Lead States. (2013). *Next Generation Science Standards: For states, by states.* Washington, DC: National Academies Press.

Norris, S. P., Phillips, L. M., & Osborne, J. F. (2007). Scientific inquiry: The place of interpretation and argumentation. In J. Luft, R. L. Bell, & J. Gess-Newsome (Eds.), *Science as inquiry in the secondary setting* (pp. 87–98). Arlington, VA: National Science Teachers Association Press.

Parent, K. (2012). The most frequent English homonyms. *RELC Journal: A Journal of Language Teaching and Research, 43*(1), 69–81.

Short, D. J., Fidelman, C. G., & Louguit, M. (2012). Developing academic language in English language learners through sheltered instruction. *TESOL Quarterly, 46*(2), 334–361.

Solís, J. L. (2017). Adaptation and the language of learning science in a bilingual classroom. In J. Langman & H. Hansen-Thomas (Eds.), *Discourse analytic perspectives on STEM education: Exploring English learner interaction in the classroom* (pp. 195–215). Cham, Switzerland: Springer International.

Solís, J., Kattan, S., & Baquedano-López, P. (2009). Socializing respect and knowledge in a racially integrated science classroom. *Linguistics and Education, 20*(3), 273–290.

Tharp, R., & Dalton, S. S. (2007). Orthodoxy, cultural compatibility, and universals in education. *Comparative Education, 43*(1), 53–70.

Thier, M., & Daviss, B. (2002). *The new science literacy.* Portsmouth, NH: Heinemann.

Yan, J. X., & Horwitz, E. K. (2008). Learners' perceptions of how anxiety interacts with personal and instructional factors to influence their achievement in English: A qualitative analysis of EFL learners in China. *Language Learning, 58*(1), 151–183.

CHAPTER 10

Amplifying Diverse Voices
with Read-Alouds in Elementary, Middle,
and High School Classrooms

Connecting Concepts to Practice

CATHERINE LAMMERT
STACIA L. LONG
JO WORTHY

There are many well-documented benefits to reading aloud to students. Some benefits are academic and lead more directly to improved literacy outcomes, while others are more social and relational. According to Laminack (2017), an advocate for reading aloud "often and well" (p. 33), reading aloud to students provides shared access to academic concepts and vocabulary; it creates opportunities to model fluent reading and reading strategies; it inspires reading by introducing students to good books; and it supports writing by providing mentor texts. Furthermore, read-alouds build a classroom community where young people are welcome to share ideas, connections, and personal responses. They engage students in purposeful dialogue about meaningful issues in the world, expose students to multiple perspectives, encourage participation in dialogue, and build a classroom environment conducive to positive social interaction. By exposing a learning community to a shared experience with text, read-alouds create a dynamic space for students to talk things out, negotiate meanings, practice language, listen, and build confidence (Worthy, Chamberlain, Peterson, Sharp, & Shih, 2012; Worthy, Durán, Pruitt, Hikida, & Peterson, 2013).

The benefits and possibilities seem endless. Over 25 years ago, Hoffman, Roser, and Battle (1993) wrote:

Reading to children is to literacy education as two aspirins and a little bed rest were to the family doctor in years gone by. Students have an impoverished vocabulary? Read to them. Students struggling with comprehension? Read to them. Students beset with negative attitudes or lacking in motivation? Read to them. Students have second language acquisition problems? Read to them. Reading to children has also been prescribed as a preventive measure: Want to ensure children's success in school? Want your children to read early? Read to them. (p. 496)

This analogy has proven prophetic. Beck and McKeown (2001, p. 10) argued that read-alouds are "probably the most highly recommended activity" for growing literacy practices with young people; however, reading aloud to children, in any shape or form, has not proven to be a cure-all. In a contemporary climate that is geared toward standards, high-stakes assessments, data-driven instruction, and measurable outcomes, practices such as read-alouds are vanishing, especially for students beyond the elementary grades.

Although young adults may be capable of reading to themselves, there are still powerful benefits to reading aloud. In particular, through the lens of culturally sustaining pedagogy (Paris, 2012), we can view read-alouds as opening spaces to center diverse experiences in the official curriculum (Apple, 2004) of schooling. Culturally sustaining pedagogy is rooted in asset-based views of students and ways of teaching. Through a stance of pluralism, culturally sustaining pedagogy connects deeply to issues of social justice, and it reinforces a commitment to change (Waitoller & Thorius, 2016). Significantly, educators need to engage in practices, such as read-alouds, that allow them to move beyond mere cultural relevance. As Bomer and Bomer (2001) explained,

Our classrooms need to be open to the outside world, to become more involved in civic conversations and community service. However, it is inside the classroom community that we learn ways of dealing with others; dispositions to negotiate; and habits of listening and talking that will allow us to be effective, strategic, and sensitive participants in public discourse. . . . Finding a voice here, developing the efficacy to speak and differ, attempting to create consensus, and building habits of civility are crucial steps in learning to create democracy moment by moment. (p. 78)

By enacting read-alouds within a culturally sustaining learning environment, teachers can create spaces ripe for negotiation and shared meaning making. Read-alouds are an invitation for students not just to be affirmed, but to have their cultural and linguistic repertoires expanded as they "create democracy moment by moment" (Bomer & Bomer, 2001, p. 78). In this chapter, we aim to honor what Calkins (2001) has described as "the exquisite intimacy and power of reading aloud, and of using the experience of that shared read-aloud time to mentor young readers in the qualities of good reading" (p. 41).

Read-Alouds Revisited

Read-aloud practices have been extensively studied under a range of names and premises, and there is "great variety" (Oyler & Barry, 1996, p. 324) in the kinds of conversations that occur in and around these structures. The diverse literature base has made it difficult to define read-alouds as a single pedagogical practice. According to Mitchell, Homza, and Ngo (2012), "the common thread of the phenomena is a fluent adult reader reading an appropriately selected text to a child or group of children" (p. 278). Reading aloud to students has been demonstrated to build interest in reading and encourage students to be more engaged in their own independent reading (Pegg & Bartelheim, 2011). Read-alouds have also been linked to growth in students' emergent literacy skills, including their vocabulary knowledge and reading and listening comprehension (Swanson et al., 2011; Teale, 1984). While all literacy practices must be understood in and adapted to different contexts and communities, the evidence in favor of read-alouds is deeply compelling. "After evaluating ten thousand research studies, the U.S. Department of Education's Commission on Reading (1985) issued a report, "Becoming a Nation of Readers," which goes so far as to state that "the single most important activity for building knowledge required for eventual success in reading is reading aloud to children" (Anderson, Hiebert, Scott, & Wilkinson, 1985, p. 23).

Although most research on the effectiveness of read-alouds has occurred in early childhood and elementary classroom settings, some teacher educators, researchers, and practitioners have written about the use of read-alouds in middle and high school classrooms (Ariail & Albright, 2006; Dreher; 2003; Laminack, 2017; Richardson, 2000; Richardson & Cantrell, 1996). The authors of these articles used read-alouds for many of the same reasons that teachers of younger students do: getting students invested in a challenging unit like poetry, making texts accessible to students, teaching strategies for working through challenging texts, and building connections to and between texts, with the ultimate goal of supporting readers to apply what they've learned from read-alouds to their independent reading. Also, "research indicates that motivation, interest, and engagement are often enhanced when teachers read aloud to middle school students" (Albright & Ariail, 2005, p. 582). For these reasons, using read-alouds in secondary settings has earned attention in informal publications, like blogs, as well as in presentations at professional conferences. In a featured presentation at the Winter Conference organized by *Journal of Language and Literacy Education*, Donalyn Miller stated that "we don't age out of the benefits of read-alouds," and we couldn't agree more.

While the early body of work surrounding read-alouds focused on narrative and storybook texts (i.e., Barrentine, 1996), more recent work has engaged in looking at how read-alouds work with informational texts (i.e., Bradley & Donovan, 2010; May, 2011; Smolkin & Donovan, 2001). This research highlights the fact that genre impacts the type of discourses produced during read-alouds, so it is important for teachers to support students in using different strategies to facilitate meaning making (Smolkin & Donovan, 2001). Similarly, thanks to an expansion of the kinds of texts that are available for reading aloud, read-alouds can occur in many different content areas (Laminack & Wadsworth, 2006), including "in support of the social studies and science curriculum" (Calkins, 2001, p. 51). In a survey of three middle schools in a single district, Albright and Ariail (2005) found that "while teachers of reading, special education, and language arts were most likely to read aloud, high percentages of teachers of other subject areas also engaged in this practice" (p. 585). Furthermore, they found that "the preponderance of reasons given by teachers indicates an emphasis on different purposes for reading" and that "these middle school teachers were concerned with facilitating their students' learning and had definitive, instrumental reasons for choosing their instructional practices" (p. 585).

The read-aloud is a powerful teaching tool, in part because reading aloud and discussing texts with students is not about a forced, or single, understanding of a text. Read-alouds should not be used to make sure everyone has read the "right" texts, or because it might make it easier to manage student behavior during a reading experience. Although it may appear didactic and teacher-centric at first, this pedagogy is well aligned with teaching that centers students as active sense makers.

Planning to use read-alouds as part of your teaching requires forethought and purpose—it is not simply reading a random book to children

(Albright & Ariail, 2005), but a structured component of a larger instructional routine and plan for teaching literacy:

> Although a simple read-aloud inserted into the classroom routine might make everyone "feel" better and give the appearance of a commitment to literature-based instruction . . . a quality read-aloud experience, well-conceived and well-constructed, is needed before the maximum effects in language, literacy, and literature growth can be realized. (Hoffman et al., p. 502)

Given all the benefits of reading aloud, and its increasing importance as a response to curricular mandates that are often stringent, we review instructional purposes and uses of read-alouds below.

Theoretical Perspectives

Culturally Sustaining Pedagogy

There have been recent calls for English language arts to become more culturally sustaining (Bomer, 2017). According to Paris and Alim (2017), culturally sustaining pedagogy "positions dynamic cultural dexterity as a necessary good" (p. 1). Culturally sustaining teachers view differences as strengths rather than deficits. Instead of continuing to work within existing educational institutions that systematically devalue the knowledge and practices of students from nondominant communities, a culturally sustaining teacher or scholar might ask, "What would our pedagogies look like if this gaze (and the kindred patriarchal, cisheteronormative, English-monolingual, ableist, classist, xenophobic, Judeo-Christian gazes) weren't the dominant one?" (p. 3).

Teachers seeking to adopt culturally sustaining pedagogy might consider how read-alouds can be used to respect and promote diversity in their classrooms (May, Bingham, & Pendergast, 2014). Pendergast, May, Bingham, and Kurumada (2015) have argued that read-alouds are particularly beneficial because they create "engaging learning opportunities for all children," (p. 65) particularly in diverse learning communities.

Ultimately, teachers who use culturally sustaining pedagogy for read-alouds acknowledge and recognize the efforts of those who have enacted change and spurred progress even as they recognize how much further we have to go as a society. In order for schools to become more equitable spaces, it is imperative for educators to value the range of knowledge and experiences students bring to any reading experience.

Reader Response Theory

Reader response theory operates on the foundational premise that "the literary text as such is not created by the author, but rather by the reader" (Nikolajeva, 2005, p. 251). Louise Rosenblatt, well known for her transactional theory of reading (1978, 1995), argued that meaning exists in a space between readers, texts, and culture, in which sense-making occurs as a "joint accomplishment" inside the transactional zone (Rosenblatt, 1978, p. 141). This transactional theory suggests that learning is mediated, or negotiated, through different modes, and that reader response can take different forms. Rosenblatt also outlined two types of reader responses, which occur on a continuum: *aesthetic,* which is more oriented toward the emotions and experience of the text, and *efferent,* which is more focused on content knowledge and understanding. Similarly, Wolfgang Iser described reading "as an active dialogue between the text and the reader" (Nikolajeva, 2005, p. 252) and argued that readers make sense of texts through their real life and literary experiences.

Reader response theory is well aligned with the practice of read-alouds. We believe that the read-aloud process invites a "kaleidoscope of perspectives, preintentions, [and] recollections" (Iser, 1972, p. 284). Read-alouds may amplify ways of coming to understand the text due to the possibilities of a shared text experience in a classroom learning community. Because read-alouds allow both teacher and students to share their understandings, all readers benefit from the multiplicity of understandings of the shared text.

Reader response theory is also well aligned with the view that "different learning outcomes may be best achieved by different reading-aloud styles" (Brabham & Lynch-Brown, 2002, p. 466). Accordingly, now we turn to the question of what different purposes teachers have for using read-alouds in their teaching practices, and how those purposes might be informed by theories of culturally sustaining pedagogy and reader response.

Purposes of Read-Alouds

When and why might we choose read-alouds for students? First, we are not advocating that all (or even most) of the reading that occurs in classrooms should take the form of a teacher reading a text aloud to students. It is important that teachers make purposeful decisions about the uses of read-alouds in their teaching. However, the uses of read-alouds are broad and varied. This seemingly simple practice can be adapted for many different purposes and genres, and can become a meaningful part of literacy instruction, as "the instruction and conversation are woven in with the reading aloud of the text" (Barrentine, 1996, p. 38). Consider the ways the following uses of read-alouds might be integrated into larger classroom structures and practices.

To Grow Discussion

To Launch a Unit

Read-alouds can be used to introduce and launch units of study and ideas or habits of mind about which students think and talk. In particular, interactive read-alouds create a space where meaning is constructed through dialogue and classroom interaction, providing an important opportunity for children to respond to literature in a way that builds on their strengths and scaffolds knowledge (Wiseman, 2011). Reading aloud a few short texts on a topic that they will encounter later can give students a chance to become familiar with content-specific vocabulary and important background information; they can then use this knowledge when reading denser texts on their own. In this way, read-alouds help fuse common reference points for students as they embark on project-based learning or inquiry explorations.

To Open Conversation

As Sipe (2000) explained, read-alouds are a key way to build an interpretive community with young children. Clearly, the importance of read-alouds lies not only in the listening "but [also] in talking about the ideas" (Beck & McKeown, 2001, p. 11). Accordingly, another important use of read-alouds is to introduce a big idea on which students will linger for an extended period of time. When we want our students to view topics in their full complexity, a shared reading of a meaty text, followed by discussion of varied perspectives, is a great place to start. Another key feature of such talk is the opportunity it provides for making connections among multiple texts, conversations, and experiences. These interactive conversations, ones that actively engage, become "an opportunity to construct shared understandings through the connections made visible by *intertextuality*" (Oyler & Barry, 1996, p. 328, emphasis added), the process of making conceptual links across multiple texts.

To Foster Purposeful Dialogue

One important use of read-alouds is to support students in having rich conversations around texts. Read-alouds create "ongoing conversations" (Pendergast et al., 2015, p. 65), but there are many aspects of purposeful dialogue that students may find challenging at first: how to start, how to dig deep and build an idea together, how to be respectful and generous listeners and conversationalists. Read-alouds invite a supportive space for students to practice these skills together. This is especially true inside interactive read-alouds. According to Maloch and Beutel (2010, p. 28), in one study,

> students contributed their thinking about text, holding their ideas up to the whole group to see if their thinking was consistent with, confirmed, or was extended by their peers or teacher. Interactive read-alouds, then, became a space for students to experiment with meaning-making, trying on their comprehension strategies in a space where there was immediate feedback from either peer or teacher. At the same time, the contributions students made became shared knowledge, or at least public knowledge, for the rest of the class and may have acted as catalysts for other students to share connections or ideas in the meaning-making discussion.

Through this kind of purposeful dialogue, students can use read-alouds as a space to move toward deeper meaning.

To Grow Reading Lives

To Inspire a Love of Literature

In their study, Albright and Ariail (2005) found that the most common reason teachers engage in read-alouds is to inspire a love of literature and reading. The reading of a well-written piece by someone who is familiar with and loves the text is one of the best advertisements for literacy there is. In fact, this kind of read-aloud, often called a *book talk* by expert practitioners such as Donalyn Miller (2009), Lucy Calkins (2001), and Nancie Atwell (1998), has been written about extensively as a way to hook kids into finding new books. In many classrooms and libraries, students often gravitate toward texts that they have been "sold" in the form of book talks and partial read-alouds. Beyond just modeling what fluent reading sounds like, reading something beautiful to students encourages them to engage with literature as art, and to read and listen as artists.

To Teach Reading Strategies

Another important use of read-alouds is to support readers' habits of mind and to provide a space for expert modeling or direct teaching of specific strategies (Calkins, 2001; Schickedanz & Collins, 2012). Important habits of mind for readers include envisioning, listening, fluency, expecting, monitoring/checking for understanding, activating knowledge, and creating relationships to characters (Bomer, 2011; Calkins, 2001). Mini-lessons using short read-alouds that simplify complex concepts can be powerful in helping students of any age understand important ideas. Through this process, readers can step back to make meaning with the text. Developing such habits often involves calling other texts to mind, remembering an autobiographical experience, developing/pursuing questions/lines of inquiring, interpreting, and critiquing social worlds and assumptions. Reading and thinking aloud can be one of the most concise ways to show a literary technique and reveal what an author is doing, so it holds powerful instructional value. Additionally, the kind of talk that happens during read-alouds can serve as opportunities "for students to be apprenticed into literary and active ways of engaging with text" (Maloch & Beutel, 2010, p. 28).

To Support Readers as Meaning Makers

Read-alouds can be used to grow the reading experience, to think, to have a written discussion, to participate in an oral discussion, to analyze a literary work, to write about a text for an audience, and to write in response to or out of inspiration from literature. "Your ability to fluently read a text that is inaccessible or challenging to many students aids their comprehension, vocabulary development, and enjoyment. Students can apply their mental effort to building meaning from the book instead of decoding the language" (Miller, 2009, p. 126). When students are engaged with the text and are interacting with one another and the teacher, they are able to "internalize the ability to use process and strategy information" (Barrentine, 1996, p. 38). The ultimate goal of read-alouds, which teach reading strategies that lead to active meaning making, is to enable students to take these ways of thinking back into their independent reading lives (Maloch & Beutel, 2010; McClure & Fullerton, 2017).

To Grow Writing Lives

To Teach Writing Strategies

An additional important place for read-alouds is inside genre study or writing cycles. In these situations, students are working with anchor texts, touchstone texts, and mentor texts (Bomer, 2011), but they may be unsure how to read those pieces in a way that helps them get a feel for a genre and to notice, analyze, and understand the writer's craft around the features and qualities of a particular kind of genre, to explore text features and how they work together, to develop a shared knowledge and language around the kinds of choices and moves writers make in a particular genre, or to dig deep into particular craft moves. Read-alouds can provide teachers with opportunities to model for students how they might use a mentor text to inspire and inform their own writing. The process of using a published text to help structure a work in progress can be especially useful for encouraging students to understand how another authors' work can inform, but not overtake, their own.

To Provide Mentor Texts

Read-alouds can also help to create a shared textual experience for students to draw on later, as they write under the influence of fantastic language (Ray, 2006). To write under this influence involves multiple steps—collecting, selecting a topic, writing like a professional writer of this genre, revising, and editing. This provides another way to describe the process of using mentor texts to inform and support our own writing, without copying them or strictly adhering to them as formulas. "Focused read-alouds can be a valuable method for scaffolding genre knowledge" (Bradley & Donovan, 2010, p. 259). They further elaborated:

> A teacher knowledgeable of genre elements, features, and organizational patterns will be able to routinely direct young students' attention to them during read-alouds within meaningful contexts, to assess student compositions for the ways in which the students apply these insights, and to invite students to examine their own texts for elements, features, and organization as well. This link between instruction and assessment has potential to improve instruction and writing, thus broadening and supporting young students' informational genre knowledge in important ways. (p. 259)

Within read-alouds, teachers can point out important features of texts and model the thought process writers use as they integrate these features into their own work.

To Celebrate Student Writing

Read-alouds do not need to be limited to published, commercial texts. Reading aloud from writing that was created by students in the learning community, sometimes described as *local texts* (Maloch, Hoffman, & Patterson, 2012), is a powerful way to engage students in learning and writing. Deb Kelt (personal communication, April 18, 2015), a former high school English teacher and the current director of a National Writing Project (NWP; 2019) affiliate site, advocates for using student work in read-alouds to teach a new writing strategy, model an effective craft move, or to celebrate the loveliness of the work. Choosing read-alouds from student writing implicitly reinforces their writer identity by placing their work alongside and in conversation with the work of (published) authors.

Implications for Practice

Read-alouds should not be the only way students engage with texts in classrooms, but they are an important pedagogical tool. In order to make sure they are effective, read-alouds should be thoughtfully planned as part of instruction, just like any other part of teaching. While some people might (mistakenly) think of read-alouds as a teacher-centered practice, they are truly a "way of apprenticing students into an active stance toward a text" as teachers engage in "making space for students' ideas and positioning students as more active participants in the reading process" (Maloch & Beutel, 2010, p. 28). When educators take the time to choose text carefully and think about their intent, read-alouds can serve as an intentional space for inviting controversy and diverse viewpoints. To consider more deeply the views represented inside of read-aloud experiences, we turn next to questions of text selection.

Selecting Diverse Books for Read-Alouds

Classrooms increasingly are becoming linguistically, racially, and ethnically diverse (National Center for Educational Statistics, 2010). Learning to teach in ways that support all students' backgrounds, communities, and identities is an essential goal for all educational enterprise, not a secondary consideration. For example, youth in lesbian, gay, bisexual, transexual, queer, and related communities (LGBTQ+) have few supports to help them navigate challenging experiences in schools. One shocking study revealed that 39% of LGBTQ+ students have heard offensive and homophobic comments made by teachers and staff (Kosciw & Diaz, 2008). Compounding this problem, studies have pointed to the absence of LGBTQ+ characters and authors in textbooks (Hermann-Wilmarth, 2007). Students who identify as being outside of the cisgender, heteronormative mainstream would benefit greatly from engaging in read-alouds that center around characters who embody similar identities; however, these books are rarely found in classrooms.

It is essential that students see themselves reflected in texts. One important point of emphasis is that most people identify with more than one group or label, and our identities are often intersectional rather than static. Smolkin and Young (2011) found that many textbooks' definition of multiculturalism or diversity are narrowly focused on representations of people of color. They further noted many missed opportunities to honor intersectional identities, stating,

> Jacqueline Woodson exemplifies complexity in diversity, existing at the intersections of race, class . . . gender . . . [and sexual orientation]. Woodson is not unique, in that other LGBT authors of color exist, but she has been outspoken about her status for quite some time, and her writings appear in journals that children's literature textbook authors generally read. (p. 223)

Still, in their analysis of elementary literature textbooks, Smolkin and Young (2011) could not find a single example that identified Woodson as a lesbian woman of color. This erasure demonstrates how intersectional positions (Crenshaw, 1989)—those that consider the relationships among race, sexual orientation, and gender expression—are still rarely communicated to students.

Regarding the importance of diverse books, Bishop (1990) wrote about the importance of providing multicultural literature, books in which students can see themselves (mirrors) and develop understandings of others (windows):

> Books are sometimes windows, offering views of worlds that may be real or imagined, familiar or strange. These windows are also sliding glass doors, and readers have only to walk through in imagination to become part of whatever world has been created or recreated by the author. When lighting conditions are just right, however, a window can also be a mirror. Literature transforms human experience and

reflects it back to us, and in that reflection we can see our own lives and experiences as part of the larger human experience. Reading, then, becomes a means of self-affirmation, and readers often seek their mirrors in books. (p. ix)

Recently, the call for multicultural literature that focuses more pointedly on issues of race, power, and oppression, and books that either focus on these issues or lend themselves to examining them, has been taken up by scholars (Brooks & Cueto, 2018). Building on Bishop's work, Tschida, Ryan, and Ticknor (2014) combined the concept of mirrors with Adichie's (2009) notion of moving beyond the *single story* or one-dimensional portrait of a group or culture. According to the authors, windows and mirrors "highlight the power of being included or excluded from the representations around you" and the notion of the single story focuses on naming "the reductive and limited stories of historical events, people, or cultural narratives, and expanding these with multiple layers of diverse perspectives" (p. 36) with the use of a variety of text types and genres.

Instructional Opportunities and Text Sets for Read-Alouds

How might this look in classrooms? Here we turn to three models: one for elementary, one for middle, and one for high school grades. We include text sets and describe ways to envision instruction.

Text Set for Elementary Grades: Migrations

The sample text set for elementary grades (see Table 10.1) focuses on *migrations*, which we define broadly as movement of people from one place to another, and how they affect children. These books are mirrors for some children and windows for others. Furthermore, exposure to many stories of migration experiences, and time to read and talk about them, help build community, develop empathy, and build multidimensional, complex portraits of the diverse peoples and their varied experience rather than a single story.

In this set, we include books that tell migration stories from a variety of countries and cultures and from various perspectives, including migrations within countries (*The Great Migration*), migrations from one country to another, and transnational or back-and-forth migrations (*Migrant*).

TABLE 10.1. Text Set for Elementary Grades: Migrations

Picture books and graphic texts fiction

Danticat, E. (2015). *Mama's nightingale: A story of immigration and separation* (L. Staub, Illus.). New York: Dial.

Diaz, J. (2018). *Islandborn* (L. Espinosa, Illus.). New York: Penguin Young Readers Group.

Kim, P. (2013). *Here I am* (S. Sánchez, Illus.). North Mankato, MN: Capstone.

Laínez, R. (2013). *From north to south/del norte al sur* (J. Cepeda, Illus.). San Francisco: Children's Book Press.

Mateo, J. (2014). *Migrant: The journey of a Mexican worker* (J. Martínez, Illus.). New York: Abrams.

Mobin-Uddin, A. (2005). *My name is Bilal* (B. Kiwak, Illus.). Honesdale, PA: Boyd's Mill Press.

Ringgold, F. (2016). *We came to America*. New York: Penguin/Random House.

Ruurs, M. (2016). *Stepping stones: A refugee family's journey* (N. Badr, Illus.). Olympia, WA: Orca.

Tarbescu, E. (1998). *Annushka's voyage* (B. Degen, Illus.). New York: Clarion.

Tonatiuh, D. (2013). *Pancho Rabbit and the coyote: A migrant's tale* (D. Tonatiuh, Illus.). New York: Abrams.

Trottier, M. (2011). *Migrant* (I. Arsenault, Illus.). Toronto: Groundwood.

Picture book information and memoir

Coy, J. (2016). *Their great gift: Courage, sacrifice, and hope in a new land* (W. Huie, photographs). Minneapolis, MN: Carolrhoda.

Landowe, Y. (Author and Illustrator). (2010). *Mali under the night sky: A Lao story of home*. El Paso, TX: Cinco Puntos.

McCarney, R. (Author and Photographer). (2017). *Where will I live?* Toronto: Second Story Press.

Novels/chapter books

Alvarez, J. (2010). *Return to sender*. New York: Yearling.

Gratz, A. (2017). *Refugee*. New York: Scholastic.

Dumas, F. (2016). *It ain't so awful, Falafel*. New York: Houghton-Mifflin.

Lai, T. (2011). *Inside out and back again*. New York: HarperCollins.

Poetry

Argueta, J. (2016). *Somos como las nubes/We are like the clouds* (A. Ruano, Illus.) Toronto: Groundwood.

Greenfield, E. (2011). *The great migration: Journey to the north* (J. Gilchrist, Illus.). New York: HarperCollins.

We include books that focus on various reasons for migration, including seeking work (*Pancho Rabbit and the Coyote: A Migrant's Tale*), and fleeing to escape war or persecution (*Annushka's Voyage, Inside Out and Back Again, Stepping Stones*). Many of the texts focus on the effects of migrations on families and children, including books about children missing or dreaming of their home countries (*Islandborn, Here I Am*), dangerous journeys (*Migrant: The Journey of a Mexican Worker*), and fears and difficult adjustments faced by refugee children and their families, including loss of identity and language, religious persecution, bullying, and racism (*My Name Is Bilal*).

In keeping with the theme of representing a range of stories, we include books from a variety of countries (e.g., El Salvador, Mexico, Russia, Iran, Syria, Vietnam, Laos) and representing multidimensional views of ethnic groups that are often *essentialized,* or viewed as all having the same narrow set of experiences and views. The books address migration stories across more than a century, including the turn of the 19th century to the 20th century (*Annushka's Voyage*), the 1920s (*The Great Migration*), the 1960s and 1970s (*Mali under the Night Sky, Inside Out and Back Again*) and the 1990s (*It Ain't So Awful, Falafel*). Modern-day accounts focus on the current political climate, in which immigrants are viewed with suspicion and are increasingly subject to racism and discrimination and the danger of deportation leading to family separations (*Mama Nightingale, From North to South, Return to Sender*).

Several books contain multiple stories. For example, *Their Great Gift: Courage, Sacrifice, and Hope in a New Land,* includes true portraits of everyday life over 30 years in one neighborhood of immigrants from a wide range of countries and cultures. The photos and lyrical text address common experiences of family and community life, along with the hardships of language and culture shifts, employment, and discrimination. Through poetic text and vibrant paintings, *We Came to America* addresses many of the same themes, along with loss of freedoms, identities, and languages.

Text Set for Middle and High School: LGTBQ+

The sample text set for middle grades (see Table 10.2) focuses on LGBTQ+ experiences. Although the prestigious Stonewall Book Award is defined as the "first and most enduring award for GLBT books" (American Library Association, n.d.), we choose the initials LGBTQ+ in our current work in recognition of the expansive, fluid, and nonbinary ways that gender and sexuality can be defined as parts of the human experience. Although we view the role of LGBTQ+ allies as essential in moving toward social progress and equity, in keeping with our emphasis on culturally sustaining practices, we have chosen to foreground books written by authors who identify as members of the LGBTQ+ community.

Some texts (e.g., *And Tango Makes Three; Will Grayson, Will Grayson*) encourage readers to consider sexual preference and identity. It is important to include representations of same-sex couples who take on

---

TABLE 10.2. Text Set for Middle and High School: LGTBQ+

Picture books

Johnson, M. E. (2015). *Large fears* (K. Daye, Illus.). No publisher identified.

Richardson, J., & Parnell, P. (2005). *And Tango makes three* (H. Cole, Illus.). New York: Simon & Schuster.

Novels

Beam, C. (2012). *I am J.* New York: Little, Brown.

Block, F. L. (2014). *Love in the time of global warming.* New York: Macmillan/Square Fish.

Brezenoff, S. (2014). *Brooklyn burning.* Minneapolis, MN: Carolrhoda Books.

Gino, A. (2017). *George.* New York: Scholastic.

Green, J., & Levithan, D. (2010). *Will Grayson, Will Grayson.* London: Penguin.

LaCour, N. (2017). *We are okay.* London: Penguin/Dutton.

Monster, S. R., & Stotts, T. (Eds.). (2015). *Beyond: The queer sci-fi and fantasy comic anthology.* Portland, OR: Beyond Press.

Murphy, J. (2017). *Ramona blue.* New York: HarperCollins Children/Balzer & Bray.

Peters, J. A. (2004). *Luna.* New York: Little, Brown.

Sáenz, B. A. (2012). *Aristotle and Dante discover the secrets of the universe.* New York: Simon & Schuster.

Wittlinger, E. (2007). *Parrotfish.* New York: Simon & Schuster.

Woodson, J. (1995) *From the notebooks of Melanin Sun.* New York: Puffin.

Informational texts

Jennings, J. (2016). *Being Jazz: My life as a (transgender) teen.* Toronto: Penguin/Random House/Ember.

Luklin, S. (2015). *Beyond Magenta: Transgender teens speak out.* Somerville, MA: Candlewick Press.

Mardell, A. (2016). *The ABC'S of LGBT+.* Miami, FL: Mango Media.

Short stories

Bauer, M. D., & Underwood, B. (Eds.). (1995). *Am I blue?: Coming out from the silence.* New York: Harper Teen.

the role of parents and caregivers, as well as texts in which same-sex couples and gay and lesbian characters exist as young people. Many of the stories on this list focus on LGBTQ+ characters as protagonists or as taking a leading role; however, it is also important to include stories in which peripheral characters and antagonists are LGBTQ+ to invite a more nuanced view of the LGBTQ+ community.

Other texts encourage readers to consider gender. For example, *Brooklyn Burning* follows "Kid" and "Scout" over two intense summers. While this may seem like a classic action/adventure story, the author never reveals the gender identity of the two main characters. This encourages readers to consider what they draw on as they envision and imagine these characters in different ways.

Some texts, both fiction and informational, highlight transgender experiences (e.g., *I am J.; Luna; Parrotfish*). *George* is a novel that focuses on a young person who is beginning to experience dissonance related to gender and uses a class production of *Charlotte's Web* as a space to enact their identity. *Beyond Magenta: Transgender Teens Speak Out* is a compilation of six biographies of transgender and/or gender-neutral teens. Both texts create spaces for read-alouds to invite reconsideration of outdated, restrictive, and oppressive conceptualizations of gender.

Text Set for High School: #BlackLivesMatter

The sample text set for high school readers and teachers (see Table 10.3) focuses on #BlackLivesMatter. Whether teaching in a school with minoritized students or in a predominately white or privileged context, texts that thoughtfully take on issues of diversity, equity, and inclusion are of the utmost importance in our current social climate. The argument for the importance of teaching about social justice through this present movement for racial justice has been made eloquently in many other places, particularly in an article by Jamilah Pitts (2017) titled "Why Teaching Black Lives Matter Matters" in *Teaching Tolerance,* so instead in this section we focus on why these particular texts have been selected and grouped together for this specific list. In compiling the list, we kept in mind Tim Wise's (2011) advice to teach about "the issue of racism and discrimination through a lens of resistance and allyship, rather than a lens of oppression and victimization" (p. 264).

Many of the books selected are picture books, but we believe that this is an important genre to bring into the secondary setting in strategic and purposeful ways through mini-lessons or in introductions to new units on

TABLE 10.3. Text Set for High School: #BlackLivesMatter

Fiction

Magoon, K. (2014). *How it went down.* New York: Square Fish.

Powell, P. H. (2017). *Loving vs. Virginia: A documentary novel of the landmark civil rights case* (S. Strickland, Illus.). San Francisco: Chronicle Books.

Reynolds, J., & Kiely, B. (2015). *All American boys: A novel.* New York: Antheneum Books for Young Readers.

Stone, N. (2017). *Dear Martin: A novel.* New York: Crown Books for Young Readers.

Thomas, A. (2017). *The hate u give.* New York: Balzer + Bray.

Graphic novels

Baker, K. (2008). *Nat Turner.* New York: Abrams ComicArts.

Coates, T. (2016). *Black panther.* New York: Marvel.

Lewis, J., Aydin, A., & Powell, N. (2016). *March.* Marietta, GA: Top Shelf Productions.

Medina, T. (2017). *I am Alfonso Jones* (S. Robinson & J. Hennings, Illus.). New York: Tu Books.

Nonfiction texts

Coates, T. (2015). *Between the world and me.* New York: Spiegel & Grau.

Hoose, P. (2009). *Claudette Colvin: Twice toward justice.* New York: Square Fish.

Partridge, E. (2009). *Marching for freedom: Walk together, children, and don't you grow weary.* New York: Viking.

Robinson, P. (2016). *You can't touch my hair: And other things I still have to explain.* New York: Plume Press.

Sheinkin, S. (2014). *The port Chicago 50: Disaster, mutiny, and the fight for civil rights.* New York: Roaring Books Press.

Picture books

hooks, b. (2004). *Skin again* (C. Raschka, Illus.). New York: Jump at the Sun.

Latham, I., & Waters, C. (2018). *Can I touch your hair: Poems of race, mistakes, and friendship* (S. Qualls & S. Aiko, Illus.). Minneapolis, MN: Carolrhoda Books.

Lester, J. (2005). *Let's talk about race* (K. Barbour, Illus.) New York: Armistad.

Nagara, I. (2013). *A is for activist.* New York: Seven Stories Press.

social justice. Books such as *A is for Activist, Skin Again, Can I Touch Your Hair: Poems of Race, Mistakes, and Friendship,* and *Let's Talk About Race* can be used to initiate important conversations about race and racism, differences and similarities, liberation movements, activism, and allyship and relationships in ways that invite all members of the classroom learning community to think together about these crucial concepts.

Other texts are more focused on contemporary issues and invite conversations about the #BlackLivesMatter movement and police brutality.

Books such as *Dear Martin, All American Boys, How It Went Down, I am Alfonso Jones,* and *The Hate U Give* are all well-regarded, widely read novels that have "gone viral" with young readers because of the honesty and sensitivity with which they deal with our current historical moment. Two of these books, *All American Boys* and *How It Went Down,* are told from multiple perspectives and invite meaningful conversations about point of view, experience, and responsibility.

Some texts in this collection look back through time to focus on important moments in civil rights history (*March; Loving vs. Virginia; Nat Turner; The Port Chicago 50; Claudette Colvin: Twice Toward Justice; Marching for Freedom*). These texts were selected because they offer up narratives of resistance that aren't often highlighted. History is taken up in other ways by *Between the World and Me,* which explores oppression and resistance through personal history, while *Black Panther* invites us into an alternative history to think about how the world could be otherwise, without the legacy of imperialism and colonization.

Conclusion

While reflecting on the text sets that we curated, we struggled with the fact that we are each white, straight, cisgender female literacy educators attempting to do this work. We each gathered together a collection books written by diverse authors that reflected lives different than our own and experiences that we may not have as a result of our privilege. We wanted to acknowledge this, while also connecting back to the importance of culturally sustaining pedagogy. In selecting these texts, we are actively choosing to create inclusive learning communities by selecting texts that offer opportunities to spend time with myriad perspectives and that are "advancing disadvantaged groups" (Bomer, 2017, p. 13). To this end, we urge you to

> trust the books, trust the students, and trust yourself. Wonderful books offer innumerable opportunities for talking about an author's work. When something is important in a book, you can be sure that children will talk about it and that you will notice it as well—if not one day, then another. Expect that you and your students will surprise and delight yourselves with your knowledge. (Eeds & Peterson, 1991, pp. 125–126)

● IMPLICATIONS FOR PROFESSIONAL LEARNING: ● FOSTERING PURPOSEFUL DIALOGUE

- Dedicate time and space for shared meaning making with text.
- Choose books carefully and intentionally by looking for well-written texts about meaningful, relevant topics.
- Emphasize active negotiation of meaning through listening to others and building on their ideas.
- Position students as capable people with positive intentions who have the capacity to "figure things out" for themselves.
- Make space for students to do most of the talking, and encourage students to initiate the conversation. Make your own voice one of many rather than dominating the conversation.
- Provide personalized space for students to express their ideas. Consider including responses through writing and composing, in addition to discussion.
- Encourage students to think and respond critically.
- Encourage diverse viewpoints, and teach students to engage respectfully when differences arise.

QUESTIONS FOR DISCUSSION

1. The basic definition of a *read-aloud* is "a fluent adult reader reading an appropriately selected text to a child or group of children" (Mitchell et al., 2012, p. 278). In what ways can we view that simple pedagogy as taking on a dynamic life inside our classrooms? How might read-alouds "look" in your classroom?

2. Why do you think read-alouds tend to disappear as students progress through school?

3. What kinds of considerations do you think are important when planning a read-aloud?

4. If you were asked by another stakeholder (parent, administrator, colleague, etc.) to defend the practice of read-alouds in your teaching context, what might you say? What kinds of reasons for engaging in read-alouds do you think are most convincing?

REFERENCES

Adichie, C. N. (2009). The danger of a single story [Video speech]. Retrieved from *www.ted.com/talks/chimamanda_adichie_the_danger_of_a_single_story.htm*.

Albright, L. K., & Ariail, M. (2005). Tapping the potential of teacher read-alouds in middle schools. *Journal of Adolescent and Adult Literacy, 48*(7), 582–591.

American Library Association. (n.d.). Stonewall Book Awards. Retrieved from *www.ala.org/rt/glbtrt/award/stonewall*.

Anderson, R. C., Hiebert, E. H., Scott, J. A., & Wilkinson, I. A. G. (1985). *Becoming a nation of readers: The report of the Commission on Reading.* Washington, DC: National Institute of Education.

Apple, M. W. (2004). *Ideology and curriculum* (3rd ed.). New York: Routledge.

Ariail, M., & Albright, L. K. (2006). A survey of teachers' read-aloud practices in middle schools. *Reading Research and Instruction, 45*(2), 69–90.

Atwell, N. (1998). *In the middle: New understandings about writing, reading, and learning.* Portsmouth, NH: Boynton/Cook.

Barrentine, S. J. (1996). Engaging with interactive read-alouds. *The Reading Teacher, 50*(1), 36–43.

Beck, I. L., & McKeown, M. G. (2001). Text Talk: Capturing the benefits of read-aloud experiences for young children. *The Reading Teacher, 55*(1), 10–20.

Bishop, R. (1990). Mirrors, windows, and sliding glass doors. *New Perspectives, 6*(3), 9–11.

Bomer, R. (2011). *Building adolescent literacy in today's English classrooms.* Portsmouth, NH: Heinemann.

Bomer, R. (2017). What would it mean for English language arts to become more culturally responsive and sustaining? *Voices from the Middle, 24*(3), 11–15.

Bomer, R., & Bomer, K. (2001). *For a better world: Reading and writing for social action.* Portsmouth, NH: Heinemann.

Brabham, E. G., & Lynch-Brown, C. (2002). Effects of teachers reading aloud styles on vocabulary acquisition and comprehension of students in the early elementary grades. *Journal of Educational Psychology, 94*(3), 465–473.

Bradley, L. G., & Donovan, C. A. (2010). Information book read-alouds as models for second-grade authors. *The Reading Teacher, 64*(4), 246–260.

Brooks, W., & Cueto, D. (2018). Contemplating and extending the scholarship on children's and young adult literature. *Journal of Literacy Research, 50*(1), 9–30.

Calkins, L. M. (2001). *The art of teaching reading.* New York: Addison-Wesley.

Crenshaw, K. (1989). Demarginalizing the intersection of race and sex: A Black feminist critique of antidiscrimination doctrine. *University of Chicago Legal Forum, 1989*, 139–168.

Dreher, S. (2003). A novel idea: Reading aloud in a high school English classroom. *English Journal, 93*(1), 50–53.

Eeds, M., & Peterson, R. (1991). Teacher as curator: Learning to talk about literature. *The Reading Teacher, 45*(2), 118–126.

Hermann-Wilmarth, J. M. (2007). Full inclusion: Understanding the role of gay and lesbian texts and films in teacher education classrooms. *Language Arts, 84*, 347–356.

Hoffman, J. V., Roser, N. L., & Battle, J. (1993). Reading aloud in classrooms: From the modal toward a "model." *The Reading Teacher, 46*(6), 496–503.

Iser, W. (1972). The reading process: A phenomenological approach. *New Literary History, 3*(2), 279–299.

Kosciw, J. G., & Diaz, E. M. (2008). Involved, invisible, ignored: The experiences of lesbian, gay, bisexual, and transgender parents and their children in our nation's K–12 schools. Retrieved from *www.glsen.org/learn/research/national/report-iii*.

Laminack, L. (2017). Read often and well. *Voices from the Middle, 24,* 33–35.

Laminack, L. L., & Wadsworth, R. M. (2006). *Reading aloud across the curriculum: How to build bridges in language arts, math, science, and social studies.* Portsmouth, NH: Heinemann.

Maloch, B., & Beutel, D. D. (2010). "Big loud voice. You have important things to say": The nature of student initiations during one teacher's interactive read-alouds. *Journal of Classroom Interaction, 45*(2), 20–29.

Maloch, B., Hoffman, J. V., & Patterson, E. U. (2012). Local texts: Reading and writing "of the classroom." In J. V. Hoffman & D. L. Schallert (Eds.), *The texts in elementary classrooms* (pp. 29–138). Mahwah, NJ: Erlbaum.

May, L. (2011). Animating talk and texts: Culturally relevant teacher read-alouds of informational texts. *Journal of Literacy Research, 43*(1), 3–38.

May, L. A., Bingham, G. E., & Pendergast, M. L. (2014). Culturally and linguistically relevant read-alouds. *Multicultural Perspectives, 16*(4), 210–218.

McClure, E. L., & Fullerton, S. K. (2017). Instructional interactions: Supporting students' reading development through interactive read-alouds of informational texts. *The Reading Teacher, 71*(1), 51–59.

McNair, J. (2016). #WeNeedMirrorsAndWindows: Diverse classroom libraries for K–6 students. *The Reading Teacher, 70,* 375–381.

Miller, D. (2009). *The book whisperer: Awakening the inner reader in every child.* San Francisco: Jossey-Bass.

Mitchell, K., Homza, A., & Ngo, S. (2012). Reading aloud with bilingual learners: A fieldwork project and its impact on mainstream teacher candidates. *Action in Teacher Education, 34,* 276–294.

National Center for Education Statistics. (2010). The condition of education 2010 (Report). Retrieved from *http://nces.ed.gov/pubsearch/pubsinfo.asp?pubid=2010028*.

National Writing Project. (2019). NWP sites. Retrieved from *www.nwp.org/cs/public/print/doc/sites.csp*.

Nikolajeva, M. (2005). *Aesthetic approaches to children's literature: An introduction.* Lanham, MD: Scarecrow Press.

Oyler, C., & Barry, A. (1996). Intertextual connections in read-alouds of information books. *Language Arts, 73*(5), 324–329.

Paris, D. (2012). Culturally sustaining pedagogy: A needed change in stance, terminology, and practice. *Educational Researcher, 41*(3), 93–97.

Paris, D., & Alim, H. S. (2017). *Culturally sustaining pedagogies: Teaching and learning for justice in a changing world.* New York: Teachers College Press.

Pegg, L. A., & Bartelheim, F. J. (2011). Effects of daily read-alouds on students' sustained silent reading. *Current Issues in Education, 14*(2), 1–7.

Pendergast, M., May, L., Bingham, G., & Kurumada, K. S. (2015). Acquiring responsive practices: Preservice teachers learn to conduct interactive read-alouds. *Action in Teacher Education, 37*(1), 65–81.

Pitts, J. (2017). Why teaching Black Lives Matter matters: Part I. Retrieved from *www.tolerance.org/magazine/summer-2017/why-teaching-black-lives-matter-matters-part-i*.

Ray, K. W. (2006). *Study driven: A framework for planning units of study in the writing workshop*. Portsmouth, NH: Heinemann.

Richardson, J. S. (2000). *Read it aloud!: Using literature in the secondary content classroom*. Newark, DE: International Reading Association.

Richardson, J. S., & Cantrell, R. J. (1996). A read-aloud for English classrooms. *Journal of Adolescent and Adult Literacy, 39*(8), 680–683.

Rosenblatt, L. M. (1978). *The reader, the text, the poem: The transactional theory of the literary work*. Carbondale: Southern Illinois University Press.

Rosenblatt, L. (1995). *Literature as exploration*. New York: Modern Language Association.

Schickedanz, J. A., & Collins, M. F. (2012). For young children, pictures in storybooks are rarely worth a thousand words. *The Reading Teacher, 65*(8), 539–549.

Sipe, L. R. (2000). The construction of literary understanding by first and second graders in oral response to picture storybook read-alouds. *Reading Research Quarterly, 35*(2), 252–275.

Smolkin, L. B., & Donovan, C. A. (2001). The contexts of comprehension: The information book read-alouds, comprehension acquisition, and comprehension instruction in a first-grade classroom. *Elementary School Journal, 102*(2), 97–122.

Smolkin, L. B., & Young, C. A. (2011). Missing mirrors, missing windows: Children's literature textbooks and LGBT topics. *Language Arts, 88*(3), 217–225.

Swanson, E., Vaughn, S., Wanzek, J., Petscher, Y., Heckert, J., Cavanaugh, C., et al. (2011). A synthesis of read-alouds interventions on early reading outcomes among preschool through third graders at risk for reading difficulties. *Journal of Learning Disabilities, 44*(3), 258–275.

Teale, W. H. (1984). Reading to young children: Its significance for literacy development. In J. Goelman, A. A. Oberg, & F. Smith (Eds.), *Awakening to literacy* (pp. 110–121). London: Heinemann.

Tschida, C., Ryan, C., & Ticknor, A. (2014). Building on windows and mirrors: Encouraging the disruption of "single stories" through children's literature. *Journal of Children's Literature, 40*, 28–39.

Waitoller, F. R., & Thorius, K. K. (2016). Cross-pollinating culturally sustaining pedagogy and Universal Design for Learning: Toward an inclusive pedagogy that accounts for dis/ability. *Harvard Educational Review, 86*(3), 366–389.

Wise, T. (2011). *White like me: Reflections on race from a privileged son* (2nd ed.). New York: Soft Skull Press.

Wiseman, A. (2011). Interactive read-alouds: Teachers and students constructing knowledge and literacy together. *Early Childhood Education Journal, 38*(6), 431–438.

Worthy, J., Chamberlain, K., Peterson, K., Sharp, C., & Shih, P. (2012). The importance of read-aloud and dialogue in an era of narrowed curriculum: An examination of literature discussions in a second-grade classroom. *Literacy Research and Instruction, 51*, 308–322.

Worthy, J., Durán, L., Pruitt, A., Hikida, M., & Peterson, K. (2013). Spaces for dynamic bilingualism in literature discussions: Developing and strengthening bilingual and academic skills. *Bilingual Research Journal, 36*, 311–328.

CHAPTER 11

What's Involved in Preparing Students for Workplace Writing Success?
Linking Conceptual and Practical Knowledge

MARIA GRANT
DIANE LAPP
THOMAS DeVERE WOLSEY

During their school years, students are often asked to share information through descriptive and argumentative essays, but once they are launched into the world of work, many also need to know how to share information through data charts, advertisements, briefs, or blogs. Each of these formats requires knowing the information well, then deciding how to communicate most effectively with the targeted audience. Stated another way, the writing tasks that occur in the workplace often integrate the type of thinking that is evident in argumentative and other critical writing tasks found in school, but they frequently take different forms for different purposes.

Given this reality, we wondered whether schools are preparing students to write within and across the disciplines using formats common in work situations. To investigate this, we asked 18 professionals from the fields of science, engineering, health and medicine, cosmetology, advertising, plumbing, music, and art two questions: "What type of writing formats do you use most frequently at work?" and "How well did school prepare you for on-the-job writing?" After interviewing each person, we listened to and coded the recordings to identify the general literacies these professionals felt were needed to successfully communicate in their work situations.

Then we listened again to more specifically identify what type of writing literacies these professionals believed they needed to succeed in their professions. Once we had completed this constant-comparative analysis of data (Bogdan & Biklen, 2002), we identified categories of writing elements needed for success in each profession and, more specifically, five common elements needed in all of the professions. We shared the common elements with 20 teachers in grades 2–12 and asked them to identify what types of instruction they believed would ensure that students learn writing skills to support their future workplace success. The answers these teachers provided can inspire fellow educators' efforts as they help students develop the conceptual knowledge they need for workplace writing. Students and employers often find a disconnect between the writing tasks in school and the writing tasks in the workplace. This disconnect need not exist. The critical and deep thinking that informs school writing tasks can be found in the workplace as well. In this chapter, we seek to bridge writing for school and writing in the workplace.

Experts Describe Workplace Literacy Practices

Finding experts from various disciplines who wanted to participate was easier than we thought it would be. We tried to identify experts who represented a broad range of disciplines. In some cases, these experts were friends or colleagues; in other cases, we simply reached out to experts who had participated in other projects in which literacy and the disciplines were represented. Similarly, we found that our literacy-minded colleagues were more than eager to participate as interviewers (Lapp & Wolsey, 2016).

Here is what the experts said about workplace literacy skills. Words have meaning; they have specific, often technical, meanings that are rooted in the discipline. The experts we interviewed expressed the notion that communication, using language from the discipline, is essential; "It's how we get things done at work," shared one scientist. In particular, what professionals write about depends on their purpose, and the content and mode of communication depend on their intent. Each of the experts highlighted the need for language precision to communicate information or ideas in ways that are unique to the discipline. For example, artists use language to describe color and to communicate with customers. The artist we interviewed shared that she uses words to clarify and develop a mutual understanding of terms such as *contemporary* and *abstract*. Because words can signal different ideas from different customers, she must move patrons from nebulous meanings to more granular, precise understandings. In this way, she can ensure that what she creates fits with customers' understandings and expectations.

Likewise, the musician might need to flesh out arrangements with bandmates, producers, or a conductor. He or she documents the arrangements using notations that are specific to the discipline. Such explicit uses of literacy were also offered by the advertising expert, who explained how she gathers information about a client and about her competitors' products to create a prototype that offers the client exactly what is needed, but with features that go beyond competitors' current models or conceptions. The cosmetologist–business owner explained that when she reads a resume, she looks for the author to be precise and to share information that is creative yet identifies the applicant's preparation in a very explicit way, while also communicating how he feels he can make a contribution through their work together. As evidenced by these professionals, when speaking to an audience of listeners or readers, one needs to know how to convey ideas in ways that are appropriate, precise, and meaningful.

As we moved from a general analysis of all of the literacies used in the workplace to a more specific analysis of the comments of each expert regarding the type of writing that is a part of his or her job, we concluded that there are five common elements informing their workplace writing. We also asked teachers to comment on these elements; the participants were generally educators we know, and in each case, they were excited about the possibilities the project offered. These teachers confirmed that the elements were considered to be major characteristics used by good writers in their disciplines and identified how these could be addressed effectively during classroom instruction. Here's what we found.

Workplace Writing

Element 1: Know Thy Purpose (for Writing)

What the Disciplinary Experts Said

As a whole, experts across the disciplines noted that effective writers must have a clear understanding of the purpose for their writing task. Whether the text is a laboratory report, a company newsletter, an online discussion with a manager, a call to service, an agenda, or a description of a piece of art, once the purpose is identified, the author is able to consider characteristics of the audience and set about crafting a piece to confirm, convince, network, or share information with like-minded individuals or ones who need to be persuaded.

Teacher Experts Responded

When asked about the importance of purpose setting for writing, teachers across the grades and disciplines agreed that knowing one's purpose is a major and initial element of any successful writing task. They identified the following ways to teach purpose setting.

VIEW MODELS

Students must be shown models of writing, including memos, blogs, e-mails, reports, and so forth. The language, the style, the need for illustrations or charts—all become apparent when appropriate models are shared and the purpose for writing is discussed. A teacher might conduct a think-aloud to illustrate how to identify purpose and audience. This information dictates the tone and the language style. One third-grade teacher explained that she has students explore gardening websites when she is asking them to propose a team design for a garden with plants that will attract butterflies and hummingbirds. Many of the websites include illustrations of plants with flowers that are enticing to these pollinators. Students get a sense of the purpose and of the options as they plan for a garden.

IDENTIFY SYNTAX AND STYLE

Students must be taught to write for the appropriate audiences by critically thinking through the process of writing and using the nuances of each text type and language style. For example, a ninth-grade math teacher stated that in order to think critically in math, students must first identify what is being asked in the problem and what type of information is needed to arrive at a solution. For example, if the problem relates to space or volume in a math task, the writer might need to craft a diagram to accompany the text. To complete a writing task like this, students must be taught to create labeled and scaled diagrams to document what they want to have the recipient visualize in real space.

Max Jones's math class (all teachers' names are pseudonyms) provides a concrete instance of this type of instruction. He shares examples of new toaster designs, complete with diagrams that indicate the height, depth, and width of the toaster ovens, and explains how designers and engineers must consider volume when creating household appliances, because some people might want a small toaster oven to fit under a low-hanging cabinet, and others might want a larger model with a greater capacity to hold various items. Just like designers do, students draw the scaled models and label them before calculating volume. They then write about the designs, stating their advantages and assets.

PRACTICE PERSPECTIVE WRITING

Students write more effectively when they have a framework that supports the perspective they should be using. Teachers mentioned using RAFT (Santa, 1988), a popular writing prompt that stands for Role, Audience, Format, and Topic. In this strategy, students are either given or they choose a role for themselves. If this were used for workplace writing, it might be used across a broad range of professions, from commercial artist to engineer to beautician. Audience is a key element in RAFT, just as it is for any professional audience. Students can utilize their understanding of audience to help fine-tune their tone and writing style. For example, if they are writing a letter to a community board to propose safety features at a busy intersection, they might use audience-friendly language to clarify technical terms. In Malia Spellman's seventh-grade class, students researched safety features and wrote to this RAFT prompt:

> R—*Role:* A citizen of the community
> A—*Audience:* The Smalltown Community Board
> F—*Format:* A letter of request
> T—*Topic:* We need a stop sign (or round-about, stoplight, crossing guard, etc.) to keep our neighborhood safe.

Element 2: Mine Resource Features

What the Disciplinary Experts Said

Experts agreed that students should listen to, read, and view authentic texts from the discipline to understand how experts make sense of them by analyzing their use of visuals, vocabulary, and sentence structure. Successful professionals and experts select credible sources, then check them carefully to ensure that they are accurate, while also considering various points of view. Credible sources should be mined to provide the information needed to inform writing.

Teacher Experts Responded

Teachers noted that they teach students across grade levels to mine resources by modeling how to consider the followings features.

NOTE THE USE OF TEXT FEATURES

Many teachers illustrate how experts make use of reports and visuals, deal with abstractions, structure sentences, and employ specific vocabulary in their writing. These authors also synthesize ideas from an array of resources, so they can draw on the best ideas when they write. One eighth-grade physical education teacher shared the procedure she uses when having students read about rehabilitation treatments for injured ankles. Students must review a minimum of six resources, with diagrams of anatomical features of the ankle or with treatment plans documented in charts. "Keeping track of ideas from an array of resources is tricky," noted the teacher. "We use small-group discussion to identify ideas from the texts and visuals, along with a graphic organizer to help synthesize a total plan."

IDENTIFY ORGANIZATIONAL STRUCTURES

One second-grade teacher explained that she provides simple sentence frames to help students clarify what they are looking for in each resource. When students study animal anatomy for the purpose of creating diagrams for a veterinarian's office, they first talk to each other about the sources, with sentence frames such as "I am looking at this picture to find the _____ [name animal part—fin, fur, hoof, tail] from the _____ [fish, dog, horse, cow]" and "The picture shows me the _____ [paws, wings, head] of the _____ [cat, bird, snake]." This tool provides the kind of guidance that helps them focus on the goals of the assignment, along with the scaffolding needed by many young learners as they develop their comfort with specific forms of writing.

READ CLOSELY AND TAKE NOTES

All of the professionals said that before they create words and paragraphs, they must have thorough knowledge of the topic. For example, the artist we spoke to noted that when she creates a design for a client, she finds herself reading about the current trends in her field and searching literature or images for inspiration.

In Dave Williams's fifth-grade classroom, we present an analogous example of bringing knowledge about a subject into the students' developing understanding of the subject. His art students are getting ready to create impressionist-style paintings. Prior to painting, Mr. Williams provides them with two articles and a website that showcases the art of Monet, Cassatt, and other Impressionists. They must take notes on both the texts they are reviewing and on the actual art they are viewing. Mr. Williams also provides them with graphic organizer templates to help them organize the notes from these three resources (see Figure 11.1). Once they finish the notetaking, they must incorporate their learnings from the provided resources about impressionism into their own paintings.

Element 3: Be Precise and Get It Right

What the Disciplinary Experts Said

A third element that the professionals identified as crucial for their writing is the ability to offer one's position or point concisely, clearly, and completely. This involves sharing information that has been checked and rechecked. Workplace writers usually rely on facts-based rather than emotional data. Wide reading from many resources allows a writer to synthesize ideas and to select areas of focus that emerge as common themes. Extraneous language is omitted to produce concise, targeted texts.

Teacher Experts Responded

There was a consensus among the teachers that in order to communicate effectively, one must build deep knowledge that is conveyed through language that informs, inspires, or convinces readers. Teachers overwhelmingly offered the following ways to support language learning and precision in use.

TEACH VOCABULARY

Teach technical and academic vocabulary by using a variety of word learning strategies (e.g., Frayer method: IRIS, n.d.; vocabulary self-collection plus: Wolsey, Smetana, & Grisham, 2015). Vocabulary learning should also provide students many opportunities, especially written

Impressionism Notes		
Article 1 Reference (use APA formatting):	Article 2 Reference (use APA formatting):	Website Resources (use APA formatting):
Key Points: • • • • •	Key Points: • • • • •	Key Points: • • • • •
Major points found in all resources:		
Ideas for my own painting:		

FIGURE 11.1. Graphic organizer for a unit on Impressionism.

opportunities, to share feedback with their peers regarding how their language is progressively similar in style, tone, and use to that used in the discipline.

Teacher Experts Responded

Although the term *academic* vocabulary might evoke visions of schools and university libraries, we note that academic vocabulary comprises the entire lexicon used on a daily basis within the classroom. In a science class, students may refer to the capacity for molecules to "adhere" to one another, rather than just "stick"; "adhere" and "adhesion" provide a greater degree of precision than does the word *cling*, for example. However, these "academic" words are not simply abandoned when students enter the workforce. Molecular biologists, medical doctors, and chemists routinely refer to substances that exhibit the characteristic of adherence. For this reason, it is vital that students become conversant with the terms that characterize informed discourse in the various professions.

In Cara Lee's 10th-grade biology classroom, students consider science terms that both relate to their study of the circulatory system and that might also be used in work done by health care providers. They create vocabulary self-awareness charts to consider these terms as they start the unit. The vocabulary self-awareness chart affords students a sense of the terminology they will be using. They are asked to tap into their background knowledge and to consider what they already know and what they will learn. They use the chart to indicate whether they can define a series of terms and give an example (see Figure 11.2). Miss Lee's chart includes both technical and academic vocabulary, because she wants students to be able to write in a precise, focused manner, using the terms of the work world. If students don't know the definition or are unable to provide an example, they indicate that on the chart; this helps them realize the unknown terms and concepts that they will learn about as part of their studies. Miss Lee uses the vocabulary self-awareness chart as a formative assessment of her students at the start of the lesson. Later, after Miss Lee has implemented the lessons, students can go back to the charts to revise and update the terms. As an assessment of what they have learned, Miss Lee asks students to write using the terms found in the chart with the following prompt:

"You are asked to communicate information about the circulatory system to a nurse at the Pear Valley hospital. Write a memo in which

Rate My Work

A. My workplace writing is similar to models from [science, math, etc.].

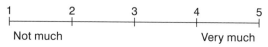

List one or two models you used to guide your writing:

B. Sources for my workplace writing are credible.

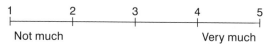

Name one or two sources you used and state why they are credible and reliable.

C. I know my purpose for writing and made that clear to my readers.

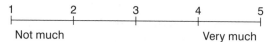

In one sentence, state the purpose for your written work.

D. I checked my sources to make sure I was precise and got the details right.

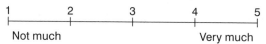

If you corrected any errors, describe them briefly.

E. The tone of my writing is conversational but also commanding. People will want to pay attention to what I wrote.

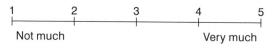

Why do you believe your writing will attract readers who want to know more about your topic?

FIGURE 11.2. Vocabulary self-awareness chart.

you succinctly and precisely explain how the circulatory system works. Use all terms in your vocabulary self-awareness chart."

INCORPORATE VISUALS

To help students appropriately support a text with figures and charts, teachers suggested having them include visuals such as inventory charts, architectural diagrams, schematics of lighting, and so forth. One fifth-grade teacher shared how his students prepared a budget chart to accompany a proposal for a client who wants to purchase musical instruments for a band program. Students then determined whether the chart would be of value to the customer. As part of their decision making, they noticed headings, labels, units, and other critical details. In this way, they were able to make a more informed decision.

GUIDE PRACTICE

Students must have opportunities to practice the stylistic elements and language of each text type until they know them well if they are going to make use of them on their own. Guided practice, with peer editing and with teacher feedback, is essential if students are to go from learning to automatic fluency when writing. For example, students in an art teacher's class, having learned about color and design, practice pitching color schemes to health care clients who are ready to hire a team to coordinate their patient waiting rooms.

Throughout this chapter, we have emphasized the need for students to experience writing in ways they may encounter in the workplace. The RAFT (Santa, 1988) approach shows us how writing prompts can be adjusted to accommodate the roles, audiences, formats, and topics student writers might encounter in the workplace. Guided practice gives students a low-risk environment in which to practice thinking about these features and building their abilities to write for varying purposes and audiences.

Element 4: Use a Conversational Yet Decisive Tone to Move Readers to Action

What the Disciplinary Experts Said

There was agreement among the disciplinary experts that writers must share their positions in a way that invites a professional response, encourages questions, and, while not off-putting, demonstrates credibility and soft command. Every word that is written should be carefully chosen with the intent of moving the recipient toward the desired action. To do so involves knowing and applying the language of the discipline.

The experts clearly identified the audience, the people they intended to address, as a keystone in any writing or other communication. Our musician, Tim Peterson (experts' names are their real names) described how he often had to find a way to describe the technical terms of his discipline to others who were not professionals in ways that both respected their intelligence and used language that would be comprehensible to them. We found this to be similarly true when Liz Jardine described her interactions with clients who commission her art. This can also be seen with the engineers we interviewed, who were very often members of interdisciplinary teams. When working with experts in other fields, they often had to communicate specific and technical details in ways that their nonengineering team members could understand, since these details were relevant to the project at hand.

Teacher Experts Responded

The teachers' examples for achieving a balance of tone for the writing in their classrooms emphasizes the power of focused, explicit instructional planning, engagement, and learning.

IDENTIFY TONE

Teachers found that having students watch commercials and speeches in various disciplines allowed them to interpret tone, meaning, and requests for action. One 10th-grade teacher, for example, had students compare elements of speeches used by three civil rights activists. Through mediated discussions, they determined the tone, mood, and message of each. The students then wrote their own messages to mirror the elements they had identified in the speeches.

KNOW THY AUDIENCE

Earlier in this chapter, we explained the RAFT (Santos, 1988) writing prompt. This approach is applicable here as well. Use of the right tone for the intended audience is a skill that writers master with practice and steady guidance from their teachers and peers. In Ms. Spellman's seventh-grade class, for example, students learned that writing to persuade the

Smalltown Community Board to improve safety at a dangerous intersection meant using a tone that conveyed the seriousness of the problem, while simultaneously using language that suggested that they and the members of the board were on the same side.

Element 5: Evaluate Progress against Success Criteria

What the Disciplinary Experts Said

The comments of the experts indicate that successful writing is achieved when the recipient of the message has been moved to action. To ensure this, writers must assess their work as they write to ensure they are achieving their desired goal. They do so by continually monitoring the intended message both for powerful words and thorough presentation of their research as a means of moving the recipient to the desired action. It is critical that they have a clearly identified target, but this is not enough. Along the way, they also have to establish clear criteria to help them determine whether they are moving toward their anticipated goal. For example, the engineer we interviewed suggested that, for him, this might involve trying out design prototypes as a means of checking steps along the way. Furthermore, reflection on their work to date was a significant belief shared by all of the experts to spur forward movement.

Teacher Experts Responded

The educators we spoke with also suggested that having success criteria allows students to think closely about their work, while simultaneously reflecting on their progress or performance toward their specified end goal. They described the following means of supporting their students' growth assessment relative to identified success criteria.

WRITE FROM A PLAN

Well-written expository text typically follows a plan the writer has prepared in advance. Prewriting is more than just a "step" in a writing process. It is an opportunity to plan the shape of the work that is to come. The popular little book *The Elements of Style* by Strunk and White (2000) suggests that writers "choose a suitable design and hold to it" (p. 26). In our experience, students often do not understand why they are asked to take notes, construct an outline, or brainstorm through freewriting. Teachers can help by making clear to students that a primary purpose of prewriting is to plan their writing. Organized writing is much more likely to convey the ideas intended in a manner that will appeal to the audience.

Top-level text structures, such as the graphic organizers in Figure 11.3, are a place to begin.

While expository writing often incorporates more than one of these organizational patterns, there is often one overarching design, such as sequence or cause and effect, that can serve to organize the flow of ideas in the writing of a particular text.

CLEAN IT UP

Encourage students to do a "final sweep" of their writing to be sure the language and meaning hit the target or meet the purpose. For example, we ask students to "read up, ask around, and double-check" (Wolsey, 2014). The point of double-checking is rereading the written piece, while looking for possibly inaccurate information. While double-checking, student writers should make sure they have a firm grasp on the sources on which they relied when making assertions, and citing those sources, if appropriate. As with any writing that is intended to be read by someone other than the author, proofreading for spelling, usage, and organizational issues is important, too.

One of the more difficult tasks facing thoughtful writers is eliminating words that do not contribute to the purpose of the writing. Models of drafts from other students and from published authors can help to demonstrate the importance of eliminating words that do not contribute directly to the purpose of a particular piece (e.g., Strunk & White, 2000).

ESTABLISH SUCCESS CRITERIA

Teachers also reiterated the idea that students should check their purpose against their actual writing as they move through the process of composing. As one middle school science teacher stated, "I ask students to identify what the goals of the writing are before they even start. If it's to convince a board room of community members that their team's design for a rec center is most suitable [for a project], they need to be sure they articulated the appropriate reasons, shared the cool features, like temperature regulated rails on the pool steps, noted how they addressed community concerns, included diagrams, and discussed budgets in an easy to comprehend format."

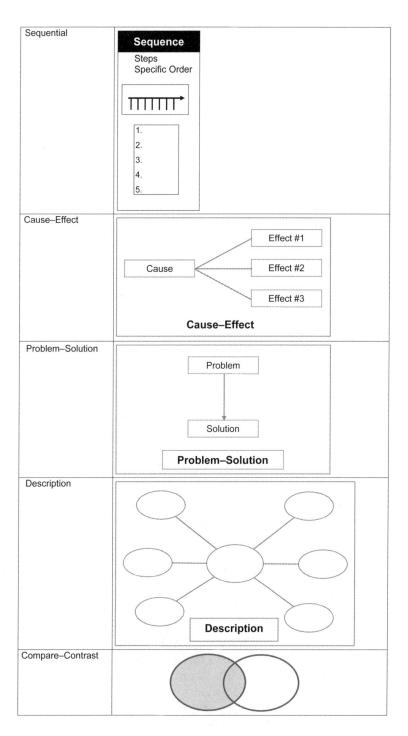

FIGURE 11.3. Types of text structures.

What Next?

Each of the five common elements are expressed in diverse ways depending on the discipline or profession. For example, knowing the writing
purpose in a science laboratory is substantially different than knowing
the purpose for writing in an advertising firm. Additionally, the types of
resources reviewed by a musician vary greatly from the briefs analyzed
by a lawyer or the notes of a colleague reviewed by a nurse who is about
to start a shift. Although different, each person's attempt to function
well in the workplace must identify and appropriately use the job-related
resources that support data collection and decision making, and promote
the way they function—and are perceived to function—as they perform
work tasks. Furthermore, the use of a conversational tone and precise
language, and the evaluation of one's progress against established success
criteria, are elements that enhance performance across disciplines. The
experts we interviewed believe that these elements ensure on-the-job
success when applied appropriately.

Feedback

As students' writing becomes increasingly more complex, particularly
those writing efforts modeled on the types of writing they will encounter
in the workplace, they need guidance from their teachers and peers. The
best time to provide that feedback is while students are actually writing;
in fact, feedback using the famous, or perhaps infamous, red pen after a
draft is complete is rarely useful. Instead, teachers should aim to meet
with their students during the writing process to provide feedback that
can be used as needed. Types of feedback include the following:

1. Simple affirmations ("Right, I agree"; "You have a well-crafted
   metaphor here").
2. Complex affirmations ("You have the right idea here
   because . . .").
3. Clarifications ("Researchers usually agree that . . ."; "In this
   context the speaker might mean . . .").
4. Observations ("I didn't know that . . ."; "Did you know
   that . . . ?").
5. Corrections to content ("When you are writing about this
   topic, you should . . ."; "Please work on or develop . . .").
6. Questions ("In this paragraph, do you mean . . . ?").

7. Corrections to spelling, usage, and style issues.
8. Exploratory ("You might also consider information from . . .").
9. Personal ("Your story reminded me of an incident when . . .").
10. Other.

Consider Writing in Digital Environments

Experts we interviewed from all of the fields noted that many of the communications they shared in workplace situations involve digital communication, including e-mail, project management software, Cloud-based word processing, and blogs. It is easy to assume that blogging or composing an e-mail is easy; however, as the experts noted, a sloppy e-mail can cause confusion, and a poorly written blog post can turn off potential customers in seconds. Precision and explicit language choices are a must across workplaces, and students need practice in how to communicate well in digital forms. Teaching them to do so requires very focused instruction. In most schools, students write digitally only when composing reports or essays. They are seldom asked to write substantive e-mails, texts, or tweets. Based on the experts' responses, we encourage a greater emphasis on these commonplace forms of written communications within school disciplines.

The experts' emphasis on expanded writing in schools is supported by information found on sites such as CoSchedule (Thakur, 2015), which identified nine types of blog posts that can increase traffic to both a blog and the company website. However, most of this writing differs substantially from typical writing assignments in schools. To be successful, content written for the Internet must attract the attention of search engines (think Google) that use algorithms to build their indices of content. This type of writing, optimized for search engines, is, by necessity, different than writing other types of content; as such, it is important that it be addressed in schools.

Conclusion

Workplace writing can be taught. It takes a concerted effort, however, one that focuses students on the aspects of writing that are essential to day-to-day communication. While we agree that it is important for all students to write compelling, evidence-based arguments, it is just as important that they be able to communicate through e-mail about a project developed by colleagues or translate a synthesis of ideas from online research to an Internet discussion forum. Writing in the post-high school realm is varied, specific, and packed with technical, discipline-specific terminology. Students who learn to write in a variety of ways for an array of audiences will have a leg up in the workplace as they seek a voice in our highly specialized world.

● IMPLICATIONS FOR PROFESSIONAL LEARNING ●

- As students learn to write a five-paragraph essay, they are taught to consider the *audience* that will be reading the essay and the appropriate *language* and *tone* to make a connection that causes audience members to want to read the essay. Invite them to choose a profession they may someday pursue. Ask them to research the *type* of writing they may be required to share in this profession. Invite them to think about their *audience*, the *tone*, and the *language* that is just right, then craft a message. For example, in a seventh-grade classroom, students identify a profession, then consider these questions related to audience: "Who is my audience?"; "What background knowledge is needed?"; "Do they have experience reading about the topic?"; "Do they have experience discussing the topic?"; "What are the points that will be new to them?"; "For what points do I need examples?"; "Will they want research documentation?"; "Will they want to be directed to additional resources?"; "What style of language will work best for them?" (Grant, Lapp, & Thayre, 2019). After addressing these questions, students are better able to craft an appropriate text for their target audience.

- Students are also taught to continually build their *bases of knowledge* in order to provide sufficient information to argue a position. Invite students to consider a future career and to craft a message on a related topic. Before they begin have them *self-assess* to determine whether they know the topic well enough to share information or whether they need to read a few resources in order to build their informational base. For example, when a 10th-grade student wanted to explore marketing and decided to craft a proposal for a team of colleagues at a marketing firm, her teacher helped her to seek out model documents to consider as she crafted her own proposal. The student then utilized a tool called Dissect a Text (Grant et al., 2019) to identify aspects of the model text, including descriptions, bullet points, literary devices, and other stylistic elements.

- Invite students to craft a list of questions they might ask a person who works in a profession they may be interested in pursuing. The questions should offer them some insights regarding the types of writing that are part of working in the profession. Once they have the information, have them craft a message that is appropriate for the career or profession. For example, students in an eighth-grade classroom were tasked with interviewing a professional in a field of interest. One student interviewed a medical student about the types of writing he commonly does in class and in his clinical work. Student questions to the medical student included the following: "What types of writing do you commonly compose at work?"; "Are there terms that people who work in your profession often use?"; "How are you learning the language of your profession?"; "Do you use different language or phrases in different situations?"

- Students who are interested in pursuing a profession need to become familiar with the language used by professionals already in that career. Have students read two or three articles that appear in journals in the related fields they are interested in pursuing. While doing so, have them identify common phrases or vocabulary, their definitions, and the way they are used to share information. Model for students, so that they know how to look for different elements in a new document or text. Think-alouds are effective ways to show students how to do the cognitive work of considering aspects of a text from a workplace environment. Then let students practice using this skill with their own text.

QUESTIONS FOR DISCUSSION

1. In what ways do schools prepare students for real-world writing situations? *Response tip:* Think about the types of writing required in workplace situations. What are you teaching students that is applicable to any type of writing?

2. After reading this chapter, how might you revamp and extend the writing curriculum at your school? *Response tip:* Work with students to have a cognitive frame of information that they draw from each time they approach a new writing task.

3. Since most students in school today probably will have more than one job during their working years, what do you think they should be taught about writing communication to support their performance in any job or profession? *Response tip:* Think about how what is learned about communicating through writing can be transferred to new workplace situation.

4. What are some basic tenets about communication that you believe support performance in any job situation? *Response tip:* Think about how you approach each writing task and identify the commonplace information that consistently applies.

REFERENCES

Bogdan, R. C., & Biklen, S. K. (2002). *Qualitative research for education: An introduction to theories and methods* (4th ed.). Boston: Allyn & Bacon.

Grant, M., Lapp, D., & Thayre, M. (2019). *Preparing students for writing beyond school.* West Palm Beach, FL: Learning Sciences International.

IRIS. (n.d.). What should content-area teachers know about vocabulary instruction? Page 7: Building vocabulary and conceptual knowledge using the Frayer model. Retrieved from *http://iris.peabody.vanderbilt.edu/module/sec-rdng/cresource/what-should-content-area-teachers-know-about-vocabulary-instruction/sec_rdng_07.*

Lapp, D., & Wolsey, T. D. (2016, April). Literacy in the disciplines. Retrieved from *https://literacybeat.com/literacy-in-the-disciplines.*

Santa, C. (1988). *Content reading including study systems.* Dubuque, IA: Kendall/Hunt.

Strunk, W., & White, E. B. (2000). *The elements of style* (4th ed.). New York: Longman.

Thakur, A. (2015, October 28). Nine types of blog posts that are proven to boost traffic [Blog post]. Retrieved from *https://coschedule.com/blog/types-of-blog-posts.*

Wolsey, T. D. (2014). Accuracy in digital writing environments: Read up, ask around, double-check. *Voices from the Middle, 21*(3), 49–53. Retrieved from *www.ncte.org/journals/vm/issues/v21-3.*

Wolsey, T. D., Smetana, L., & Grisham, D. L. (2015). Vocabulary Plus Technology: An after-reading approach to deep word learning. *The Reading Teacher, 68*(6), 449–458.

Index

Note. *f* or *t* following a page number indicates a figure or a table.

Abstract questions, 23–24. *See also* CAR (Competence, Abstract, and Relate) Quest

Academic discourse, 129–130

Academic vocabulary. *See also* Vocabulary
dual-meaning words, 177–178, 181–182
elements of workplace writing and, 217, 219–221, 220*f*
informational texts and, 38–39
overview, 37–38
scaffolding oral language for ELLs with science texts and, 175–176, 178

Achievement gap, 2

Agentic learning experiences, 50–51

Analogical reasoning, 66, 68–69, 68*t*

Anchor text, 85–87

Anticipation guides, 176

Argument overlap, 113

Argument schema theory, 60–61

Argumentation, 169–170

Argumentative essays, 6–7. *See also* Writing Assessment
elements of workplace writing and, 223
English language learners (ELLs) and, 172–173

Attitudes, 76–77

Audience, 213–214, 222–223, 228

Author's craft or metatextuality, 150–151

B

Background knowledge. *See* Prior knowledge

Basic Interpersonal Communicative Skills (BICS), 175–176

Bidirectional expertise, 121–122, 126–129, 137–138

#BlackLivesMatter, 204–206, 205*t*

Book centers, 25

Book selection. *See* Text selection

Brown Bag Exam, 86–87

Building Bridges
conversations with children and, 11–16, 17
vocabulary learning and instruction and, 25, 26*f*

C

CAR (Competence, Abstract, and Relate) Quest
example of PAVEd for Success in action and, 27–29
overview, 10, 17
vocabulary learning and instruction and, 22–24, 25, 26*f*

Cartoons, political, 95–96, 97*f*